Post-communist Regime Change

This book seeks to explain the divergent political pathways of 26 post-communist states, following the breakdown and eventual collapse of communism in 1989–91.

Considering the trajectories of these states between 1990 and 2007, this book challenges two central bodies of theory relating to democratization and regime change. Through a sustained analysis of global and post-communist developments within this time period, the author shows that claims of an increasing asymmetry between the 'electoral' and 'liberal' elements of modern democracy have been greatly exaggerated. The author goes on to contend that in accounting for the geographical dispersion of post-communist regime forms, deeper structural factors should be considered as crucial. The book is divided into two parts:

- Part I demonstrates how different conceptualizations of democracy can lead to very different conclusions about the empirical dynamics of democratization.
- Part II contrasts different explanations of post-communist political change and provides an integrated framework for explaining the political pathways encountered within the former Eastern Bloc.

This book will be of interest to students and scholars of post-communist studies, democratization studies, comparative politics and regime change.

Jørgen Møller is Assistant Professor at the Institute of Political Science, University of Århus, Denmark.

Routledge research in comparative politics

1   Democracy and Post-communism
    Political change in the post-communist world
    Graeme Gill

2   Sub-state Nationalism
    A comparative analysis of institutional design
    Helena Catt and Michael Murphy

3   Reward for High Public Office
    Asian and Pacific Rim states
    Christopher Hood and B. Guy Peters

4   Social Democracy and Labour Market Policy
    Developments in Britain and Germany
    Knut Roder

5   Democratic Revolutions
    Asia and Eastern Europe
    Mark R. Thompson

6   Democratization
    A comparative analysis of 170 countries
    Tatu Vanhanen

7   Determinants of the Death Penalty
    A comparative study of the world
    Carsten Anckar

8   How Political Parties Respond to Voters
    Interest aggregation revisited
    Kay Lawson and Thomas Poguntke

9 Women, Quotas and Politics
Drude Dahlerup

10 Citizenship and Ethnic Conflict
Challenging the nation-state
Haldun Gülalp

11 The Politics of Women's Interests
New comparative and international perspectives
Louise Chappell and Lisa Hill

12 Political Disaffection in Contemporary Democracies
Social capital, institutions and politics
Mariano Torcal and José Ramón Montero

13 Representing Women in Parliament
A comparative study
Marian Sawer, Manon Tremblay and Linda Trimble

14 Democracy and Political Culture in Eastern Europe
Hans-Dieter Klingemann, Dieter Fuchs and Jan Zielonka

15 Social Capital and Associations in European Democracies
A comparative analysis
William A. Maloney and Sigrid Roßteutscher

16 Citizenship and Involvement in European Democracies
A comparative analysis
Jan van Deth, José Ramón Montero and Anders Westholm

17 The Politics of Foundations
A comparative analysis
Helmut K. Anheier and Siobhan Daly

18 Party Policy in Modern Democracies
Kenneth Benoit and Michael Laver

19 Semi-presidentialism Outside Europe
A comparative study
Robert Elgie and Sophia Moestrup

20 Comparative Politics
The principal-agent perspective
Jan-Erik Lane

21 **The Political Power of Business**
Structure and information in public policymaking
Patrick Bernhagen

22 **Women's Movements**
Flourishing or in abeyance?
Marian Sawer and Sandra Grey

23 **Consociational Theory**
McGarry and O'Leary and the Northern Ireland conflict
Rupert Taylor

24 **The International Politics of Democratization**
Comparative perspectives
Nuno Severiano Teixeira

25 **Post-communist Regime Change**
A comparative study
Jørgen Møller

Post-communist Regime Change

Change

A comparative study

Jørgen Møller

Routledge
Taylor & Francis Group

LONDON AND NEW YORK

First published 2009
by Routledge
2 Park Square, Milton Park, Abingdon, Oxon OX14 4RN

Simultaneously published in the USA and Canada
by Routledge
711 Third Avenue, New York, NY 10017

*Routledge is an imprint of the Taylor & Francis Group, an informa
business.*

First issued in paperback 2013

© 2009 Jørgen Møller

Typeset in Sabon by Swales and Willis Ltd, Exeter, Devon

British Library Cataloguing in Publication Data
A catalogue record for this book is available from the British Library

Library of Congress Cataloging in Publication Data
Møller, Jørgen.
Post-communist regime change : a comparative study / Jørgen Møller.
p. cm.—(Routledge research in comparative politics ; 25)
Includes bibliographical references and index.
1. Former communist countries—Politics and government. 2. Post-communism. I. Title.
JN96.A58M64 2009
320.9171'7—dc22
2008047756

ISBN13: 978-0-415-85010-0 (pbk)
ISBN13: 978-0-415-48339-1 (hbk)
ISBN13: 978-0-203-87807-1 (ebk)

To Erik, my son.

Contents

List of figures xi
List of tables xii
Acknowledgements xiii

Introduction: the puzzle of the post-communist tripartition 1

PART I
Unfolding the tripartition 9

1 The gap between electoral and liberal democracy revisited: some
conceptual and empirical clarifications 11

*Considerations about the gap between electoral and
liberal democracy 12*
Conceptualization – why and how? 15
Conceptualizing democracy 17
A reappraisal of the third wave of democracy 29
*Concluding on the gap between electoral and liberal
democracies 36*
*Appendix 1.1: Counting rules for the typology of
political regime forms 38*
*Appendix 1.2: A critical note on 'The Rise of Illiberal
Democracy' 39*

2 The post-communist tripartition described 45

Dealing a new deck of cards 46
A second glance at the realities on the ground 51
Conclusions 57
*Appendix 2.1: Counting rules for the classification of
political regime forms 59*

PART II
**A cross-temporal and cross-spatial analysis of patterns
of post-communist political change**   61

3   **An actor-centred analysis of post-communist political pathways**   63

*Three dominant actor-centred explanations in the literature
    on post-communism 65
A preliminary methodological discussion 75
A typological analysis of post-communist political pathways 81
Conclusions 87
Appendix 3.1: Using a statistical cluster analysis as a
robustness test 90*

4   **A structural analysis of post-communist political pathways**   93

*Identifying structural factors in the literature on
    post-communism 94
A typological analysis of post-communist political pathways 102
Conclusions 108*

5   **Contrasting structures, actors and diffusion**   111

*Piecing the general picture together 111
Integrating the packages 118
Enter diffusion 122
Conclusions 130*

Conclusions   133

**Endnote: Montesquieu's 'General Rule' and the rule of law in
the post-communist setting**   141

Notes   153
Bibliography   165
Index   173

List of figures

1.1   Diamond's original typology of political regime forms   13
1.2   Levels of conceptualization and measurement   17
1.3   A typology of political regime forms   23
1.4   The elaborated Dahlian model   26
1.5   Comparing the two analyses of the empirical gap   32
1.6   The bivariate correlations between 'political rights'
      and 'civil liberties', 1990–2005   34
2.1   The relative distribution of cases in the three classes on
      the dependent variable, 1990–2007   54
3.1   The full typology with empirical referents, 1997   82
3.2   The full typology with empirical referents, 2002   84
3.3   The full typology with empirical referents, 2007   86
4.1   The full typology with empirical referents, 1992   104
4.2   The full typology with empirical referents, 1997   105
4.3   The full typology with empirical referents, 2002   106
4.4   The full typology with empirical referents, 2007   107
5.1   A typology of the possible combinations on the actor-centred
      package and the structure-based package   113
5.2   The general causal chain emerging from the typological analyses   121
6.1   A scatter plot of the linear regression of TAX1996 and RL1996   148
6.2   A scatter plot of the linear regression of TAX2000 and RL2000   148

List of tables

1.1 Diamond's account of political regime forms, 1990–7   30
1.2 The alternative account of political regime forms, 1990–7   31
1.3 The alternative account of political regime forms, 1998–2007   32
1.4 The alternative typological account of political regime
forms in the post-communist setting, 1990–2007   35
1.5 Redoing Zakaria's analysis, 1990–2007   42
1.6 The alternative typological account of political regime forms,
1990–2005   44
2.1 The classificatory account of political regime forms on
the global level, 1990–2007   52
2.2 The classificatory account of political regime forms in the
post-communist setting, 1990–2007   54
2.3 The empirical distribution of political regime forms
within the post-communist setting, 1992–2007   56
3.1 An overview of the scoring on the proximate variables   75
3.2 K-means analysis for 1997, 2002 and 2007   91
4.1 An overview of the scoring on the 'deep' variables   102
5.1 The types that have empirical referents, 1997   115
5.2 The types that have empirical referents, 2002   116
5.3 The types that have empirical referents, 2007   117
5.4 The tripartite orderings on Fish's independent and
dependent variable   124
6.1 Pearson's r for the robustness test   149

Acknowledgements

This book was conceived in the context of a three-year stay at the European University Institute in Florence, from where I obtained my doctorate in 2007. A number of people have helped me traverse the territories of post-communism.

At the Institute, I am particularly indebted to László Bruszt and Peter Mair. László was supervisor beyond compare. Always generous with his time, he constantly practised 'creative destruction' when reading my various drafts. Also, his general cheerfulness and sense of humour made me look forward to our almost weekly sessions. Though not formally my co-supervisor, Peter at times functioned as one – reading the numerous drafts I sent him and constantly encouraging me that, to quote (or maybe rather paraphrase), 'something could be publishable here'.

Outside of the EUI, scholars such as Larry Diamond, Guillermo O'Donnell and Philippe Schmitter – who is at the EUI most of the time – have been kind enough to comment on particular pieces that I sent them. I have also benefited much from the critical comments of anonymous reviewers at journals such as *Acta Politica*, *British Journal of Political Science*, *Comparative Political Studies*, *Democratization*, *Comparative Politics*, *East European Politics and Society*, *Journal of Democracy* and *World Politics* – as well as the *EUI Working Paper Series*.

Also, my warm thanks go to Assistant Professor Svend-Erik Skaaning from my home University of Århus, who has not only read a number of drafts over the last three years, but has also helped me strengthen the analysis in a common project. Notwithstanding these manifold contributions, the sole responsibility for any shortcomings or outright errors rests with me.

Finally, I wish to thank various publishers and journals for allowing me to reproduce earlier published articles. An earlier and less elaborate version of Chapter 1 has been published as Møller, Jørgen, 'The Gap between Electoral and Liberal Democracy Revisited: Some Conceptual and Empirical Clarifications', *Acta Politica*, Vol. 42, Issue 4, 2007, reproduced with permission of Palgrave Macmillan. An earlier version of the second appendix in Chapter 1 has been published as Møller, Jørgen, 'A Critical Note on "The Rise of Illiberal Democracy"', *Australian Journal of Political Science*, Vol.

43, No. 3, 2008, reproduced with permission of Taylor and Francis Group (for the website of the journal, see http://www.informaworld.com). Parts of the endnote can be found in the article Møller, Jørgen, 'Wherefore the Liberal State? Post-Soviet Democratic Blues and Lessons from Fiscal Sociology', *East European Politics and Society*, Vol. 21, No. 2, 2007, reproduced with permission of Sage. Also, I have been permitted to reproduce Diamond, Larry, *Developing Democracy: Toward Consolidation*, pp. 28, Table 2.4, 1999, published by The Johns Hopkins University Press.

Introduction
The puzzle of the post-communist tripartition

When communism broke down, two conflicting voices were heard within the study of regime change. From one corner of the ring the optimists predicted the coming of a glorious democratic future. Francis Fukuyama's (1992) thesis on *The End of History and the Last Man* captured most headlines. Fukuyama's argument was both lucid and complex, emphasizing the *longue durée* only. His claim was that a Hegelian 'struggle of recognition' was pushing the countries of the world toward liberal democracy in an almost teleological manner. However, Fukuyama's assertion was quickly translated into a short-term notion about the inexorable advent of democratic regime change.

Also, the optimism was not confined to the deliberately provoking view of his proselytes. The school of Transitology, which was very influential at the time, may have had low expectations concerning the spread of democracy at heart (see in particular O'Donnell and Schmitter 1986), but it also stressed that in the heat of the transition from authoritarianism it was only the actors' choices that were of vital importance. Larry Diamond (1999: 193) later termed this '[. . .] the thesis of the causal primacy of political factors'. This short-term actor perspective led many to adopt a comforting long-term message that 'when it comes to democracy, anyone can do it'.[1]

Staunchly opposed to this view, the pessimists argued that the history of these countries, and the communist legacy in particular, more or less ruled out a steady movement toward liberal democracy. Most famous, perhaps, was Samuel P. Huntington's (1996) thesis on *The Clash of Civilizations*, which claimed that a fundamental gap separated at least half of the former communist countries from the West and, by extension, from democracy. But others went even further than that: witness Ken Jowitt's (1992) warning that 'the Leninist Legacy' had nothing but misery to offer its freed slaves. To quote one (1992: 300) of his many trenchant phrases:

> Allow me to continue with my 'catholic heresy' and suggest that in this setting it will be demagogues, priests, and colonels more than democrats and capitalists who will shape Eastern Europe's general institutional identity. Most of the Eastern Europe of the future is likely to resemble the

Latin America of the recent past more than the Western Europe of the present.

Jowitt was not alone in striking these tones. Adam Przeworski (1991), too, hinted that the East was more likely to copy the South than to join rank with the West, and Claus Offe (1991) maintained that the social atomization bequeathed by communism provided barren soil for the democratic seeds. Valerie Bunce (1999: 758) has captured this dichotomy elegantly:

> Thus, there were those whose scenario for postsocialism was gloomy, with images of disarray, despair, and despots as the 'civilizations' of liberalism and state socialism clashed with one another. The picture that emerged in other investigations was a rosy one, however. Here, the argument was either that certain elements of the socialist past were helpful to a liberal outcome, or that the socialist past, while illiberal, had been decisively defeated. In either event, the premise, if not the promise, was that eastern Europe was well positioned to become precisely that: the eastern half of Europe.

Throughout the first two decades of post-communism, reality conformed to neither of these views, however. Rather, it placed itself squarely between them. First, the setting came to exhibit a fairly systematic partition between democracies and autocracies; the former cluster situated on the western fringes of the old empire, the latter cluster mostly inhabiting the eastern territories. Second, quite a number of post-communist states – very conveniently situated between the two other clusters geographically – drifted toward a third alternative. Rather than closing rank with either their democratic or their autocratic counterparts, these 'hybrid regimes' came to be caught midstream.

In other words, less than a decade[2] after the upheaval of 1989–91, the post-communist edifice was strikingly similar to the global one with regard to the basic distinction between political regime forms. To quote Valerie Bunce (1999: 760) yet again: 'The postsocialist experience, therefore, exhibits considerable economic and political diversity. Indeed, once a cohesive area representing an alternative world order, this region has become – and very quickly – a microcosm of the larger world within which it resides'.

In fact, we can go further than that. As Herbert Kitschelt (2003: 49) has noted, '[m]easured in terms of civic and political rights indexes developed by the Freedom House, there is no region or set of countries on earth with a currently larger diversity of political regimes'.

In this book, I set out to account for the combination of synchronic and diachronic variation in post-communist political regime forms. That is, I deliberately construe time and space as dimensions of variation. The objective is to expound both the political pathways of post-communism and the cross-case divisions at different points in time along these paths. I open right after the genesis of 1989–91 but my aim is to trace the political developments into the present.

The period in question, 1992–2007, was the one in which the respective scenarios of doom or deliverance were expected to unfold. Also, as indicated above, this 16 years stretch did indeed see significant political developments, although neither the scenario of the pessimists nor that of the optimists seized the day. Thus, from a common political point of departure – that of autocracy – in the late 1980s, the post-communist countries went their separate ways. Anticipating the empirical findings of Chapters 1 and 2, a tripartition or trichotomy between democracies, hybrid regimes and autocracies quickly became the reality.[3]

This combination of cross-temporal and cross-spatial variation is interesting in its own right – and it very much invites a comparative analysis (cf. Bartolini 1993). My first puzzle can thus be expressed in terms of three particular questions which, by zooming in on the described outcomes on the dependent variable, spell out the general problem of this book:

1   Which factors account for the presence or absence of democracies in the post-communist setting since the upheavals of 1989–91?
2   Which factors account for the presence or absence of hybrid regimes in the post-communist setting since the upheavals of 1989–91?
3   Which factors account for the presence or absence of autocracies in the post-communist setting since the upheavals of 1989–91?

Yet there is more to it than this. I am especially keen on explaining the fact that the variation in political regime forms that has locked in across the setting since the 1990s has, from a geographical point of view, been very systematically dispersed. To reiterate and elaborate a point made above, no East-Central European[4] country has failed to reach the destination of democracy since the breakdown of communism. Conversely, no Central Asian country has consistently[5] withstood the pull of autocracy. Finally, most of the remaining countries have (for the better part of the period) lingered in a hybrid state. This brings me to my second puzzle: Which factors account for the systematic combination of intra-subregional similarities and inter-subregional differences in post-communist political regime forms that has locked in since the early 1990s?

The term 'intra-subregional' is basically meant to capture the two extreme clusters of East-Central Europe and Central Asia. However, as we shall see, an intermediate area comprising the Western parts of the former Soviet Union and much of the Balkan Peninsula can also be construed as a subregional cluster. Inter-subregional refers to the distinction between these clusters.

When speculating about the origins of dividing lines such as these, the tentative conclusion that comes to mind is a simple one: the political pathways are so strikingly similar within the three said clusters of post-communist countries that this pattern questions the causal importance of the actors, at least in the longer term.[6] To phrase it differently, it seems obvious that the point of departure of these three groups – the factors that tied each cluster together and set the three clusters apart on the eve of the transition – carries explanatory weight. Furthermore, it is remarkable that the actors, with a few notable and very interesting exceptions, have not been able to break what almost seem to equal a 'geographical iron law of political change'.[7] Both the optimists and the pessimists obviously brushed over these inter-subregional differences during and in the immediate aftermath of the upheavals of 1989–91.[8]

All of this seemingly justifies opting solely for a structural investigation. Furthermore, it is tempting to do so for the simple reason that the actor-centred explanations have dominated the study of regime change since at least the mid-1980s. It used to be very different. Upon its conception and birth after the Second World War, the democratization literature was deliberately cast in a structural guise. Most notable were the two very different but equally influential studies of Seymour Martin Lipset (1959a) and Barrington Moore (1991 [1966]). Lipset pointed to the overriding importance of structural preconditions of democratization: in his case the economic level of development or, more generally, 'modernization'. Barrington Moore emphasized the historical paths that brought about the respective outcomes of democracy and autocracy in the world of yesterday, thus tracing the present into the past. Whereas Lipset inaugurated the so-called 'functional school', Barrington Moore sparked off the manifold attempts to explain democratization from the viewpoint of 'historical sociology'.

Early criticisms of these approaches were aired by Dankwart Rustow in 1970 and Juan J. Linz in 1978. However, it was not until the mid-1980s that the pendulum really swung with the publication of Guillermo O'Donnell and Philippe Schmitter's (1986) path-breaking conclusions on *Transitions from Authoritarian Rule*. O'Donnell and Schmitter found that countries with very diverse starting points were able to reach the same outcome – democracy – which spoke against the fixation on the structural point of departure. Also termed 'Transitology', this strand within the literature stresses the uncertainty prevailing in the transition phase; a state of flux in which actors make often unintended (and sometimes unwanted) choices about institutions in the context of strategic interaction between contending groups. Focus is, in other words, placed on the importance of the actor-choices, especially those of political elites, during periods of radical change. In this guise, Transitology dominated the study of regime change well into the 1990s.

Not surprisingly, then, in the post-communist subsetting, such actor-centred approaches have been very influential. The causal factors emphasized by these approaches are, *inter alia*, the outcome of the initial elections, constitutional engineering and the character of the economic reform process (e.g. Roeder 1994, Fish 1998a, 1998b, 2006; Ishiyama and Velten 1998; McFaul 2002; Fish and Choudhry 2007). Generally speaking, the derivative causal chain leads from actor-choices to political outcomes. More particularly, these explanations of regime change share two propositions concerning social change – and in doing so they are heavily indebted to Transitology. The first proposition is that the important factors shaping the political outcomes dated from the transitional upheavals, not from antecedent structural factors. The second, and consequent, proposition is that these constraints were put in place by actors in a relatively voluntaristic way (e.g. Fish 1998a: 77–8 and Fish 2006: 11–12).

However, another explanatory paradigm has crystallized in the latest decade. Spearheaded by Herbert Kitschelt's (1993, et al. 1999, 2003) forceful critique of these very theories, a cohort of students of post-communism have been turning their attention to the way historical legacies and other structural factors have shaped the scope of choice.[9] Kitschelt (2003: 74–5) distinguishes between deep, structural explanations on the one hand and shallow, proximate explanations on the other. He anchors the separation temporally, underlining that the deeper the causes, the more distant they are from the *explanandum* and the more blurred the affiliated causal mechanisms tend to be.

Conversely, proximate causes are situated relatively close to the outcome on the dimension of time and provide explicit causal mechanisms. At first sight, they thus have a competitive edge as *explanans*. But looks may be deceptive. Kitschelt's ontological point is that the proximate explanations are often too closely – at times almost tautologically – connected with the outcome to be causally interesting vis-à-vis their deeper counterparts.

This does not imply that the actor-centred attributes, as causes, are worthless; only that it is more appropriate to view them as links in a chain that leads from the deep factors to the outcome. This equals saying that the most important theoretical and empirical task is not one of assessing the relative explanatory power of competing bids – and even less of opting for one over the other at the outset of an empirical investigation – but rather one of theoretical integration.

In the context of the former communist countries there is, somewhat surprisingly, a lack of research dedicated to assessing the empirical relevance of Kitschelt's fundamental critique. In fact, his propositions have not really been tested by juxtaposing deep and proximate causes in a unified explanatory framework, thereby assessing their mutual relationship as well as their particular political effects.

Translated into genuine hypotheses, Kitschelt's assertions imply two sets of expectations:

1   As 'packages',[10] both the deep and the proximate explanatory variables largely account for the present variation in post-communist political regimes.

2   As a 'package', the deep explanatory variables largely account for the variation in the proximate explanatory variables.

In this book, these two hypotheses will be systematically tested. Rather than choosing the narrow structural focus only, I will contrast the two approaches in order to examine how each of them bear upon the outcome on the dependent variable of post-communist political regime forms and how they bear upon each other in the post-communist setting.

Is it wise to zoom in on the post-communist setting only? The mid-1990s saw a trenchant methodological debate on the fruitfulness of carrying out interregional comparisons, in particular of comparing the 'East' (the post-communist countries) with the 'South' (either the Southern European or Latin American countries). This debate was centred around the opposing views of, on the one hand, Philippe Schmitter and Terry Karl (1994) and, on the other hand, Valerie Bunce (1995).

Schmitter and Karl's message was a simple one: only by comparing very different regions is it possible to establish the presence of regional idiosyncrasies (or the lack thereof). Bunce's reaction to this plea for conceptual travels was to point out that the post-communist region is so unique that it makes much more sense to contrast the countries of this setting with each other, in particular because it contains the optimal combination of similarities and differences for engaging in comparative endeavours.

Theoretically, there is much to recommend in Bunce's stand. Her premise is of the same ilk as Kitschelt's: structural factors are extremely important for the political and economic potential of the respective post-communist countries. *A fortiori*, these antecedents render actor-centred comparisons with regions with completely different legacies of state formation and democratization – such as Latin America – almost nonsensical.

Yet somewhat paradoxically, methodologically Schmitter and Karl have the upper hand in this debate, at least according to my view. Uniqueness should be established through empirical comparisons – *a posteriori* – not assumed *a priori*. Conceptual stretching is less of a problem than Bunce makes it out to be since it can be remedied by a zealous use of the ladder of abstraction (i.e. by opting for more general concepts when travelling (cf. Sartori 1970)).

In all events, it does not make much sense to construe the post-communist setting as a 'region' if this term denotes the presence of a relatively homogenous cluster. As already noted – and in spite of what seemed a common politico-economic point of departure in 1989–91 – the former communist bloc is today among the most heterogeneous, with respect to political outcomes, globally. Hence, when comparing the post-communist countries which each other, one may in fact do what Schmitter and Karl recommend: contrast intra- and inter-(sub)regional similarities and differences. This is what I aim to do in this book, and this is why I will stick to the post-communist setting, but include as much of the setting as possible.

Regarding this latter point, one further question must be tackled straight away: Which countries to choose? Obviously, it would be preferable to zoom in on the entire population, discussing all 28 post-communist countries (not counting newly independent Montenegro). I have, however, been forced to exclude Bosnia-Herzegovina and Serbia-Montenegro.

Other scholars have excluded even bigger parts of the former Yugoslavian whole from similar analyses, arguing that due to pernicious internecine strife the four countries of Croatia, Bosnia-Herzegovina, Macedonia and Serbia-Montenegro have followed a very unflattering political path throughout most of post-communism for reasons that are not necessarily linked to general factors of political change. The causal mechanisms at work in this corner of post-communism are likely to be very idiosyncratic, the argument goes (e.g. Kopstein and Reilly 2000: 25).

As I am on the stakeout for more general mechanisms, this may seem a valid argument. That is not the case. The Ex-Yugoslavian wars ended quite some time ago and in the longer run, the countries should – if the structural expectations are on target – conform to the same patterns as the rest of the setting. As such, these countries can in fact be construed as 'critical cases' for Kitschelt's propositions, and I have done my best to include them. This has not proven possible for Bosnia-Herzegovina and Serbia-Montenegro for one pragmatic, but also very important, reason: I have not been able to obtain comparable data with respect to the indicators that I use to measure the deep and proximate variables. That leaves us with a set of 26 countries, ranging from the Czech Republic in the west to Mongolia in the east.

A few words on the structure of the book might seem appropriate at this point. In the subsequent two chapters – Part I – I will conceptualize, operationalize and order the empirical referents on the dependent variable, bearing the stated problem in mind. In doing so, I will also test a descriptive argument that rose to prominence in the late 1990s: an increasing global gap between the electoral and the liberal property of modern or liberal democracy has come into existence.[11]

Part II, which is made up of Chapters 3 to 5, represents the bulk of the book as this is where I engage the *explanans*. In Chapters 3 and 4 I analyse the causal merits of actor-centred and structural explanations of post-communist political diversity, respectively. On the basis of these analyses, I contrast the two approaches in Chapter 5 and add a discussion of yet a third alternative explanation: diffusion.

Finally, in the Endnote I attempt to substantiate the legacies-approach to post-communism that underpins the structural explanations. This short elaboration, however, has more to do with descriptive than causal inference.

Enough said – let us get into the ring.

Part I
Unfolding the tripartition

1 The gap between electoral and liberal democracy revisited

Some conceptual and empirical clarifications

The general objective of Chapters 1 and 2 is to provide a useful conceptualization of the dependent variable of political regime forms. To be more specific, the aim is to arrive at an edifice that sets dissimilar post-communist countries apart while bringing similar post-communist countries together – with regard to the explanandum.[1] Reinventing the wheel is seldom advisable and the proper point of departure is the existing literature on democracy or, more generally, on political regime forms.

The contemporary literature teems with new conceptualizations of democracy. Glancing back at the literature of the 1950s, 1960s and 1970s, this development is striking. In those days, the non-democratic part of the spectrum was where the important political variation was sought, conceptually as well as empirically. Recall Juan J. Linz's famous effort to provide a conceptual separation between 'totalitarianism' and 'authoritarianism', Giovanni Sartori's (1987) protracted endeavours to elucidating 'What Democracy Is Not' and Linz and Stepan's (1978) influential volume on *The Breakdown of Democratic Regimes*. This non-democratic bias (or pivot) of scholarship held sway even as the new focus on democracy was inaugurated in the 1980s. Witness only the title of Guillermo O'Donnell, Philippe Schmitter and Laurence Whitehead's path-breaking four-volume work from 1986: *Transitions from Authoritarian Rule*.

But these days it is the democratic part of the spectrum that is being dissected.[2] Peter Mair (2008) has pointed to two reasons lying behind this new scholarly agenda. First, and empirically, the ascendancy of what Samuel P. Huntington (1991) has termed the 'third wave of democratization' means that what used to be a relatively homogenous class subsuming empirical referents situated in the north-western quadrant of the world has become a heterogeneous one, containing a large number of quite dissimilar countries encountered in virtually every corner of the globe.[3] Second, and theoretically, the literature on regime change has moved to a lower level of abstraction since the early 1980s, highlighting the political consequences of different kinds of democracy rather than merely seeking to explain democracy *in toto*, as used to be the case.

Hence both the proliferation of 'democracy with adjectives' that Collier and

Levitsky (1997) so superbly identified and diagnosed a decade ago and hence the relevance of focusing on the new conceptualizations of democracy in the first place.

Most prominently, a number of scholars have advanced an interesting claim: that it is necessary to make a conceptual and empirical distinction between the faces of democracy. This distillation of democracy into electoral and liberal components primarily builds on inductive arguments. For these formerly Siamese twins are seemingly, so the claim goes,[4] being torn apart by the third wave. If this is indeed the case, then we do need to embed the electoral vis-à-vis liberal distinction into the conceptualization of the political regime form. Otherwise, we cannot appreciate the dominant empirical dynamics of political change taking place in the world of today. So, let us start out by elucidating and testing this claim.[5]

Considerations about the gap between electoral and liberal democracy

Almost a decade ago Larry Diamond published *Developing Democracy*. In this book, he carefully developed a distinction between electoral and liberal democracy and then went on to demonstrate that most of the recent instances of democratization belong in the electoral category, separated by a significant gap from their liberal betters. To quote from his (1999: 10) account, '[. . .] the gap between electoral and liberal democracy has grown markedly during the latter part of the third wave, forming one of its most significant but little-noticed features'.

Diamond has not been alone in staking this claim. Guillermo O'Donnell's notion of 'delegative democracy' is very much based on the existence of such a gap, albeit with a narrower empirical context in mind, viz. that of Latin America. To quote from his (1992: 7) original working paper on this new concept, '[d]elegative democracy [. . .] is more democratic, but less liberal, than representative democracy'. In his later writings, this assertion has been elaborated further. In an attempt to direct attention to the intimate relationship between the state and democracy, O'Donnell (1993: 11–12, emphasis in original) thus writes that '[. . .] in many areas the *democratic*, participatory rights of polyarchy are respected. But the *liberal* component of democracy is systematically violated'.

Fareed Zakaria has been even more outspoken. In a recent book with the telling title *The Future of Freedom: Illiberal Democracy at Home and Abroad*, he argues that electoral (termed 'illiberal' by Zakaria) and liberal components of democracy have more or less parted ways in today's world. Quoting one of his (2003: 17) trenchant passages: 'Over the last half-century in the West, democracy and liberty have merged. But today the two strands of liberal democracy, interwoven in the Western political fabric, are coming apart across the globe. Democracy is flourishing; liberty is not'.

A strong theoretical argument does, in fact, favour spelling out the merits of modern democracy with reference to both an electoral and a liberal element. As we shall see, the two dimensions cover distinct aspects of modern democracy. In other words, both regimes that combine the presence of the electoral component with the absence of the liberal equivalent and vice versa are conceptually meaningful. Also, the distinction aptly captures the lineage of democracy. The electoral element dates back to ancient Greece. The liberal element neatly covers the much more recent Anglo-Saxon addition, empha-sizing – at the very least – the constitutional qualifications of freedom rights and the rule of law. If a significant gap is separating the two, then it is indeed an important observation.

Be that as it may, the assertions about electoral and liberal democracy of Diamond, O'Donnell and Zakaria are tied together not by common theoret-ical premises but by inductive reasoning. When looking at the world, they simply identify a gap between the two constructs. This inductive emphasis is no mere coincidence. At the end of the day, the justification for separating the two components must be empirical. If we do not obfuscate the dynamics of regime change in the present world by collapsing the two dimensions, then there is no reason to separate them since this only increases the conceptual complexity. More technically, if we can translate 'thicker' concepts into 'thin-ner' concepts without notable validity problems, parsimony dictates that we do so (cf. Gerring 1999).

This is the test then: whether the conceptual separation assists us in capturing the empirical variation – the most salient dividing lines – on, first, the global level and, second, with regard to the post-communist subset. Diamond's account of the gap is the most ambitious in the literature, theoretically as well as empirically. Hence, I will stick to him throughout this chapter. (See Appendix 1.2 for a discussion of Zakaria's work.)

Diamond's actual conceptualization is, however, less convincing than his point of departure. He goes on to develop a fourfold 'typology' of political regime forms, as illustrated in Figure 1.1.

As the one-dimensionality of Figure 1.1 indicates, Diamond's edifice is not what we would normally term a typology. Rather, it is a classification or, at the very most, a matter of 'quasi-types' (cf. Lazarsfeld and Barton 1951).[6] One may feel inclined to ask 'So what?'. The consequent conceptual problem is, however, a very tangible one. A pure classification only covers one

| Liberal democracy | Electoral democracy | Pseudo-democracy | Non-democracy |

Figure 1.1 Diamond's original typology of political regime forms.

dimension; it is an ordering – based on mutually exclusive classes – that refers to one attribute only. In other words, Diamond has drawn a line with 'very democratic' on one end and 'very undemocratic' on the other end with four types in between.

In doing so, Diamond is unable to carry his distinction between the electoral and the liberal dimensions of liberal democracy over into his actual conceptualization of political regime forms. In his typology, the two dimensions are not conceptually independent of each other. Rather, they are covered by one and the same attribute. Hence, a country moves from electoral democracy to liberal democracy not by adding liberal merits only but by either doing somewhat better with regard to both the electoral and the liberal criteria or doing much better with regard to any of the two. In other words, the two quasi-types or classes are separated by a difference in degree, not a difference in kind.[7] This is also obvious when reading Diamond's subsequent scoring of selected countries, an issue to which I will return. Taken together, Diamond's conceptualization simply cannot appreciate his own distinction between the electoral and liberal components of liberal democracy.

To be fair, Diamond has somewhat changed his conceptual scheme since the publication of *Developing Democracy* (see Diamond 2002 and 2003). First, he has proposed to operate with one dimension only, namely the electoral one. Second, he has rebuilt his typology. Third, he has changed the thresholds between the quasi-types or classes. This third point, the modification of thresholds, is only a technicality, albeit a very pertinent one. (I myself will mention and adhere to it later on.) But let us discuss the two first corrections in turn. Starting with the former point, sticking to the electoral dimension definitely presents a way to circumvent the logical problems identified above. In this manner, it is possible to rely on a purely electoral classification, i.e. it is possible to classify countries independently of the liberal dimension, thus abandoning the very notion of two components. Doing so means that we cannot capture any gap, though, and this strategy is not very congenial to the agenda he has himself staked out.

This is probably why Diamond does not stop here – and this brings us to the second point. Immediately after classifying countries on the electoral dimension only, he (2003: 8) reintroduces the notion of conceiving '[. . .] of democracy in terms of two thresholds'. The first is that of electoral democracy: that '[. . .] principal positions of political power are filled through regular, free, fair, and competitive (and, therefore, multiparty) elections'. The second is that of liberal democracy:

> Beyond the electoral arena, it features a vigorous rule of law, with an independent and non-discriminatory judiciary; extensive individual freedoms of belief, speech, publication, association, assembly, and so on; strong protections for the rights of ethnic, cultural, religious, and other

minorities; a pluralistic civil society, which affords citizens multiple channels outside the electoral arena through which to participate and express their interests and values; and civilian control over the military.

(2003: 9)

The two dimensions are back in, and Diamond's consequent new typology of political regime forms – consisting of the six quasi-types of 'Liberal Democracy', 'Electoral Democracy', 'Ambiguous Regimes', 'Competitive Authoritarian', 'Electoral, Uncompetitive Authoritarian' and 'Politically Closed Authoritarian' – is merely an elaboration of his former edifice. This is underlined by the fact that the countries once again move from the 'electoral' to the 'liberal' quasi-types not exclusively by adding liberal merits but by doing better on both of the two dimensions. Also, the connotations[8] of the latter four constructs do not as such carry any semantic reference to a logical distinction between the two attributes.

In a nutshell, the logical problem of identifying two relevant theoretical dimensions and then building an ordering that refers to one attribute only remains. In this chapter, I will seek to remedy that problem by creating a conceptualization that does indeed capture these two dimensions. To be more precise, I will build up an ordering of 'attribute compounds', i.e. a genuine typology (cf. Lazarsfeld and Barton 1951). Throughout these endeavours, I will build on Diamond's 'theoretical' argumentation about or distinction between the two dimensions of liberal democracy – it is the taxonomical[9] exercise that I intend to adjust. However, as will be demonstrated, this has significant consequences for the actual scoring of the cases and, by extension, for the conclusions about the direction of the current of the third wave of democratization. Let us start out at the proper point: discussing the very technique of conceptualization.

Conceptualization – why and how?

In his seminal article on conceptualization, Giovanni Sartori (1970: 1038) asserts that '[C]oncept formation stands prior to quantification'. Sartori's point is straightforward: before we can even think about measurement – in order to verify or falsify a given causal claim – we must solve the logical problems of conceptualization. Quoting John Gerring (1999: 357–8):

'Concept formation' conventionally refers to three aspects of a concept: (a) the events or phenomena to be defined (the extension, denotation, or definiendum), (b) the properties or attributes that define them (the intension, connotation, definiens, or definition), and (c) a label covering both *a* and *b* (the term).

It is widely acknowledged that the ability to navigate between the three corners of this triangle – also known as the Ogden-Richards Triangle – is extremely important. Yet the opinions differ when it comes to the question of 'how to?'. Sartori champions a very rigorous approach. His (1970: 1041) focal point is the so-called 'ladder of abstraction': 'We make a concept more abstract and more general by lessening its properties or attributes. Conversely, a concept is specified by the addition (or unfolding) of qualifications, i.e., by augmenting its attributes or properties'. To solve the corresponding problems, Sartori proposes ten demanding rules for concept formation.

Sartori has subsequently been criticized for his uncompromising attitude to the rigour of concept formation. Gerring (1999) has pointed out that the relevance of a concept hinges on the particular research project. This is so because concept formation is an uncertain process driven by choices, or 'trade-offs', to use his term. Gerring proposes a 'criterial' corrective, i.e. he directs attention to the many different (and often mutually conflicting) criteria that must be observed. Concept formation is, in his opinion, a struggle between eight competing *desiderata*, these being familiarity, resonance, parsimony, coherence, differentiation, depth, theoretical utility and field utility. To quote him (1999: 367), '[c]oncept formation is a fraught exercise – a set of choices which may have no single "best" solution, but rather a range of more-or-less acceptable alternatives'.

It is therefore pretentious – and flawed – to seek to provide the ultimate clarification, valid through space and time, of a given concept. Instead, Gerring advocates, the scholar should reveal all his interim considerations and thus ensure that the process of concept formation is transparent. To paraphrase, the validity of the definitions depends in the last instance on whether it is possible to understand the researcher's goals and the way these are produced.

Gerring's criticism of Sartori's rigid scheme makes sense. But this does not mean that Sartori's 'ladder of abstraction' is not useful. It is only his affiliated rules that are unnecessarily demanding. Hence, throughout this book the notion of the ladder of abstraction will act as a pivot for the conceptual considerations, but Sartori's various rules will not be observed in any systematic way. Instead, I will keep in mind Gerring's emphasis on the intimate link between the definition and the actual field of research, *in casu* the third wave of democratization in general and the post-communist experience in particular.

This equals saying that the inverse relationship between 'connotation' or 'intension' (the meaning of the concept) and the 'denotation' or 'extension' (the cases subsumed by the concept), which provides the nexus of Sartori's ladder, has to be zealously appreciated throughout the conceptual stage. Robert Adcock and David Collier (2001) have devised a 'model of layered concept formation' (see Figure 1.2) which facilitates such an appreciation.

Adcock and Collier's objective is to safeguard 'measurement validity' when moving from the concepts to the reality on the ground. To quote: 'Valid

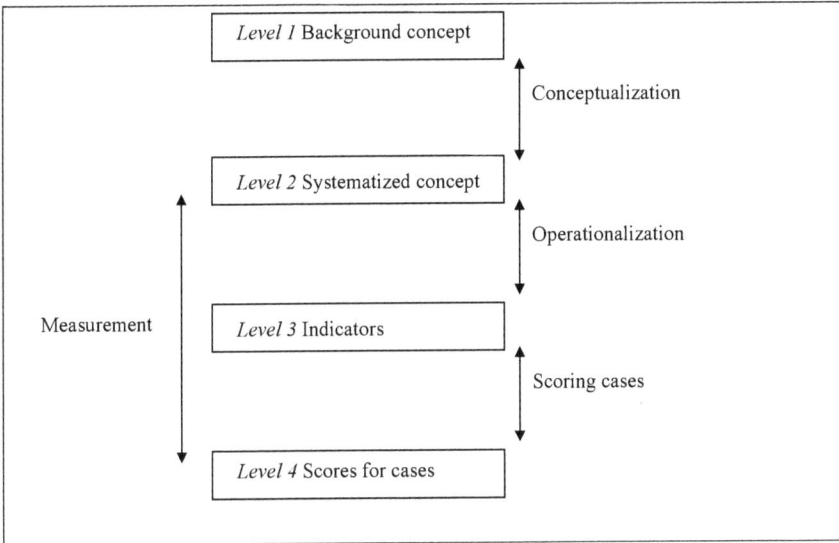

Figure 1.2 Levels of conceptualization and measurement.

Source: adapted from Adcock and Collier (2001)

measurement is achieved when scores (including the results of qualitative classification) meaningfully capture the ideas contained in the corresponding concept' (2001: 530). I find this construct very useful because it allows us to separate conceptual issues from measurement and it makes for moving back and forth between concepts and operationalizations – an option that will be used to good effect in Chapter 2.

The most abstract – or general, as Adcock and Collier prefer to term it – level is that of the background concept. This is a playground where little disagreement exists because the concept carries almost nothing with regard to negation, i.e. what it is not.[10] Descending to the next rung – i.e. moving down the ladder of abstraction – we reach the level of the systematized concept. Here, the researcher is compelled to take a stand, to clearly specify what the connotations of the concept are not capturing. Taking another step, we arrive at the levels of the indicators, the operationalization of the concept that is. At this point, we must declare the denotations of the concept before finally presenting a way to measure it.

Conceptualizing democracy

Defining democracy from scratch would be a bold but also a foolish quest. A plethora of competing definitions already exists within the literature and is impossible to escape as a theoretical frame of reference. In the subsequent pages, I will descend the ladder of abstraction, in turn elucidating the dominant definitions of democracy found within the literature. Starting with the most modest connotation, I will discuss the advantages of moving (or not moving) towards 'thicker' definitions. In doing so, I will – as already indicated – very much walk down the same aisle as Larry Diamond did in *Developing Democracy*. But I feel that it is necessary to lay bare this path to avoid any confusion about the subsequent empirical analysis.

The background concept

Tackling the level of the background concept should not cause much confusion.[11] Little disagreement exists with regard to the most abstract definition of democracy. Quoting Diamond (1999: 8, emphasis in original):

> By and large, most scholarly and policy uses of the term *democracy* today refer to a purely political conception of the term, and the intellectual shift back to an earlier convention has greatly facilitated progress in studying the dynamics of democracy, including the relationship between political democracy and various social and economic conditions.

Defining democracy as 'a political regime form' is in line with the tradition reaching back to Joseph A. Schumpeter – what I perceive to be the most promising understanding given the empirical setting under scrutiny. In *Capitalism, Socialism and Democracy*, originally published during the Second World War, Schumpeter (1974 [1943]: 242, emphasis in original) famously wrote:

> [d]emocracy is a political *method*, that is to say, a certain type of institutional arrangement for arriving at political – legislative and administrative – decisions and hence incapable of being an end in itself, irrespective of what decisions it will produce under given historical conditions. And this must be the starting point of any attempt at defining it.

I find this point of departure very appealing. Even on the most abstract level such a definition paves the way for assessing the importance of socio-economic factors as independent variables of democracy – something that is obviously not possible when these are included directly into the dependent variable (cf. also Adcock and Collier 2001: 533). Hence, I will simply stick to this understanding of democracy on the most general level.[12] We still have a long way to travel conceptually, though. At the present stage, our problem is the very tangible one that democracy, whatever it may be, is logically only one status (or outcome) on the variable of the political regime form. In order to capture the dependent variable, we need to spell out what democracy, as a political regime form, is and is not[13] in detail, also as regards the connotative definition. This forces us to move to the level of the systematized concept.

The systematized concept

Schumpeter (1974 [1943]: 269) went on to define democracy as '[. . .] that institutional arrangement for arriving at political decisions in which individuals acquire the power to decide by means of a competitive struggle for people's vote', i.e. the free competition for the free vote. Elections have often been the cardinal point in definitions of democracy (e.g. Huntington 1991; Przeworski et al. 1996); Schumpeter's is merely the seminal – and, *ipso facto*, most influential – of these. The electoral current within the theoretical literature simply argues that free contestation for political leadership is what, at the end of the day, separates democracies from autocracies.

Viewing democracy as a pure electoral engine may facilitate empirical endeavours, yet it is not unproblematic in the world of today. To quote Diamond (1999: 9): '[. . .] such formulations may still fail to give due weight to political repression and marginalization, which exclude significant segments of the population – typically the poor or ethnic and regional minorities – from exercising their democratic rights'.

Recall that the connotation (the intension) of a definition is inversely related to the denotation (the extension). To translate Diamond's objection into this language, with such a modest (purely electoral) intension, the extension is likely to cover a very large cluster of countries that have very little in common. Hence, it makes sense to expand the connotation of the concept of democracy. Before doing so, one thing should be made clear. It is possible to maintain Schumpeter's 'realistic' vein of thinking, i.e. to keep his interpretation of democracy as a method, while expanding the connotation of the concept. Like pearls on a string, we keep the one necklace, yet add new content to it. (Using Collier and Levitsky's 1997 terminology, we 'precise the definition'.) This is obviously only possible for so long, however, since, at some point, we will in fact be toying with another kind of beads, and hence a different necklace. This cut-off point should not go unnoticed.

The most influential elaboration of the Schumpeterian definition dates back to 1971 when Robert A. Dahl conceived his concept of *Polyarchy* (revisited in 1989), crafted as an empirical approximation of the ideal notion of democracy. Quoting him (1989: 220):

> [p]olyarchy is a political order distinguished at the most general level by two broad characteristics: Citizenship is extended to a relatively high proportion of adults and the rights of citizenship include the opportunity to oppose and vote out the highest officials in the government.

To spell out this combination of participation and contestation, Dahl augments the definition into seven institutional criteria: elected officials; free and fair elections; inclusive suffrage; right to run for office; freedom of expression; alternative information; associational autonomy (see Figure 1.4). The former four criteria can be construed as capturing the electoral component of democracy, whereas the latter three capture the liberal equivalent, and in the Dahlian edifice any political regime form capable of fulfilling all of these earns the status of polyarchy.[14]

Dahl's conceptual edifice has many merits, adding liberal components to the electoral ones as it does. However, it also suffers from some of the same problems as its Schumpeterian predecessor. Dahl, too, emphasizes the procedural aspects in themselves while neglecting the capacity to uphold these procedures. To be fair, he (1989: 221) asserts that:

> It is important to understand that these statements characterize actual and not merely nominal rights, institutions, and processes. In fact, the countries of the world may be assigned approximate rankings according to the extent to which each of the institutions is present in a realistic sense.

However, Dahl does not include this requirement directly into his list of criteria; it remains a background condition or premise. If this were in itself sufficient, he might just as well have defined polyarchy as a regime form where both contestation and participation (and hence the affiliated electoral and liberal rights) are facts of life, without spelling it out into seven requirements or subcomponents. Once again we encounter a need to augment the connotation. What we need at this point is some thorough theorizing about the state and democracy or, to be more precise, about constitutional liberalism. As Diamond (1999: 11–12) rightly tells us:

> Freedom and pluralism, in turn, can be secured only through a 'rule of law', in which legal rules are applied fairly, consistently, and predictably across equivalent cases, irrespective of the class, status, or power of those subject to the rules [. . .] This in turn requires a legal and judicial system and, more broadly, a state with some capacity. Thus Juan Linz's dictum: 'no state, no *Rechtsstaat*, no democracy'.

Before we proceed any further, it is interesting to hark back to Schumpeter's original definition for a moment. One of his (1974 [1943]: 271) main points stands in stark contrast to the one about to be made here: 'We have seen that the democratic method does not necessarily guarantee a greater amount of individual freedom than another political method would permit in similar circumstances'. To illustrate this, he (1974 [1943]: 243) delivers a quasi-historical example in the footnotes:

> In particular it is not true that democracy will always safeguard freedom of conscience better than autocracy. Witness the most famous of all trials. Pilate was, from the standpoint of the Jews, certainly the representative of autocracy. Yet he tried to protect freedom. And he yielded to a democracy.

This quotation pinpoints the difference between the Schumpeterian definition and that of his successors. Today, while still defining democracy as a political method, it is most often perceived as a method that safeguards certain liberties; it is perceived as a constitutional aegis against arbitrary, and therefore limitless, power, including the power of the majority (see also Sartori 1987 on this point). By implication, mob rule is no more democratic than tyranny. This brings us to the next stop on our theoretical journey: Guillermo O'Donnell.

In 1993, O'Donnell published a working paper titled *On the State, Democratization and Some Conceptual Problems*. His point of departure is an observation akin to that of Diamond, namely that many polyarchies are not very liberal. On this background, O'Donnell (1993: 10) invites us to remember the most critical aspect of a genuinely liberal state: the existence of a universalistic legal order, one that '[. . .] can be successfully invoked by anyone, irrespective of her position in society'. Subsequently, O'Donnell has expanded these thoughts in the article 'Democracy, Law, and Comparative Politics'. Herein, he (2001: 14) stresses that '[. . .] the combined effect of the freedoms listed by Dahl and other authors (expression, association, and access to information) cannot fully guarantee that elections will be fair', thus advertising for an additional criterion, viz. 'a legal system that enacts and backs – at least – the rights included in the definition of a democratic regime; and [. . .] prevents anyone from being *de legibus solutus*' (24).

The rule of law, in its classical liberal interpretation, is exactly the criterion that needs to be added to Dahl's concept of polyarchy in order to arrive at a fuller coverage of what is most properly termed 'liberal democracy' (but could just as well be termed 'democracy proper').

Having gone this far, should we proceed further, enriching the connotation even more? A number of oft-cited scholars have, in fact, done so. In their tour de force, *Problems of Democratic Transition and Consolidation*, published in 1996, Juan Linz and Alfred Stepan define consolidated democracy as a political situation in which democracy has become 'the only game in town' – behaviourally, attitudinally and constitutionally.

I have so far stopped short of any attitudinal requirements. The reason is simple: adding attitudes does not represent an elaboration of democracy as a method or as a political regime form; it represents an entirely different theoretical track. As Schumpeter rightly pointed out more than 60 years ago, travelling down this path is not desirable, and it is a subject that is today best treated in the so-called Quality of Democracy discussion (see Diamond and

Morlino 2004). This is not really surprising considering that Linz and Stepan focus on the 'consolidation' of democracy rather than on democracy as a political regime when stating this requirement. But my purpose in raising the issue is merely to explain why no attitudinal properties have been deemed relevant for the purpose at hand.

The same objections apply to that distant relative of the attitudinal component: the focus on civil society. The most important contemporary author espousing the 'civil society view' is Robert Putnam (1993, 2000). One sarcastic reference to the Schumpeterian conception of democracy effectively elucidates his (otherwise not very systematically treated) elaboration of the Schumpeterian concept of democracy:

> That democratic self-government requires an actively engaged citizenry has been a truism for centuries. (Not until the middle of the twentieth century did some political theorists begin to assert that good citizenship requires simply choosing among competing teams of politicians at the ballot box, as one might choose among competing brands of toothpaste.)
> (2000: 336)

Once again, the requirement theoretically covers a different aspect. What it is important to emphasize is the extent to which the state secures a free space for such organizational activity (and through Dahl and O'Donnell we have already covered that aspect). Again, what matters is the presence of what has been termed 'the rule of law', not the extent to which people actually engage in independent organizational activities. And hence we end our side trip through the theoretical literature.

With the theoretical discussion of the preceding sections in mind, I have thus far advocated an understanding of liberal democracy that has two requirements: the first is fulfilled by Schumpeter's electoral criterion; the second by the combination of Dahl's criteria concerning free expression and associational autonomy and O'Donnell's criterion of the presence of a rule of law to uphold these rights.

What logically follows from this is that I have conceptualized the political regime form as having two dimensions: one electoral and one liberal. This is the property space that I cover at the level of the systematized concept and it can be captured using two separate classifications. The first concerns the electoral component of democracy. Here, a country either fulfils the Schumpeterian criterion of free and fair elections for political leadership or it does not. The second concerns the liberal component. Here, a country either fulfils the criterion that the state apparatus is capable of upholding certain liberal rights (Dahl) through a rule of law (O'Donnell) or it does not. When fusing these two categorical classifications, a typology covering the political regime form emerges (see Figure 1.3).[15]

Before proceeding, it is necessary to say a few words about the notion of the presence or absence of the the rule of law as a property covering part of the

	+ *Freedom* rights and rule of law	− *Freedom* rights and rule of law
+ *Free and* fair elections	Liberal democracy	Electoral democracy
− *Free and* fair elections	Liberal autocracy	Illiberal autocracy

Figure 1.3 A typology of political regime forms.

serial operations on one of the two attributes of the political regime attribute compound. Collier and Levitsky (1997: 445–6) have proposed that O'Donnell is shifting his background – or 'overarching', as they term it – concept of democracy from 'regime' to 'state' when including the rule of law into his definition. As already mentioned, O'Donnell does in fact attribute the legal characteristics to the state. Yet this does not alter the fact that his main point seems to be that the electoral rights will never be effective without the support of the rule of law. In other words, when following in O'Donnell's footsteps it is possible to retain the Schumpeterian concept of democracy as a political regime form but – as is also done by borrowing from the Dahlian elaboration – add requirements.[16]

Thus, I have developed an analytical scheme that exhausts the background concept and spells out the possible variants in a systematic manner. At this point, a few words on the nomenclature seem appropriate.[17] I have chosen to name the four consequent types 'liberal democracy', 'electoral democracy', 'liberal autocracy' and 'illiberal autocracy'. The two polar types (type 1 and type 4) are easily understandable as they combine either the presence of both the electoral and the liberal property (liberal democracy) or the absence of both properties (illiberal autocracy). Type 2 and type 3 are more complicated matters. Electoral democracy, on the one hand, describes a country in which free elections take place in an illiberal state, i.e. in the absence of freedom rights and the rule of law. This is the species of democracy that

Diamond, O'Donnell and Zakaria perceive to be on the increase. Liberal autocracy, on the other hand, describes a country characterized by liberal constitutionalism but where free elections do not take place. This type was, with certain qualifications due to the more limited scope and/or effectiveness of the rights, a salient phenomenon in nineteenth-century Western Europe. It has been argued that it may re-emerge in the near future (see, for example, Mair 2005 on the EU), but, as we will see, in the present world it is a very rare species.

This typology allows us to capture the electoral and the liberal attributes (each of which can be present or absent) as independent dimensions, i.e. the two dimensions can vary separately. For that very reason, it provides a vehicle for assessing whether an empirical gap between the two dimensions is salient and whether it is increasing. To elaborate, such a gap is salient if the empirical referents found in the type of liberal democracy constitute a relatively low proportion of all the countries that have the attribute of free and fair elections, i.e. the absolute number of referents found in type 1 (liberal democracy) and type 2 (electoral democracy).[18] And the gap is increasing if the number of referents in the type of electoral democracy grows relatively compared with the number of empirical referents in the type of liberal democracy. In what follows, I will use this typological construct to carry out an empirical (re)assessment of Diamond's analysis.

The last thing remaining on this level is to specify the connotative or conceptual definitions of the four types, i.e. to exhaust the attribute space of the typology. On the basis of the preceding sections, I propose the following definitions:

1   *Liberal democracy* is a political regime form that combines i) the presence of free electoral competition for political leadership with ii) the presence of a liberal state upholding certain liberal rights through the rule of law.

2   *Electoral democracy* is a political regime form that combines i) the presence of free electoral competition for political leadership with ii) the absence of a liberal state upholding certain liberal rights through the rule of law.

3   *Liberal autocracy* is a political regime form that combines i) the absence of free electoral competition for political leadership with ii) the presence of a liberal state upholding certain liberal rights through the rule of law.

4   *Illiberal autocracy* is a political regime form that combines i) the absence of free electoral competition for political leadership with ii) the absence of a liberal state upholding certain liberal rights through the rule of law.

Indicators

We have now reached the denotative side of the conceptual coin, i.e. the operational level. Operational definitions (definitions that by themselves incorporate the identification of the empirical referents) are complicated matters, not least within the study of regime change. I follow Sartori (1984: 34) in arguing that the social scientist is faced with three separate operational problems:

1   the border problem (to be settled by denotative definitions);
2   the membership problem (to be settled by precising definitions);
3   the measurability problem (to be settled by operational definitions).

All three problems must, in turn, be tackled.

The border problem

As a first step, I will seek to solve the border problem for each of the four types identified at the level of the systematized concept. I will do so by employing an elaborated version of Dahl's criteria for polyarchy. Luckily, it is only necessary to recast (i.e. expand) the denotative definitions with one category: the rule of law. Instead of coming up with my own formulation, I will use O'Donnell's (2001: 24) aforementioned criterion, viz. whether '[. . .] the legal system enacts and backs – at least – the rights included in the definition of a democratic regime and prevents anyone from being *de legibus solutus*'. This criterion can be added to the Dahlian list, as demonstrated in Figure 1.4.

The membership problem

Having solved this problem, I proceed by targeting the membership problem. What is necessary here is to ensure that all scrutinized countries or cases will fit logically into the proposed typology and, by extension, that the types and underlying classes are mutually exclusive. Crossing self-imposed conceptual thresholds is oftentimes a somewhat arbitrary matter. What are we to do in the present case?

Sheer common sense tells us that it is only meaningful to classify a country as either having an electoral democracy or a liberal state if the requirements pertaining to this dimension are more fulfilled than they are violated. This brings me to the following precising definitions with respect to the four types:

1   *Liberal democracy* is a political regime form where both the former four criteria and the latter four criteria are more fulfilled than violated.

1. Elected officials	Control over government decisions about policy is constitutionally vested in elected officials.
2. Free and fair elections	Elected officials are chosen in the frequent and fairly conducted elections in which coercion is comparatively uncommon.
3. Inclusive suffrage	Practically all adults have the right to vote in the election of officials.
4. Right to run for office	Practically all adults have the right to run for elective offices in the government, though age limits may be higher for holding office than for the suffrage.
5. Freedom of expression	Citizens have a right to express themselves without the danger of severe punishment on political matters broadly defined, including criticism of officials, the government, the regime, the socio-economic order and the prevailing ideology.
6. Alternative information	Citizens have a right to seek out alternative sources of information. Alternative sources of information exist and are protected by laws.
7. Associational autonomy	To achieve their various rights, including those listed above, citizens also have a right to form relatively independent associations or organizations, including independent political parties and interest groups.
8. The rule of law	The legal system enacts and backs, at least, the rights included in the definition of a democratic regime and prevents anyone from being *de legibus solutus*.

Figure 1.4 The elaborated Dahlian model.

2   *Electoral democracy* is a political regime form where the former four criteria are more fulfilled than violated, whereas the latter four criteria are more violated than fulfilled.

3   *Liberal autocracy* is a political regime form where the former four criteria are more violated than fulfilled, whereas the latter four criteria are more fulfilled than violated.

4   *Illiberal autocracy* is a political regime form where both the former four and the latter four criteria are more violated than fulfilled.

The measurability problem

Finally, it is necessary to solve, or at least settle, the measurability problem. What is at stake here is both the validity and the reliability of the scoring. A high validity will only be achieved insofar as it is meaningful to claim that the data employed measure the eight criteria listed above (and, thus, the overarching systematized concept). A high reliability requires that the data employed actually measure what they posit to measure.

The claim that I intend to defend here is that the Freedom House ratings of 'political rights' and 'civil liberties' will serve me better than any available alternative. This assertion sounds somewhat defensive. It does so because using the Freedom House ratings to measure 'democracy' is very much a point of controversy within the democratization literature (see, in particular, Munck and Verkuilen 2002).

Concerning the reliability of the data, the ratings are without doubt more reliable than anything I would be able to produce on my own, especially since I need diachronic data. More to the point, the validity of the alternative indices of democracy differ more from my definition than those of Freedom House do. To give but one example, the POLITY IV index, which has been hailed as one of the best on the marketplace, does not directly touch upon the criteria of the rule of law and civil liberties. To quote from the POLITY IV data users' manual:

> Democracy is conceived as three essential, interdependent elements. One is the presence of institutions and procedures through which citizens can express effective preferences about alternative policies and leaders. Second is the existence of institutionalized constraints on the exercise of power by the executive. Third is the guarantee of civil liberties to all citizens in their daily lives and in acts of political participation. *Other aspects of plural democracy, such as the rule of law, systems of checks and balances, freedom of the press, and so on are means to, or specific manifestations of, these general principles. We do not include coded data on civil liberties.*
>
> (Marshall and Jaggers 2002: 12, my emphasis)

In other words, the issue of the validity of the data favours the Freedom House ratings.[19] This index is divided into questions concerning two dimensions: one covering political rights and one covering civil liberties. To describe this distinction, a quotation from Karatnycky (2003: 102) – the president of Freedom House – will suffice:

> A country grants its citizens political rights when it permits them to form political parties that represent a significant range of voter choice and whose leaders can compete for and be elected to positions of power in government. A country upholds its citizens' civil liberties when it respects and protects their religious, ethnic, economic, linguistic, and other rights, including gender and family rights, personal freedoms, and freedoms of press, belief, and association.

This separation is well suited for my purposes because it mirrors the distinction between the electoral and the liberal dimensions captured by the typology crafted above. In fact, the Freedom House index is built around a number of questions that are remarkably like my elaborated Dahlian criteria (cf. Figure 1.4). Consequently, the index captures the respective properties emphasized by Schumpeter, Dahl and O'Donnell.

Having said that, on both the electoral and the liberal dimensions the Freedom House questions go somewhat beyond these properties. For instance, to measure the attribute of political rights questions on whether the government is accountable to the electorate between the elections and whether the government is free from pervasive corruption are included. Likewise, to measure the attribute of civil liberties questions concerning personal autonomy and other more private rights are included. None of these properties are relevant for my purposes, and they do of course weaken the validity of using the measure to order the cases within my typology. However, these particular validity problems do not undermine the general distinction between an electoral and a liberal dimension, and I will ignore them in the following analysis. Using the Freedom House ratings has one further great advantage: it will allow me to compare my findings with those of Diamond since he, too, employs these figures. Note that this is in itself a weighty (albeit pragmatic) argument favouring the choice of the Freedom House ratings.

I will let my two dimensions of democracy be covered by the corresponding two dimensions of the Freedom House ratings. The electoral dimension will be measured using the values for political rights; the liberal dimension will be measured using the values for civil liberties. My precising definitions rest on the conceptual claim that in order to qualify as having free and fair elections and freedom rights and the rule of law, respectively, the foursome of criteria pertaining to each of these dimensions should be more fulfilled than violated. But what are the consequent thresholds?

The Freedom House ratings assign scores between 1 and 7 on both the electoral and the liberal dimensions of democracy, with 1 indicating the highest degree of 'freedom'. With regard to their own classification of political regime forms, the most important cut-off point is situated at 2.5 (on the average value of political rights and civil liberties). This threshold separates 'free' countries from 'partly free' countries and it is the threshold that Diamond relied on in *Developing Democracy*.

I cannot rely upon this scheme as I seek to order on two equally important dimensions that must carry equal weight. Two requirements must thus be observed. First, I must have the same threshold on both attributes. Second, a country must pass each of these thresholds to reach the type of 'liberal democracy'. The question is, however, whether I should choose the value of 3 or 2 as the threshold on each of the dimensions. As touched upon earlier, in some of his more recent pieces Larry Diamond has changed his threshold. Whereas he relied upon the Freedom House's cut-off point between free and partly free in *Developing Democracy*, he now only lets countries scoring 2 or better on both political rights and civil liberties obtain the predicate of liberal democracy. Diamond's argument is that this is necessary to avoid classifying countries with severe political shortcomings as liberal democracies. He makes a convincing case for this and I will follow in his footsteps on this point. This brings us to the following operational definitions:[20]

1   *Liberal democracy* is a political regime form in which both the former four criteria and the latter four criteria carry an average value that equals or is less than 2 when using the values of political rights and civil liberties reported by the Freedom House.
2   *Electoral democracy* is a political regime form in which the former four criteria carry an average value that equals or is less than 2, whereas the latter four criteria carry an average value of more than 2 when using the values of political rights and civil liberties reported by the Freedom House.
3   *Liberal autocracy* is a political regime form in which the former four criteria carry an average value of more than 2, whereas the latter four criteria carry an average value that equals or is less than 2 when using the values of political rights and civil liberties reported by the Freedom House.
4   *Illiberal autocracy* is a political regime form in which both the former four criteria and the latter four criteria carry an average value of more than 2 when using the values of political rights and civil liberties reported by the Freedom House.

A reappraisal of the third wave of democracy

It is time to return to Diamond's empirical observations concerning the gap between electoral and liberal democracy in the 1990s. I will (re)test his claim in two empirical contexts, viz. the global setting and the post-communist subset, respectively. The first test will clarify the general validity of Diamond's conclusions. The second test will examine whether the conclusions are valid with respect to the explanandum of this book.

In doing so, I will solely employ his original analysis – the one from *Developing Democracy* – for two reasons. First, as already argued, his elaborated typology basically suffers from the same logical problem of mixing together the two dimensions of democracy. Second, and more pragmatically, his original edifice is that which is easiest to compare with my typology because it contains fewer quasi-types or classes.

The global setting

A typological comparison

Diamond's empirical claim about the gap is not based on an actual comparison between the two quasi-types of liberal democracy and electoral democracy. Rather, he employs a proxy, namely Freedom House's distinction between 'free states' (i.e. liberal democracies) and 'formal democracies' (i.e. electoral democracies).[21] Referring to these data, he (1999: 28) points out that,

> [a]s a proportion of all the world's democracies, free states declined from 85 percent in 1990 to 65 percent in 1997 [. . .] The proportion inched back up to 69 percent in 1997 (and close to 75 percent in 1998). But it remains to be seen whether this is a harbinger of a new trend of democratic deepening or just oscillation within a new equilibrium.

The data series that he refers to are presented in Table 1.1, adapted from his own account.

Table 1.1 Diamond's account of political regime forms, 1990–7

	Formal democracies (N, %)	Free states/liberal democracies (N, %)	Free states as percentage of formal democracies	Total N
1990	76 (46.1)	65 (39.4)	85.5	165
1991	91 (49.7)	76 (41.5)	83.5	183
1992	99 (53.2)	75 (40.3)	75.8	186
1993	108 (56.8)	72 (37.9)	66.7	190
1994	114 (59.7)	76 (39.8)	66.7	191
1995	117 (61.3)	76 (39.8)	65.0	191
1996	118 (61.8)	79 (41.4)	67.0	191
1997	117 (61.3)	81 (42.4)	69.2	191

Source: Adapted from Diamond 1999: 28.

Table 1.2 The alternative account of political regime forms, 1990–7

	Liberal democracies (N, %)	Electoral democracies (N, %)	Liberal autocracies (N, %)	Illiberal autocracies (N, %)	Liberal democracies as percentage of all electoral democracies	Total N
1990	51 (30.9)	14 (8.5)	2 (1.2)	98 (59.4)	78.5	165
1991	52 (28.3)	26 (14.1)	1 (0.5)	105 (57.1)	66.7	184
1992	57 (30.6)	19 (10.2)	3 (1.6)	107 (57.5)	75.0	186
1993	57 (30.0)	19 (10.0)	1 (0.5)	113 (59.5)	75.0	190
1994	57 (29.8)	22 (11.5)	2 (1.0)	110 (57.6)	72.2	191
1995	63 (33.0)	18 (9.4)	0 (0.0)	110 (57.6)	77.8	191
1996	64 (33.5)	22 (11.5)	0 (0.0)	105 (55.0)	74.4	191
1997	64 (33.5)	21 (11.0)	0 (0.0)	106 (55.5)	75.3	191

Table 1.1 clearly demonstrates that the gap between free states (i.e. liberal democracies) and formal democracies (i.e. electoral democracies) was widening throughout the 1990s. But what happens when the Freedom House numbers are reanalysed using the fourfold typology conceptualized in this paper? The corresponding figures are depicted in Table 1.2.

Three trends are worth elucidating. First, at the outset liberal democracies constitute a lower proportion of all electoral democracies (i.e. of all countries that have free and fair elections) in my edifice than when relying on Diamond's analysis: 78.5 per cent as opposed to 85.5 per cent. But then the relationship is turned upside down from 1993 onwards. Whereas Diamond's numbers hit a rock bottom of 65 per cent in 1995, my numbers only reach 72.2 per cent in 1994.

Second, and more importantly, according to my typology there is no increasing gap between the number of referents in the type of 'electoral democracy' and the type of 'liberal democracy' in the period 1990–7. With the sole exception of 1991 – the ultimate year of political change[22] – liberal democracies as a proportion of all electoral democracies are fixed close to 75 per cent throughout the period.

Third, pure electoral democracies are not a very common species. In absolute numbers, the membership of this political regime form only oscillates from a low of 14 in 1990 to a high of 26 in 1991; from then on it hovers around 20. Related to this, I find some liberal autocracies in most of this period, ranging from a high of three in 1992 to a low nil in 1995, 1996 and 1997. The scant membership and volatile nature of the 'liberal autocracy' type go to show that this is not a stable political regime form. But neither is electoral democracy. It is in fact very difficult to find stable specimens of either of these two types over the period in question.

What emerges from these differences? When the electoral and the liberal dimensions of liberal democracy are systematically conceptualized as independent of each other, Diamond's increasing gap does not exist.

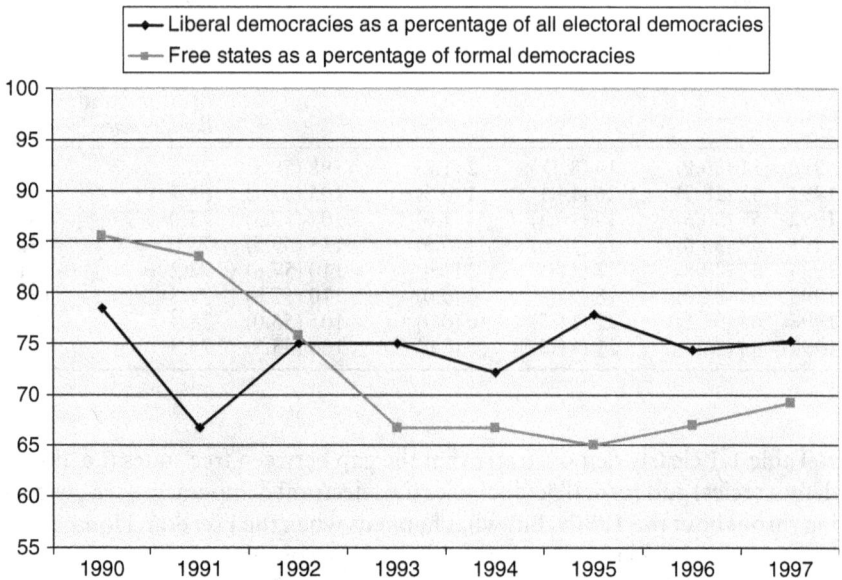

Figure 1.5 Comparing the two analyses of the empirical gap.

Throughout the period in question, the countries almost always move in the same direction on both the electoral and the liberal dimensions. True, there are exceptions to this pattern, but they are indeed exceptions. Figure 1.5 depicts the observed misfit between the two empirical appraisals of the gap.

Table 1.3 The alternative account of political regime forms, 1998–2007

	Liberal democracies (N, %)	Electoral democracies (N, %)	Liberal autocracies (N, %)	Illiberal autocracies (N, %)	Liberal democracies as percentage of all electoral democracies	Total N
1998	64 (33.5)	24 (12.6)	1 (0.5)	102 (53.4)	72.7	191
1999	67 (34.9)	19 (9.9)	0 (0.0)	106 (55.2)	77.9	192
2000	69 (35.9)	19 (9.9)	1 (0.5)	103 (53.6)	78.4	192
2001	66 (34.4)	20 (10.4)	2 (1.0)	104 (54.2)	76.7	192
2002	72 (37.5)	15 (7.8)	3 (1.6)	102 (53.1)	82.8	192
2003	75 (39.1)	11 (5.7)	3 (1.6)	103 (53.6)	87.2	192
2004	76 (39.6)	11 (5.7)	2 (1.0)	103 (53.6)	87.4	192
2005	79 (41.1)	7 (3.6)	3 (1.6)	103 (53.6)	91.9	192
2006	78 (40.2)	10 (5.2)	3 (1.5)	103 (53.1)	88.6	194
2007	78 (40.4)	10 (5.2)	2 (1.0)	103 (53.4)	88.6	193

Diamond did not have the possibility of analysing the subsequent years of 1998–2007.[23] What happens if we extend the analysis to this period? The empirical distribution of Table 1.3 appears.

As can be seen, the gap between electoral and liberal democracies has shrunk significantly in the new millennium. Since 2000, liberal democracies as a proportion of all electoral democracies have risen above the former pinnacle of 78.5 per cent in 1990, even clearly surpassing it since 2002. Also, and related to this, the number of purely electoral democracies has hit a low of around ten in the most recent years.

The empirical conclusion of the typological exercise is therefore twofold. First, the orderings on the electoral and the liberal dimensions overwhelmingly co-vary (i.e. not much of a gap exists). Second, even the limited differences between the two are not on the rise in the period of 1990–2007; the gap actually decreases. In other words, the conclusion is that there is no increasing number of countries in which free elections take place in an illiberal state, neither absolutely nor relatively.

One may, however, object that the crude thresholds used to separate the classes on each of the dimensions could disguise the actual differences between the scores on the electoral and the liberal dimensions. After all, none of the previous taxonomical orderings allow us to make any distinction between a country scoring 3 and a country scoring 7 on either of the two dimensions. In both instances, the properties are absent.

To appreciate this point, I will retest the empirical conclusions by statistically correlating the respective Freedom House scores of 'political rights' (the electoral dimension) and 'civil liberties' (the liberal dimension), i.e. by treating the differences on each dimension as differences of degree only. A twofold conclusion appears. First, Pearson's r,[24] measuring the global relationship between political rights and civil liberties, is situated between 0.907 and 0.952 throughout the period in question (1990–2007). This is a very strong correlation which shows that the scores on the two dimensions normally go hand in hand. Second, there is only a slight drop in the late 1990s and the highest correlations are found at the end of the period, demonstrating that the relationship is strengthening over time.

This assertion needs to be qualified on one account, however. A modest fall is visible after 2005 as Pearson's r decreases from 0.952 in that year to 0.943 in 2007. The small setback is mirrored in the above typological analysis in which the liberal democracies as a percentage of all electoral democracies declined from 91.9 per cent to 88.6 per cent in this period. This recent negative change does not question – or even alter – the general conclusions of the empirical analysis of this chapter. However, it is nevertheless interesting and I will return to it in Chapter 2. What is important here, however, is that the statistical investigation corroborates the findings of the taxonomical exercises: the countries almost always travel in the same direction on both of the two dimensions and that this co-variation has increased, not decreased, over time.

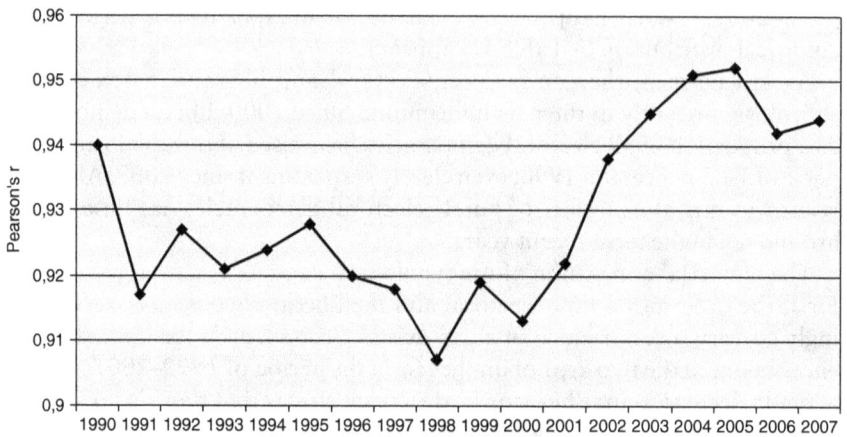

Figure 1.6 The bivariate correlations between 'political rights' and 'civil liberties', 1990–2005.

The post-communist setting

One thing needs to be settled before we can dismiss the empirical value of the theoretical distinction between the electoral and liberal dimensions of liberal democracy. The world's a stage, but it is not the stage of this book. The empirical context covered herein is limited to the post-communist countries. The distinction between the electoral and the liberal component may, of course, capture important dividing lines in the post-communist setting even though it does not do so on the global level.

This must be checked. However, to keep this chapter from becoming too tedious, I will solely carry out the typological exercise this time. Table 1.4 repeats the investigation of political regime forms in the post-communist quarter only. (Recall that I deliberately exclude Bosnia-Herzegovina and Serbia-Montenegro.) What do the numbers show?

Table 1.4, which depicts the development in the period 1990–2007, gives rise to two observations. First, we see that there is no increasing gap between liberal and electoral democracy in the 1990s. Strikingly parallel to the global level, the year 1991 is the only exception to this pattern. The genesis of so many post-communist countries in that year created a situation in which liberal democracies were outnumbered two-to-one by their electoral counterparts. After 1991, however, the situation reversed as the liberal democracies have outnumbered the electoral democracies by at least two-to-one. The dominance of the liberal democracies is a trifle lower than that found at the global level, but the important thing is that the gap is not on the rise.

Table 1.4 The alternative typological account of political regime forms in the post-communist setting, 1990–2007

	Liberal democracies (N, %)	Electoral democracies (N, %)	Liberal autocracies (N, %)	Illiberal autocracies (N, %)	Liberal democracies as percentage of all electoral democracies	Total N
1990	3 (37.5)	0 (0.0)	0 (0.0)	5 (62.5)	100.0	8
1991	3 (12.5)	6 (25.0)	0 (0.0)	15 (62.5)	33.3	24
1992	4 (16.0)	2 (8.0)	2 (8.0)	17 (68.0)	66.7	25
1993	5 (19.2)	3 (11.5)	1 (3.8)	17 (65.4)	62.5	26
1994	5 (19.2)	3 (11.5)	2 (7.7)	16 (61.5)	62.5	26
1995	8 (30.8)	2 (7.7)	0 (0.0)	16 (61.5)	80.0	26
1996	7 (26.9)	4 (15.4)	0 (0.0)	15 (57.7)	63.6	26
1997	8 (30.8)	3 (11.5)	0 (0.0)	15 (57.7)	72.7	26
1998	9 (34.6)	3 (11.5)	0 (0.0)	14 (53.8)	75.0	26
1999	9 (34.6)	3 (11.5)	0 (0.0)	14 (53.8)	75.0	26
2000	9 (34.6)	4 (15.4)	0 (0.0)	13 (50.0)	69.2	26
2001	10 (38.5)	3 (11.5)	0 (0.0)	13 (50.0)	76.9	26
2002	12 (46.2)	0 (0.0)	0 (0.0)	14 (53.8)	100.0	26
2003	12 (46.2)	0 (0.0)	0 (0.0)	14 (53.8)	100.0	26
2004	11 (42.3)	0 (0.0)	1 (3.8)	14 (53.8)	100.0	26
2005	12 (46.2)	0 (0.0)	1 (3.8)	13 (50.0)	100.0	26
2006	12 (46.2)	0 (0.0)	1 (3.8)	13 (50.0)	100.0	26
2007	12 (46.2)	0 (0.0)	1 (3.8)	13 (50.0)	100.0	26

Second, in the 2000s we find a pattern reminiscent of, but more clearly marked than, that identified on the global level. The illiberal autocracies are able to hold their own: their proportion never falls below 50 per cent. But the liberal democracies are the only democracies left standing at the end of the period: as a proportion of all democracies they reach 100 per cent in the period of 2002–7. Over time, the post-communist countries simply move toward, and clump in, the two extremes. In other words, the electoral democracies die out in the new millennium; their extinction mirrors the victory of their liberal counterparts.

To sum up, although we find a different distribution of political regime forms in the post-communist microcosm of the third wave universe, we find very much the same trends. Hence we find no differences with regard to any gap between electoral and liberal democracies. With this in mind, it is time to gather the threads.

Concluding on the gap between electoral and liberal democracies

In this chapter, I have attempted to develop a conceptualization capable of making a systematic distinction between the electoral and the liberal components of so-called 'liberal' or 'modern' democracy. This conceptualization and the subsequent empirical analysis of the third wave of democratization follow in the footsteps of that crafted by Larry Diamond in *Developing Democracy*. However, I part ways with Diamond by operationalizing the electoral and liberal dimensions as different attributes which are independent of each other.

To do this theoretically, I have departed from Schumpeter's classical electoral definition, yet I have maintained his emphasis on democracy as a method. Assisted by Dahl's notion of polyarchy and O'Donnell's focus on a liberal state capable of upholding the rule of law, I have arrived at a fourfold typology of political regime forms. In emphasizing both the electoral and the liberal element of democracy, this typology exhausts the dependent variable of the political regime form.

When I reanalyse the period placed under scrutiny by Diamond (i.e. 1990–7), I find myself forced to qualify his conclusions concerning the current – and, in particular, the illiberal – undertow of the third wave. Treated as independent attributes, the gap between the electoral and the liberal components is not on the increase – neither globally nor with regard to the post-communist subset. This pattern is only strengthened in the subsequent period (i.e. 1998–2007), where it is more or less disappearing. Otherwise said, Diamond's pivotal type of 'electoral democracy' makes up a Procrustean bed, which the empirical referents can only lie down in if their heads are chopped off.

To a large extent, the same logical flaw seems to lie behind the aforementioned observations of Guillermo O'Donnell[25] and Fareed Zakaria (on

Zakaria, see Appendix 1.2). The conceptual conclusion is, therefore, inescapable. If we are to operate with two independent dimensions of democracy (i.e. one electoral and one liberal) and if we trust that the Freedom House ratings actually measure what they claim to measure, then there is no increasing gap between the electoral and the liberal components of democracy – and there has not really been one during the latest two decades. To be sure, these are big 'ifs'. However, the result of the analysis should still be noted because a lot of recent writings on democracy, which do in fact accept these 'ifs', obscure these empirical facts as they do not pay heed to the taxonomical logic.

To drive the conclusion home, the corrective to the conventional wisdom about a gap between electoral and liberal democracies presented in the preceding analyses is not a product of employing different thresholds. Rather, it is the product of keeping conceptually independent dimensions empirically independent (as they must be, according to the underlying systematized concept). This is, arguably, what makes this chapter's categorization more valid than that of Larry Diamond.

All of this can be appreciated by paraphrasing Shakespeare: although the distinction between the electoral and liberal components of democracy may be full of sound and fury conceptually, empirically it has lately been signifying nothing. Doing better with regard to one element most often means doing better with regard to the other.

Appendix 1.1

Counting rules for the typology of political regime forms

With a Freedom House ratings threshold of 2 on both the electoral dimension ('political rights') and its liberal equivalent ('civil liberties'), the counting rules of my typology are very simple.

A Freedom House score that:

- equals or is lower than 2 on both political rights and civil liberties provides for the political regime form of 'liberal democracy' [+ electoral property; + liberal property] for any given country;
- equals or is lower than 2 on political rights but higher than 2 on civil liberties provides for 'electoral democracy' [+ electoral property; – liberal property] for any given country;
- is higher than 2 on political rights but that equals or is lower than 2 on civil liberties provides for 'liberal autocracy' [– electoral property; + liberal property] for any given country;
- is higher than 2 on both political rights and civil liberties provides for 'illiberal autocracy' [– electoral property; – liberal property] for any given country.

The first four empirical examples from the data series:
Afghanistan 1990 (PR = 7; CL = 7): Illiberal Autocracy
Antigua and Barbuda 1990 (PR = 3; CL = 2): Liberal Autocracy
Argentina 1990 (PR = 1; CL = 3): Electoral Democracy
Australia 1990 (PR = 1; CL = 1): Liberal Democracy

Appendix 1.2

A critical note on 'The Rise of Illiberal Democracy'

In 1997, Fareed Zakaria published the oft-cited article 'The Rise of Illiberal Democracy' in *Foreign Affairs*. In the article, an early version of his influential book, *The Future of Freedom* (2003), Zakaria carefully develops a conceptual distinction between the electoral and the liberal components of liberal democracy. The electoral attribute is construed as 'free and fair elections', whereas the liberal equivalent – what he also terms 'constitutional liberalism' – includes 'the rule of law, a separation of powers, and the protection of basic liberties of speech assembly, religion and property'.

Bearing this distinction in mind, Zakaria (1997: 23) eloquently notes that '[t]oday the two strands of liberal democracy, interwoven in the Western political fabric, are coming apart in the rest of the world. Democracy is flourishing; constitutional liberalism is not'. On the basis of this inductive observation, Zakaria reaches two deductive theoretical conclusions. First, that the consequent new illiberal species of democracy is relatively stable (it constitutes a dysfunctional equilibrium, so to speak). Second, that the increase in 'illiberal democracies' that took place in the 1990s is a harbinger of what is to come. Zakaria (1997: 24) touches upon both of these points in the following sentences:

> Illiberal democracy is a growth industry [. . .] And to date few illiberal democracies have matured into liberal democracies; if anything, they are moving toward heightened illiberalism. Far from being a temporary or transitional stage, it appears that many countries are settling onto a form of government that mixes a substantial degree of democracy with a substantial degree of illiberalism.

In this short appendix, I will reassess Zakaria's conceptual treatment of the electoral and liberal attributes and his consequent empirical analysis, just as I have done with Diamond's in Chapter 1 proper. The aim is to probe i) whether what Zakaria terms 'illiberal democracy' – when operationalized systematically – was in fact on the rise in the 1990s and ii) whether it has been on the rise (i.e. whether it has indeed established itself as a new species of democracy) since Zakaria's contribution was published in 1997.

A conceptual critique

Zakaria (1997: 23) uses the Freedom House ratings to illustrate 'the rise of illiberal democracy'. His point of departure is that the '[. . .] separate ratings for political liberties and civil liberties [. . .] correspond roughly with democracy and constitutional liberalism, respectively'. Visiting the Freedom House

Survey of 1997, which covers the year of 1996, Zakaria (1997: 24) finds that still more 'democratizing' countries are faring worse on the latter, liberal dimension than on the former, electoral dimension, culminating at the time of writing: 'Of the countries that lie between confirmed dictatorship and consolidated democracy, 50 per cent do better on political liberties than on civil ones. In other words, half of the "democratizing" countries in the world today are illiberal democracies'.

Zakaria spells out his operationalization of democratizing states and illiberal democracy in an associated footnote. In brief, he has added up the Freedom House ratings on 'political rights' and 'civil liberties' (both 7-point scales), thus creating a one-dimensional index which ranges from a low of 2 (the highest degree of freedom) to a high of 14 (the lowest degree of freedom). Zakaria considers any country scoring between 5 and 10 to be democratizing. Half of these are then, to reiterate, illiberal democracies in the 1997 survey because their political rights scores are better (i.e. lower) than their civil liberties scores.

Let us try to reflect a bit on this conceptual exercise. As already emphasized, Zakaria deliberately advances a purely electoral definition of democracy. The noun 'democracy', on the one hand, thus denotes the presence of free and fair elections and nothing else. The adjective 'liberal', on the other hand, denotes the presence of constitutional liberalism, particularly the rule of law and certain freedom rights. If a country has both the electoral and the liberal attributes, then it is a liberal democracy. If it only has the electoral attribute, then it is an illiberal democracy.

This means that any country scoring between 5 and 10 (when adding up the two attributes) is considered to be a democracy by Zakaria. Otherwise, it is not possible to identify illiberal democracies within this terrain. That is almost exactly the class that Freedom House terms 'partly free' and almost exactly the class that I term 'hybrid regime' in Chapter 2. Since democracy, to Zakaria, basically denotes the presence of the electoral attribute, this means that these countries are posited as having, at least to a large extent, free and fair elections.

That seems faulty considering that this class (in the survey covering 1996 that Zakaria employs) contains countries such as Burkina Faso (PR = 5, CL = 4), Eritrea (PR = 6, CL = 4), Gabon (PR = 5, CL = 4), Kuwait (PR = 5, CL = 5), Morocco (PR = 5, CL = 5), Tanzania (PR = 5, CL = 5), Zambia (PR = 5, CL = 4) and Zimbabwe (PR = 5, CL =5). None of these countries figure on the Freedom House's own, rather lax list of electoral democracies for the same year. There is one very good reason for that: they do not, according to any meaningful criterion, have free and fair elections.

These are only the most extreme particular examples, but the point I wish to make here is a more general one: that Zakaria commits a clear case of conceptual stretching by subsuming empirical referents under a concept that does not cover these by his own definition (i.e. free and fair elections) when he uses the term 'illiberal democracy' to cover some of the referents in this class.[26] Arguably, he is merely showing that many of the countries that are hybrid regimes, not democracies, do better on the electoral dimension than the liberal dimension in 1996. The conceptual stretching is then further enhanced in the text where Zakaria discusses a number of countries which are not even covered by Freedom House's class of 'partly free' as examples of illiberal democracies (e.g. Iran, Kazakhstan and Belarus); he acknowledges this himself in the aforementioned footnote.[27]

That is not the only conceptual problem. The other, equally salient one is that Zakaria, too, uses a one-dimensional classification to identify democratizing states by collapsing the electoral and the liberal attributes. Otherwise said, the democratic merits are determined on the aggregate score of 'electoralness' and 'liberalness'. But recall that Zakaria makes a clear distinction between these two components of liberal democracy and emphasizes that democracy rests on an electoral criterion only. If he were to follow a stringent logic of conceptualization, then he would, arguably, end up with a fourfold typological edifice mirroring that crafted in Chapter 1: a compound made of electoral and a liberal dimensions, thus creating a property space of the four types of 'liberal democracy', 'illiberal democracy',[28] 'liberal autocracy' and 'illiberal autocracy'.

Following Zakaria, whether a country is an electoral democracy here only depends upon the presence or absence of the electoral component of free and fair elections. Likewise, whether a country is characterized by 'constitutional liberalism' only depends upon the presence or absence of the electoral component of rule of law and freedom rights.

This typological construct provides a pivot for checking whether illiberal democracy is, relatively speaking, on the rise in a given period. If this is the case then the empirical referents in type 2 (illiberal democracy) should increase as a proportion of the empirical referents in type 1 (liberal democracy) and type 2 taken together, i.e. of all the countries that are electoral democracies. The Freedom House ratings can once again be employed as indicator. 'Political rights' cover the electoral component, whereas the 'civil liberties' cover the liberal component. As in Chapter 1, the threshold of 2 in the Freedom House ratings of political rights and civil liberties is used to denote the presence of the electoral and the liberal properties, respectively.

Let us, with this twofold conceptual critique in mind, revisit the empirics to see if Zakaria's observations about the increase of illiberal democracy did really play out in the 1990s and whether it has increased in the 2000s. To do so I will employ both Zakaria's own operationalization and the alternative one that is built up around my conceptual critique.

An empirical re-evaluation

In Table 1.5 I have extended Zakaria's analysis both back in time (to 1990) and into the present (to 2007). What can we say about the dynamics of what

Table 1.5 Redoing Zakaria's analysis, 1990–2007

	Democratizing states	Democratizing states with PR < CL	Democratizing states with PR > CL	Democratizing states with PR = CL	Democratizing states with PR < CL as % of all democratizing states
1990	54	18	16	20	33.3
1991	76	31	21	24	40.8
1992	76	29	23	24	38.2
1993	71	34	11	26	47.9
1994	74	38	14	22	51.4
1995	71	32	12	27	45.1
1996	70	35	12	23	50.0
1997	70	34	14	22	48.6
1998	75	36	19	20	48.0
1999	73	33	12	28	45.2
2000	65	29	12	24	44.6
2001	69	28	13	28	40.6
2002	69	25	12	32	36.2
2003	67	17	15	35	25.4
2004	66	16	17	33	24.2
2005	68	12	20	36	17.6
2006	71	20	22	29	28.2
2007	72	18	23	31	25.0

Note
PR = Political rights; CL = Civil liberties.

Zakaria terms 'democratizing states' (i.e. roughly the countries belonging to Freedom House's class of 'partly free')?

We see that the number of what Zakaria terms 'democratizing states' has been rather stable, only oscillating between a low of 65 and a high of 76 in the entire period of 1991–2007.[29] The number of democratizing states doing better on political rights than civil liberties (Zakaria's 'illiberal democracies') has not been very stable in the same period, however. In absolute terms, the number has oscillated between 36 (1998) and 12 (2005). In relative terms, i.e. as a proportion of all democratizing states, the oscillation is also very large: from a high of 51 per cent in 1994 to a low of 18 per cent in 2005.

Two points can be made with regard to these trends. First, they underline that the illiberal species of democracy – which, using Zakaria's conceptualization, is really a species of hybrid regime – is not a stable political regime form over the period; no dysfunctional equilibrium seems to exist in this grey zone between democracy proper and autocracy proper. Second, it turns out that 'illiberalness' of these countries has not been on the rise since Zakaria vented his warning; rather, it has clearly been on the wane. In the period 2004–7 countries that do better on civil liberties (the liberal attribute) even outnumber those doing better on political rights (the electoral attribute).

The drop in illiberal democracies became quite salient as early as 2002. It thus seems to be a bit of an overstatement when Zakaria (2003: 99), having scrupulously noted that the number is on the decrease, remarks that '[s]till, as of this writing close to half of the "democratizing" countries in the world are illiberal democracies'. On one account Zakaria was right, though. The illiberal democracies did grow as a proportion of all democratizing states in the period leading up to the publication of his 1997 article. But does this conclusion hold if we instead use the alternative conceptualization of the typology of political regime forms?

Table 1.6 shows that the number denoting illiberal democracies as a proportion of all electoral democracies was in fact a very stable one during the period 1990–7. With the sole exception of 1991, it lay relatively close to 25 per cent. In plain English, when the electoral and illiberal attributes are kept conceptually independent of each other, we do not really find any rise of illiberal democracy over the period. Furthermore, the figures show the tendency also evinced in the prior extension of Zakaria's analysis: the relative frequency has been very much on the wane since the late 1990s, albeit with a minor increase at the very end of the period (2006 and 2007).

Thus, once again, we see that the gap – which is, to reiterate, really a hybrid regimes gap in Zakaria's case – dissolves over time. This conclusion very much echoes the one I arrived at when revisiting Diamond's analysis from *Developing Democracy*.

Table 1.6 The alternative typological account of political regime forms, 1990–2005

	Liberal democracies (N, %)	Electoral democracies (N, %)	Liberal autocracies (N, %)	Illiberal autocracies (N, %)	Liberal democracies as percentage of all electoral democracies	Total N
1990	51 (30.9)	14 (8.5)	2 (1.2)	98 (59.4)	21.5	165
1991	52 (28.3)	26 (14.1)	1 (0.5)	105 (57.1)	33.3	184
1992	57 (30.7)	19 (10.2)	3 (1.6)	107 (57.5)	25.0	186
1993	57 (30.0)	19 (10.0)	1 (0.5)	113 (59.5)	25.0	190
1994	57 (29.8)	22 (11.5)	2 (1.1)	110 (57.6)	27.8	191
1995	63 (33.0)	18 (9.4)	0 (0.0)	110 (57.6)	22.2	191
1996	64 (33.5)	22 (11.5)	0 (0.0)	105 (55.0)	25.6	191
1997	64 (33.5)	21 (11.0)	0 (0.0)	106 (55.5)	24.7	191
1998	64 (33.5)	24 (12.6)	1 (0.5)	102 (53.4)	27.3	191
1999	67 (34.9)	19 (9.9)	0 (0.0)	106 (55.2)	22.1	192
2000	69 (35.9)	19 (9.9)	1 (0.5)	103 (53.6)	21.6	192
2001	66 (34.4)	20 (10.4)	2 (1.0)	104 (54.2)	23.3	192
2002	72 (37.5)	15 (7.8)	3 (1.6)	102 (53.1)	17.2	192
2003	75 (39.1)	11 (5.7)	3 (1.6)	103 (53.6)	12.8	192
2004	76 (39.6)	11 (5.7)	2 (1.0)	103 (53.6)	12.6	192
2005	79 (41.1)	7 (3.6)	3 (1.6)	103 (53.6)	8.1	192
2006	78 (40.2)	10 (5.2)	3 (1.5)	103 (53.1)	11.4	194
2007	78 (40.4)	10 (5.2)	2 (1.0)	103 (53.4)	11.4	193

2 The post-communist tripartition described

The paradoxical conclusion of Chapter 1 is that a conceptualization that is actually able to appreciate the distinction between the electoral and the liberal components of democracy is worth little empirically. Beyond the finding that there is no gap between the electoral and liberal dimensions, the constructed typology tells us precious little about the political dynamics on the ground. The reason is straightforward: while the polar type of 'liberal democracy' is empirically useful, its opposite number – the polar type of 'illiberal autocracy' – becomes a residual category which contains a large number of countries that have very little in common politically. By implication, the only gap elucidated by the preceding analysis seems to be between stable liberal democracies on the one hand and countries moving to and fro between all the three other types in the typology – or at least staying within the 'lower' regions of the illiberal autocracy type – on the other hand.

It is really this gap that Diamond homes in on. In his reading of the numbers, it becomes a gap between electoral and liberal democracies because these two quasi-types are operationalized using one dimension only. Situated in the middle of the one-dimensional continuum, they logically tend to fall into the class of electoral democracy as this class is based not only on electoral merits, but on the combination of electoral and liberal characteristics. That the actual gap is of this kind also seems to be Diamond's (at least implicit) conclusion in some of his later pieces. Instead of talking about the electoral and liberal democracies partings ways, he refers to the increase of 'pseudo-democracies'. To quote: 'Thus the trend toward democracy has been accompanied by an even more dramatic trend toward pseudodemocracy' (2002: 27). Anticipating the reconceptualization of this chapter, one could also speak about a trend toward 'hybrid regimes', which is indeed the very headline Diamond is working under in the said article.

Only an additional empirical analysis can determine whether such a dividing line between democracy proper and semi-democracy – or between liberal democracy and hybrid regimes – is indeed a salient phenomenon and whether it has been on the increase throughout the 1990s and 2000s. But the conceptual stadium precedes the empirical, and to capture this distinction it is necessary to conceptualize and measure democracy using one dimension only.

This can be done either by referring to the electoral attribute, or dimension, only – as Diamond has proposed in his more recent writings – or by demonstrating that the electoral and liberal attributes are in sync and can thus be collapsed. This latter way out of the conceptual mess is pointed to by the preceding analysis.

There is really little new in this. Michael Coppedge and Wolfgang H. Reinicke advocated the use of a one-dimensional measurement as early as 1990, noting that the 'separate indexes for political rights and civil liberties . . . are very highly correlated' and that

> [c]ommen sense dictates that a one-dimensional phenomenon be measured with a one-dimensional indicator. Once the unidimensionality of the phenomenon has been established, insisting on two-dimensional indicators is like trying to measure length in acres.
>
> (1990: 56)

Chapter 1 established such empirical one-dimensionality. The preceding analysis demonstrated that the proposition about a gap between electoral and liberal democracies has tended to ignore the intimate empirical relationship between liberal constitutionalism (the liberal property) on the one hand and free and fair elections (the electoral property) on the other hand. Simply stated, the liberal attribute must – empirically, if not theoretically – be present for the elections to be free and fair (cf. Elklit and Svensson 1997). Needless to say, this conclusion is only valid for the examined years and settings. Yet these are exactly the years that interest me, and the post-communist setting has been thoroughly scrutinized above. In the subsequent sections, I will therefore develop a new conceptualization along the lines proposed here.

Dealing a new deck of cards

In a 2004 article on 'Comparative-Historical Methodology' James Mahoney discusses some of the main advantages of paying intimate attention to matters of concept formation. One of the advantages is, he argues, that it is possible to revisit the point of departure should one's first conceptual track prove a dead-end or not to be up to the task, empirically. To quote him (2004: 95):

> [. . .] researchers can easily move back and forth between conceptual definitions, indicators, and scores for cases in many rounds of iteration. Operational definitions and indicators can be refined in light of initial efforts to score cases; likewise, conclusions about the inadequacy of indicators can lead scholars to revisit the very definitions of the concept being measured.[1]

This is exactly what I aim to do here. Notice that my criticism of Diamond – and of other proponents of making a conceptual and operational separation between the electoral and liberal dimensions when using the Freedom House ratings – is situated from the level of the systematized concept and downward. Hence, it is neither necessary to revisit the background concept nor to change much with regard to the systematized concept. With this in mind, let us enter at the appropriate level.

The systematized concept

Conceptually, the electoral and the liberal attributes of democracy are separate things. But on the basis of the analysis of Chapter 1, I now argue that they can be added up as one attribute because they are almost always in sync empirically – at least in the period and setting that interest me. This move is quite straightforward. As Gerardo L. Munck has pointed out, a clear correlation between any two dimensions (*in casu* along the diagonal of the typological property space of Figure 1.3) justifies collapsing them. To quote (2006: 36–7):

> [. . .] the closer the data are aligned on the diagonal linking the bottom left corner to the top right corner of the property space, the more correlated the data are and the less of a loss of information is incurred in aggregation – in other words, the less the view of the trees will get lost in the picture of the forest.

In the present case, where the countries cluster overwhelmingly along the diagonal (i.e. in the respective types of liberal democracy and illiberal autocracy), the trees are likely to remain clearly discernable.

Notice that there is no need whatsoever to expand the connotations of the term 'democracy'. The gist of the matter is that the taxonomical exercise must be altered. The reason is a simple one. Working with a compound of attributes, as I have done in Chapter 1, makes for a typology, i.e. an ordering on more than one dimension. Working with serial operations on one attribute, on the contrary, makes for a pure classification, i.e. an ordering based on one dimension only. To state it somewhat more particularly, the move from two dimensions implies that we discard the distinction between the electoral and liberal components of the political regime form. Instead, focus is placed on the dimension that captures the general distinction between democracy and autocracy. Yet to appreciate the actual empirical gap – the one Diamond identified yet mislabelled – it is necessary to insert a class between these two opposites, namely that of hybrid regime.[2]

Why is that? Recall that one of the shortcomings of the preceding typology was that the polar type of illiberal autocracy swallowed up a large number of countries that in fact differed significantly politically. In other words, it became a residual category when it should not have been. There were simply far too many illiberal autocracies which had far too little in common, not least in the post-communist setting where, throughout the period 1992–2007, at least half of the countries belonged to this class.[3] Consequently, I will carve out the three classes of 'democracy', 'autocracy' and 'hybrid regime' along the dimension covering the political regime form. How do these fill out the connotative space of the systematized concept?

First, a country may be classified as a democracy if it, when these are treated as a whole, fulfils i) the Schumpeterian criterion of free and fair elections for political leadership and ii) the Dahlian criterion of certain liberal rights through the O'Donnelian criterion of the rule of law. Second, a country may be classified as an autocracy if it, when these are treated as a whole, falls short with regards to i) the Schumpeterian criterion of free and fair elections for political leadership and ii) the Dahlian criterion of certain liberal rights through the O'Donnelian criterion of the rule of law. Third, a country may be classified as a hybrid regime if it is situated between these two classes. That is, it must, when these are treated as a whole, go some way towards fulfilling i) the Schumpeterian criterion of free and fair elections for political leadership and ii) the Dahlian criterion of certain liberal rights through the O'Donnelian criterion of the rule of law but still fall short with regard to the operationalized threshold.[4]

Obviously, harking back to Munck's argument about the correlation between the two dimensions stated above, this tripartite division on the dependent variable ultimately rests on the claim that the empirical referents would also clump along the diagonal if I were to trichotomize the electoral and the liberal dimensions respectively, thus creating a property space consisting of nine types. The very strong statistical cross-temporal correlations between the Freedom House's own orderings on the two dimensions (cf. Figure 1.6 in Chapter 1) indicate that this is indeed the case. To reiterate, this is not surprising considering that the cases clump along the diagonal when crafting a typology consisting of four types. Hence, this demonstration seems superfluous in the present case.

Once again, I have thus developed a scheme that exhausts the background concept and spells out the possible variants in a systematic manner. The last thing remaining on this level is to specify the connotative definitions of these three classes, i.e. to exhaust the attribute space of the classification. I propose the following three definitions:

1   *Democracy* is a political regime form that, when collapsing the attributes, clearly combines the presence of i) free electoral competition for political leadership with the presence of ii) a liberal state able to uphold certain liberal rights through the rule of law.

2   *Hybrid regime* is a political regime form that, when collapsing the attributes, neither clearly combines the presence nor the absence of i) free electoral competition for political leadership with the presence or absence of ii) a liberal state able to uphold certain liberal rights through the rule of law.

3   *Autocracy* is a political regime form that, when collapsing the attributes, clearly combines the absence of i) free electoral competition for political leadership with the absence of ii) a liberal state able to uphold certain liberal rights through the rule of law.

Indicators

Once again, it is necessary to move from the connotative definitions to their denotative equivalents, hence tackling Sartori's (1984) three operational problems: the border problem (to be settled by denotative definitions); the membership problem (to be settled by precising definitions); and the measurability problem (to be settled by operational definitions).

This time around, however, these problems are easier to handle. Since it is only the taxonomical exercise that has changed, there is no need to change the solution to the border problem. Suffice to say that the 'elaborated Dahlian model' with its eight criteria (see Figure 1.4) still does the trick.

The membership problem is a more complicated matter. To reiterate, what is necessary here is to ensure that all scrutinized countries, or referents, will fit logically into the crafted classification, including the requirement that the classes are mutually exclusive. I propose the following very simple, precising definitions with respect to the four classes:

1   *Democracy* is a political regime form in which the eight criteria, when added up,[5] are clearly fulfilled.
2   *Hybrid regime* is a political regime form in which the eight criteria, when added up, are neither clearly fulfilled nor clearly violated.
3   *Autocracy* is a political regime form in which the eight criteria, when added up, are clearly violated.

Notice that the definitions thus delimit the classes using averages instead of stressing that all eight criteria must – as bounded wholes (cf. Sartori 1987) – be fulfilled in the case of democracy, whereas none must be fulfilled in the case of autocracy. By implication, and referring to note 4 on p. 158, I do not stipulate that the hybrid regimes connote a situation where a logical *or* is used to underline that some but not all criteria are fulfilled. This may seem problematical considering the classificatory logic. Giovanni Sartori (1970) has famously – and forcefully – warned against the exercise of 'degreeism', i.e. to construct classes with a reference to differences in degree rather than differences in kind and, by extension, to rely on detailed rank orderings rather than a dichotomous equivalent when constructing them. As Michael Coppedge has counter argued, however, '[i]f one wanted a categorical measure, it could always be derived from the continuous one by identifying more thresholds that correspond to the desired categories'. The only logical requirement for doing so is that

> [. . .] the analyst examines the strength of association among the compo-
> nents to discover how many dimensions are represented among them and
> in the mother concept [. . .] components that are very strongly associated
> with one another are treated as one-dimensional, that is, as all measuring
> the same underlying dimension, and may be combined.
>
> (Coppedge 1999: 469–70. See also Munck 2006)

This is exactly what I have done in Chapter 1 and why using the averages makes sense.

Finally, there is the measurability problem. This is where the real issue is at stake. I have already argued for relying on the Freedom House ratings concerning political rights and civil liberties to measure the eight criteria, and I will not repeat my discussion of the validity and reliability of these scores. Needless to say, the problems that were identified in this discussion are relevant for the new classification, just as they were for the preceding typology.

My precising definition rests upon, on the one hand, the conceptual claim that in order to qualify as a democracy, the eight criteria must, when added up, be clearly fulfilled. On the other hand, they must, when added up, be clearly violated for a country to qualify as an autocracy. Every combination in between logically makes for a hybrid regime. What does this entail with regard to thresholds?

Recall that the Freedom House index assigns scores between 1 and 7 on both the electoral and the liberal dimensions of democracy. Their own thresholds are worth revisiting since i) they also divide the countries into three classes, namely 'free', 'partly free' and 'not free' and ii) these are oftentimes construed as measuring democracy, hybrid regimes and autocracy, respectively.

As mentioned in Chapter 1, the first of their thresholds (between free and partly free) is situated at 2.5. My new class of 'democracy' basically covers what 'liberal democracy' covers in the typology. The one and only difference is that it is now possible for a country to pass the threshold of this class on the average score of political rights and civil liberties, rather than having to pass each of the thresholds of the subcomponents separately. Having said that, because the logic is the same, the general threshold should likewise be the same. With this in mind, only countries that score 2 or better (my threshold from Chapter 1) on the average of political rights and civil liberties will earn the predicate of 'democracy'.

What about the threshold between hybrid regime and autocracy? Freedom House's second threshold, the one separating the classes of partly free and not free is situated at 5.5. I see no reason to alter this line of demarcation. Since I now rely on the average value on the two dimensions, there is no logical problem of using a 0.5 cut-off point. Also, keeping the threshold will allow me to stay close to the categories suggested by the Freedom House ratings. Hence, only countries that receive an average score on political rights and civil liberties of 5.5 or higher will be classified as autocracies. This brings us to the following three operational definitions:

1 *Democracy* is a political regime form in which the average value of the eight criteria equals or is less than 2 when using the aggregate scores of political rights and civil liberties reported by the Freedom House.
2 *Hybrid regime* is a political regime form in which the average value of the eight criteria is higher than 2 but lower than 5.5 when using the aggregate scores of political rights and civil liberties reported by the Freedom House.
3 *Autocracy* is a political regime form in which the average value of the eight criteria equals or is higher than 5.5 when using the aggregate scores of political rights and civil liberties reported by the Freedom House.

Any thresholds along one dimension will only be somewhat arbitrary; the same goes for these ones. Yet notice two arguments favouring them. First, the threshold delimiting the class of democracy almost mirrors that used to delimit liberal democracy in the preceding typological analysis. Otherwise said, what I have done is basically to unpack the type of illiberal autocracy, which – I have argued – became a residual type when it should not have been (due to the very significant diversity or dissimilarity within this category). Second, the three classes almost cover the same empirical referents as the Freedom House categories of free, partly free and not free. The new operationalization therefore passes what may most suitably be termed a 'taxonomical field test'.[6] Having thus descended the ladder of abstraction again, let us take a second look at the empirical world to test the value of this new conceptual and classificatory scheme.

A second glance at the realities on the ground

What happens when we repeat the empirical investigation equipped with the new classification of political regime forms? The consequent global distribution for the period 1990–2007 is illustrated in Table 2.1.

The revealed global pattern is a very stable one. Take the democracies, for instance. From an initial peak of almost 50 per cent of all non-autocracies[7] in 1990, the proportion fell to around 40 per cent in the subsequent years, only to climb back to around 50 per cent by the late 1990s and even to surpass this proportion in the 2000s. Table 2.1 thus demonstrates that the tide of the third wave of democratization was not falling in the dying years of the 1990s and that it has actually been rising in the new millennium. Hence, and to reiterate, the third wave of democracy has not been hollowing out as Larry Diamond warned or even prophesized in *Developing Democracy*.

There is one minor *aber dabei* to this. Notice that a small hiccup seems to occur at the very end of the period. The number indicating democracies as a proportion of all non-autocracies decreases a trifle, from 53.8 in 2004 to 52.0 in 2007. This development is also visible, although less so, in the typological analysis of Chapter 1 – in the context of which I promised to reflect upon it in

Table 2.1 The classificatory account of political regime forms on the global level, 1990–2007

	Democracies (N, %)	Hybrid regimes (N, %)	Autocracies (N, %)	Democracies as a proportion of non-autocracies	Total N
1990	53 (32.1)	54 (32.7)	58 (35.2)	49.5	165
1991	54 (29.3)	76 (41.3)	54 (29.3)	41.5	184
1992	57 (30.6)	76 (40.9)	53 (28.5)	42.9	186
1993	62 (32.6)	71 (37.4)	57 (30.0)	46.6	190
1994	62 (32.5)	74 (38.7)	55 (28.8)	45.6	191
1995	67 (35.1)	71 (37.2)	53 (27.7)	48.6	191
1996	68 (35.6)	70 (36.7)	53 (27.7)	49.3	191
1997	69 (36.1)	70 (36.7)	52 (27.2)	49.6	191
1998	69 (36.1)	75 (39.3)	47 (24.6)	47.9	191
1999	71 (37.0)	73 (38.0)	48 (25.0)	49.3	192
2000	74 (38.6)	65 (33.9)	53 (27.6)	53.2	192
2001	73 (38.0)	69 (35.9)	50 (26.0)	51.4	192
2002	73 (38.0)	69 (35.9)	50 (26.0)	51.4	192
2003	76 (39.6)	67 (34.9)	49 (25.5)	53.1	192
2004	77 (40.1)	66 (34.4)	49 (25.5)	53.8	192
2005	79 (41.1)	68 (35.4)	45 (23.4)	53.7	192
2006	78 (40.2)	71 (36.6)	45 (23.2)	52.3	194
2007	78 (40.2)	72 (37.3)	43 (22.3)	52.0	193

this chapter. It has not gone unnoticed in the literature, and it deserves a small digression. Both Larry Diamond and Arch Puddington, Director of Research at Freedom House, have used the new trend to predict the coming of what, in Huntington's (1991) terminology, is a possible reverse wave of democratization. Witness only the title of two articles published in spring 2008: Puddington's 'Is the Tide Turning?' in *Journal of Democracy* and Diamond's 'The Democratic Rollback' in *Foreign Affairs*.

Diamond and Puddington use the Freedom House numbers to underpin their conclusions. In unison, they note that 2007 was the second year in a row in which the average scores for political rights and civil liberties developed in a negative direction, globally. Such a situation has not occurred in one and a half decades. This trend is visible at the end-points of the typological and the classificatory analyses of Chapters 1 and 2.

How convincing are the warnings of Diamond and Puddington? First, using their own conceptual schema, it is interesting to note that the so-called 'democratic rollback' has not left its imprint in the orderings of the countries within the Freedom House's own classes of free, partly free and not free. On the contrary, the number of free countries did not change in 2007, whereas two countries moved from not free to partly free and only one country followed the opposite itinerary. The net development within this classification has been positive, then. It is only within the three categories that relatively more countries have worsened their scores: 38 countries compared to ten that saw improvements. Generally speaking, therefore, and to return to

Huntington's metaphor, the present development so far presents nothing more than a ripple.

Second, one cannot help recalling that Diamond has warned about reverse waves since at least the late 1990s. The assertion about a gap between electoral and liberal democracies reviewed in Chapter 1 provides the centrepiece of these forebodings. However, as early as 1996 Diamond published an article entitled 'Is the Third Wave Over?'. A few years later he used General Musharraf's coup in Islamabad to send the same message in the article 'Is Pakistan the (Reverse) Wave of the Future?'.

There is in fact nothing new in this disposition, which can be traced all the way back to Huntington's 1991 book. In this book he implied that the third wave was in the process of being replaced by a third reverse wave.[8] Taken together, it therefore seems premature to accept the argument about a turning tide.

But all of this is by the way. What is important here is the empirical value of the new intermediate category. The class of hybrid regime claims membership of more than one-third of all countries throughout the period. This quite even distribution across the categories is the most salient difference from the distribution of empirical referents identified by the preceding typology and goes to show the analytical merits of the new classification. At the global level, the classification thus has a clear competitive edge when compared with the preceding typological schema. Most importantly, it captures the dividing line between democracies and hybrid regimes – the gap that Diamond correctly identified yet erroneously characterized as a gap between the liberal and the electoral aspects of democracy. As this analysis has demonstrated, it is a dividing line operating on both the electoral and the liberal dimensions of democracy – which is why it makes sense to collapse these two dimensions into a single attribute. Having said that, it is not a gap that is on the increase; it is its magnitude, not its momentum, which is empirically interesting.

The object of this study is to explain the diverging political paths found within the post-communist microcosm (or subset) of the global universe. Let us therefore zoom in on this setting to see if the classification stands the ultimate test of relevance.

Table 2.2 shows that the post-communist setting was not in sync with global dynamics in the 1990s. Instead of a relatively even tripartition, the class of hybrid regime housed more than half of all post-communist countries in the period 1991–4. However, after the mid-1990s the democratic wave did really take off: democracies have outnumbered hybrid regimes since 2000. This is illustrated in Figure 2.1 where the relative weight of the empirical referents that fall in each class is depicted cross-temporally. The figure also shows that the cases cluster at the extremes of democracy and autocracy over time (at the expense of the class of hybrid regime).

These very tangible dynamics only strengthen the analytical leverage of the classification. In the post-communist setting, the early 1990s did witness a

Table 2.2 The classificatory account of political regime forms in the post-communist setting, 1990–2007

	Democracies (N, %)	Hybrid regimes (N, %)	Autocracies (N, %)	Democracies as a proportion of non-autocracies	Total N
1990	3 (37.5)	3 (37.5)	2 (25.0)	50.0	8
1991	3 (12.5)	18 (75.0)	3 (12.5)	14.3	24
1992	4 (16.0)	18 (72.0)	3 (12.0)	18.2	25
1993	6 (23.1)	16 (61.5)	4 (15.4)	27.3	26
1994	6 (23.1)	15 (57.7)	5 (19.2)	28.6	26
1995	8 (30.8)	13 (50.0)	5 (19.2)	38.1	26
1996	7 (26.9)	13 (50.0)	6 (23.1)	35.0	26
1997	8 (30.8)	13 (50.0)	5 (19.2)	38.1	26
1998	9 (34.6)	12 (46.2)	5 (19.2)	42.9	26
1999	9 (34.6)	12 (46.2)	5 (19.2)	42.9	26
2000	9 (34.6)	10 (38.5)	7 (26.9)	47.4	26
2001	11 (42.3)	8 (30.8)	7 (26.9)	57.9	26
2002	12 (46.2)	7 (26.9)	7 (26.9)	63.2	26
2003	12 (46.2)	7 (26.9)	7 (26.9)	63.2	26
2004	11 (42.3)	7 (26.9)	8 (30.8)	61.1	26
2005	12 (46.2)	7 (26.9)	7 (26.9)	63.2	26
2006	12 (46.2)	7 (26.9)	7 (26.9)	63.2	26
2007	12 (46.2)	7 (26.9)	7 (26.9)	63.2	26

salient gap between democracies and hybrid regimes. Since then the trend has reversed in that the democracies have outnumbered the hybrid regimes by almost two to one since 2002. Such temporal variation facilitates studying the causes of the divergent political paths. Furthermore, no class is even close to emptying out over the entire period of 1990–2007, so we clearly have a tripartition. In other words, the cross-temporal variation goes hand in hand

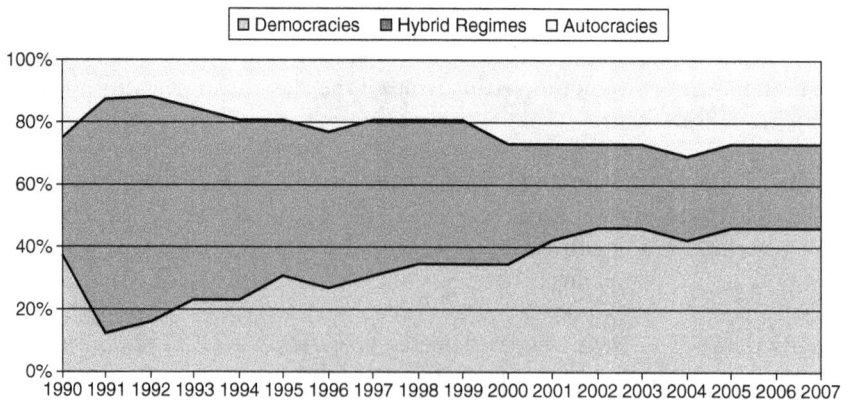

Figure 2.1 The relative distribution of cases in the three classes on the dependent variable, 1990–2007.

with cross-sectional variation – which is a great advantage for anyone who wishes to use the comparative method.

In sum, this classification provides a suitable pivot for analysing and explaining the divergent political paths found within the post-communist setting – which is the very object of this study. Using the proper names of the empirical referents, the final section of this chapter illustrates the cross-sectional and cross-temporal differences and similarities within the post-communist setting that I wish to cover, i.e. those found in the period after the upheavals of 1989–91. This will also allow me to briefly reintroduce the geographic dimension and the matching differences between subregional clusters.

Post-communist political regime forms, 1992–2007

To make the combination of variation across space and time more manageable, i.e. to reduce the complexity of the presentation, I will only include the empirical distribution of the four years of 1992, 1997, 2002 and 2007, respectively. (These are the four points in time on which I will focus in the comparative analyses of subsequent chapters.) The temporal demarcation line of 1992 has been chosen because the breakdown of the Soviet Union only finished in the preceding year. Generally speaking, 1992 is the first genuine year of post-communism. Other than that, 1992, 1997, 2002 and 2007 have been selected not for some intrinsic qualities but to elucidate i) the early outcome of the transition (1992), ii) the mid-term occurrences (1997 and 2002) and iii) the longer-term[9] developments (2007) in a symmetric fashion. These years are used to explain both the political pathways of post-communism and the cross-case divisions at different temporal points along these paths.

Unfortunately, as will be demonstrated in Chapter 3, some of the actor-centred variables that I use have to be measured as late as the mid-1990s. Hence, in the initial actor-centred analysis I will not be able to include the year of 1992 on the dependent variable because of what John Gerring (2001: 125–7) terms 'priority', viz. that the cause(s) must predate the effect on the dimension of time. In the subsequent structural analysis, however, I am able to include all four years. Let us take a look at the distribution on the dependent variable in the period of 1992–2007. Are there any noticeable cross-spatial patterns? Do they change cross-temporally?

Table 2.3 sends two clear messages. First, after communism had been relegated to the 'ash heap of history', hybrid regimes dominated the setting. In 1992, 18 out of 25 post-communist countries belonged in this class. Only four were democracies, whereas another three had never embarked from their autocratic point of departure. Second, the geographical distribution was not very clear-cut back then. A harbinger of what was to come, the three democracies were in East-Central Europe and the three autocracies were in Central Asia. But the hybrid regimes could be encountered in many different places.

Table 2.3 The empirical distribution of political regime forms within the post-communist setting, 1992–2007

	Democracies	*Hybrid regimes*	*Autocracies*
1992	Czechoslovakia, Hungary, Poland, Slovenia	Albania, Armenia, Azerbaijan, Belarus, Bulgaria, Croatia, Estonia, Georgia, Kazakhstan, Kyrgyzstan, Latvia, Lithuania, Macedonia, Moldova, Mongolia, Romania, Russia, Ukraine	Tajikistan, Turkmenistan, Uzbekistan
1997	Czech Republic, Estonia, Hungary, Latvia, Lithuania, Poland, Romania, Slovenia	Albania, Armenia, Azerbaijan, Bulgaria, Croatia, Georgia, Kyrgyzstan, Macedonia, Moldova, Mongolia, Russia, Slovakia, Ukraine	Belarus, Kazakhstan, Tajikistan, Turkmenistan, Uzbekistan
2002	Bulgaria, Croatia, Czech Republic, Estonia, Hungary, Latvia, Lithuania, Mongolia, Poland, Romania, Slovakia, Slovenia	Albania, Armenia, Georgia, Macedonia, Moldova, Russia, Ukraine	Azerbaijan, Belarus, Kazakhstan, Kyrgyzstan, Tajikistan, Turkmenistan, Uzbekistan
2007	Bulgaria, Croatia, Czech Republic, Estonia, Hungary, Latvia, Lithuania, Mongolia, Poland, Romania, Slovakia, Slovenia	Albania, Armenia, Georgia, Kyrgyzstan, Macedonia, Moldova, Ukraine	Azerbaijan, Belarus, Kazakhstan, Russia, Tajikistan, Turkmenistan, Uzbekistan

By 1997, the empirical distribution had become more balanced. First, 13 countries could be classified as hybrid regimes, eight as democracies and five as autocracies. Second, this variation in political regime forms was becoming more subregionally (geographically) fixed. All the democracies were still found in East-Central Europe. Also (with the sole exception of Belarus), all autocracies were Central Asian or Caucasian countries, and only Kyrgyzstan was still capable of breaking free of the autocratic air of Central Asia. But – and this is the most important change vis-à-vis 1992 – most of the hybrid regimes were now geographically situated between these two subregions.

The situation in 2002 only reinforced these trends. The East-Central European countries were democracies and the Central Asian republics were, together with Azerbaijan and Belarus, autocracies; the countries geographically situated between them were hybrid regimes. Most notably, not a single country in the subregions of East-Central Europe and Central Asia, respectively, was a hybrid regime. Notice, however, that Mongolia, which is a country that does not have any East-Central European flavour to it, moved into the class of democracy.

Finally, by 2007 the dynamics of political change had, to some extent, re-entered the picture. First, the very tripartition of political regime forms of 2002 was no longer as salient as before (though it was still relatively salient). In particular, the hybrid regime class was seemingly running dry. Only seven of 26 countries were hybrid regimes, whereas 12 were democracies and seven were autocracies. Second, even though the intra-subregional divisions were still relatively stable, this box had opened up, too. Mongolia still resided in the class of democracy. Conversely, Russia had become an autocracy and Kyrgyzstan had reverted to the class of hybrid regime. Notice, however, that even in 2007 the empirical puzzle of divergent political pathways was rather clear-cut. This puzzle is that I set out to solve in the subsequent chapters.

Conclusions

Based on the analysis in Chapter 1, I have stressed that in order to appreciate the actual gap between democracies and hybrid regimes that Larry Diamond (1999) identified (but misnamed), it is necessary to conceptualize and measure democracy using only one dimension. Otherwise said, I have objected to Diamond's nomenclature and his associated claim (based on the Freedom House ratings) about the dynamics of the electoral and the liberal components, not to his actual empirical dividing lines.

When redoing the taxonomical exercise to capture these dividing lines, i.e. when collapsing the electoral and liberal attributes and carving out thresholds along the consequent dimension, I arrive at a tripartite classification of political regime forms. The matching distinction between the three classes of democracy, hybrid regime and autocracy allows me to exhaust the dependent variable of political regime form in a way that does indeed capture the dominant political trends of the third wave of democratization. This applies both globally and with regard to the post-communist subset.

Concerning the former setting, the classification demonstrates that a relatively even tripartition, or trichotomy, between the three regime forms has been in existence during the third wave, but the democracies have been gaining ground in the 2000s. In short, then, Diamond's prophesy about an increasing gap is discounted even when collapsing the two attributes. Bearing this in mind, his new warning that the (still rather modest) negative trend of 2006 and 2007 marks the coming of the reverse wave (which did not materialize in the late 1990s) brings to mind Aesop's fable about the boy who cried wolf. As documented above, and considering the empirical feet of clay it – so far – builds on, it is hard to take Diamond's warning seriously because he has cried out so many times.[10]

Concerning the latter setting, which is the subject of this book, the early 1990s was a period of upheaval in which hybrid regimes dominated the setting. This state of disruption only lasted a few years, however. By the mid-1990s the post-communist countries were also beginning to cluster in a relatively even manner in the three classes, a pattern that came into its own by the end of the decade.

Also, the variation in political regime forms had a peculiar intra-subregional flavour to it: all democracies inhabited East-Central Europe; all autocracies (save Belarus) were in Central Asia and the Caucasian regions; and the hybrid regimes were, generally speaking, situated in between. This pattern has changed a bit in the 2000s, most notably by Mongolia becoming a democracy and by Russia becoming an autocracy. However, and to conclude, from a bird's-eye view the dividing lines are unmistakable, even in the most recent years. This is the pattern I will seek to explain in subsequent chapters.

Appendix 2.1

Counting rules for the classification of political regime forms

With a Freedom House threshold of 2 and 5.5 on the average of the electoral dimension ('political rights') and its liberal equivalent ('civil liberties'), the counting rules of my classification are very simple.

A Freedom House score that:

- equals or is lower than 2 on the average of 'political rights' and 'civil liberties' (i.e. the Freedom House ratings *tout court*) provides for the political regime form of 'democracy';
- is higher than 2 but lower than 5.5 on the average of 'political rights' and 'civil liberties' provides for the political regime form of 'hybrid regime';
- equals or is higher than 5.5 on the average of 'political rights' and 'civil liberties' provides for the political regime form of 'autocracy'.

Three empirical examples:

Afghanistan 1990 (PR = 7; CL = 7; average = 7): Democracy
Algeria 1990 (PR = 4; CL = 4; average = 4): Hybrid Regime
Argentina 1990 (PR = 1; CL = 3; average = 2): Autocracy

Part II

A cross-temporal and cross-spatial analysis of patterns of post-communist political change

3 An actor-centred analysis of post-communist political pathways

Until now, this book has only provided descriptive inference.[1] Having done so with respect to the dependent variable of the political regime form, it is time to target the issue of causal inference.[2]

To reiterate, we need to answer three empirical questions, thereby testing two theoretical hypotheses. First, why does democracy reign supreme in East-Central Europe? Second, why has autocracy held its own in Central Asia? Third, why are so many of the countries that are situated in between hybrid regimes? The hypotheses formulated in the Introduction posit that i) both proximate and deep explanations within the literature enable us to account for these empirical regularities and, critically, that ii) the deeper or structural factors also account for the proximate or actor-centred choices, therefore allowing us to create an integrated explanatory paradigm.

To test these hypotheses, Part II of the book will be wedded to carrying out three separate analyses of post-communist regime change: first, from a proximate perspective, thereby testing whether the actor-centred approaches account for the variation on the dependent variable (Chapter 3); second, from a deep perspective, thereby testing the relevance of a structural corrective (Chapter 4); third, from a joint, or juxtaposed, perspective, thereby construing each of the two dimensions as packages (i.e. composite indices) and contrasting them, in turn testing the general relevance of Kitschelt's theoretical recommendations (Chapter 5).

This equals saying that I set out to identify and test relevant explanatory factors (i.e. to provide causal inference) bearing these questions in particular and the described variation on the dependent variable in general in mind. As Arend Lijphart (1971: 683) stressed three and a half decades ago, any comparative endeavour that aims at scientific explanation,

> [. . .] consists of two basic elements: (1) the establishment of general empirical relationships among two or more variables, while (2) all other variables are controlled, that is, held constant. These two elements are inseparable: one cannot be sure that a relationship is a true one unless the influence of other variables is controlled. The *ceteris paribus* condition is vital to empirical generalizations.[3]

Lijphart's yardstick is, however, as demanding as it is necessary. The social world is riddled by factors that might be relevant but normally are not. How do we tackle this dilemma, this helter-skelter of possible explanatory variables? While acknowledging that there is no one single answer to that question, my preferred remedy is one that is often invoked. As Alexander George and Andrew Bennett (2005: 30) have expressed it, '[t]he pragmatic (but not necessarily incomplete) approach we and others suggest is that researchers limit themselves to testing alternative theories, which individuals have proposed, rather than worrying over the infinite number of potential theories that lack any proponent'.[4]

Travelling down this road, I will now pay the theoretical literature a visit, identifying, operationalizing and measuring the dominant actor-centred explanations that have been proposed with respect to the study of post-communism. In doing so, I am interested in identifying factors that, when present in the post-communist setting, theoretically provide for the described package of electoral and liberal rights (i.e. those which make for 'democracy') and when absent in the post-communist setting theoretically do not provide for the package of electoral and liberal rights (i.e. those which make for 'autocracy'). In other words, I will divide each variable into a dichotomous classification on the basis of either the presence or the absence of a particular, theoretically relevant attribute.

Notice that the consequent analysis is very theory-driven. The purpose of it being so is twofold: first, to capture and contrast the competing offers on the explanatory marketplace; second, to embed the comparative method that I will opt for at a later stage in theory; something that is very important when using simple dichotomies. This also means that, where at all possible, I will use the data and the cut-off points of existing explanations. The objective is, to reiterate, to contrast the competing explanations and come up with a general position of my own, not to minutely criticize the causal claims staked and the data employed. This is also reflected by the fact that I dichotomize ordinal- or interval-scaled variables using cut-off points justified by the extant theories, not around means (as done by, for example, Kitschelt 1988) or medians. Concerning the use of dichotomies, a word of caution is nevertheless pertinent. As Giovanni Sartori (1976: 147) has reminded us with respect to categorical classifications, '[w]hile the cases can be moved from one class to another, nonetheless a classification imputes permanence and boundedness. If no such imputation is justified, the ever-changeable rank orderings and more sensitive indexes would be more attuned to the real world'.

When I opt for the dichotomous classifications at this point (and, later on, for a typological schema), it is on the basis of the pre-eminent observation of Chapter 1: the dependent variable is characterized by a very salient tripartition which has been reproduced over time since the mid-1990s. This seems to indicate that the setting is indeed characterized by stable differences in kind, rather than unstable differences in degree and, therefore, by form rather than formlessness. However, should the empirical analysis of the independent variables show that this is only the case on the surface, i.e. in case the regularities on the dependent variable do not extend to the independent variables, it would undermine the merits of the classificatory and typological schema, at least vis-à-vis standard statistical procedures. I will come back to this after having engaged the reality on the ground.

It is necessary to consider one more issue. As King, Keohane and Verba (1994: 79) have emphasized, social science is burdened by what they term 'the fundamental problem of causal inference': '[. . .] we can never hope to know a causal effect for certain'. However, with systematic comparisons, we can render the existence of such an effect probable. Four criteria have to be observed here (Agresti and Finlay 1986: 357)[5]: first, there has to be an empirical relationship between the cause(s) and the effect(s) (i.e. we need to establish some sort of co-variation); second, it is necessary to control for other causes (i.e. we must avoid spuriousness); third, the cause must predate the effect (i.e. 'priority' must be observed); and fourth, the relationship must be supported by a viable theoretical argument (i.e. we need to explain why a relationship is to be expected).

The first two conditions are, in effect, those mentioned by Lijphart above. These matters must be left to the empirical analysis and I have already indicated how I will approach them. The last two conditions, however, are to be solved in the theoretical arena. Hence, these must be observed in the subsequent discussions. Otherwise said, an independent variable (i.e. a potential cause) will only be included in so far as it i) is linked to the dependent variable (the effect) by a convincing theoretical explanation and ii) predates the effect on the temporal dimension.

Three dominant actor-centred explanations in the literature on post-communism

According to my reading, the theoretical literature on political change in the post-communist setting is dominated by three somewhat intertwined actor-centred perspectives. First, we have what I will term the 'political competition explanation'. This is the assertion that the political pathways of the former communist countries were shaped by the character and outcome of the first election which, in turn, depended on the mobilization of oppositional forces during the transition. This perspective has, with some significant differences in emphasis, been recommended by scholars such as M. Steven Fish, Valerie Bunce,[6] Michael McFaul and Milada Anna Vachudova.

Second, and closely related, we have what I will term the 'economic reform explanation'. This assertion points to the clash between the proponents of shock therapy and gradualism in the 1990s. The argument promoted by the shock therapists was that a speedy process of economic liberalization and privatization would empower the reform-friendly, liberal strata of society, in turn facilitating democratization. In the aftermath of the breakdown of communism, economists such as Jeffrey Sachs, Anders Åslund and Andrei Shleifer promoted this point of view; recently it has been picked up by M. Steven Fish and Omar Choudhry.

Third, we have what I will term the 'constitutional engineering explanation'. This proposition is linked with scholars such as M. Steven Fish and Timothy Frye.[7] The hypothesis holds that the initial constitutional choices, whether operationalized along the dimension of power distribution or parliamentary contra presidential power, are what accounts for the subsequent variation in political regime forms. Needless to say, this factor can also be construed as institutional rather than actor-centred as it kicks in via the mechanism of institutional freezing. I will come back to that. When I group it as actor-centred, it is to underline the fact that the institutional choices are exactly that: choices made by the actors during the transition.

Taken together, these three 'proximate' explanations capture the logic of the dominant actor-centred perspectives on post-communism.[8] Furthermore, they can be construed as a coherent threesome because they reflect different aspects of the same phenomenon: the actor-choices of the early 1990s. I will therefore confine my attention to them in this chapter. Translated into the language of independent variables, each of the three explanations offers a prediction of the political pathways of the respective post-communist countries. Beyond being somewhat intertwined, they have two important postulates in common about political change in the post-communist setting: first, the important factors shaping the outcome on the political regime form date from the transitional upheavals, not from antecedent structural factors; second, and partly related, that these constraints were put in place by actors in a relatively voluntaristic way (see, for example, Fish 1998a: 77–8 and Fish 2006: 11–12). I will revisit, discuss, operationalize and measure[9] the three associated variables in turn.

The political competition variable (displacement)

In 1998, M. Steven Fish (1998a) published the article 'The Determinants of Economic Reform in the Post-Communist World'. The message of this article is both tangible and simple: the properties (i.e. the outcome and the character) of the initial elections after the breakdown of communism laid out the tracks of the concomitant or subsequent economic reform process. Also, Fish emphasizes that the initial elections were not shaped by 'deeper' factors. Rather, the outcome and character of the elections were relatively voluntaristic in that they depended upon the political elites. To quote from the article (1998a: 77–8, emphasis in original):

> The outcome of the initial elections certainly cannot readily be traced to a particular structural, cultural, or institutional factor. It is not out of the question that some explanation for the outcome of the initial elections may be found in the *availability of alternative leadership* at the moment of the elections.

The fact that founding elections are no small matter is not a novel insight within the study of regime change (e.g. O'Donnell and Schmitter 1986: 61–3). However, most anterior contributions which can be grouped under the headline of Transitology emphasized that either some sort of stalemate or even a win for the outgoing autocrats favours democracy, whereas a clear-cut oppositional win may trigger a reaction, possibly culminating in a democratic breakdown. As such, the Transitology-sponsored reading of the consequences of the first elections contrasts head-on with that of Fish (cf. also McFaul 2002). This equals saying that Fish's perspective presents a novel contribution.

What is more, others have elaborated and confirmed his assertions. The most notable support has been rendered by Valerie Bunce. In a very interesting overview of the economic and political occurrences after the breakdown of communism, Bunce (1999) both broadens and extends the causal chain developed by Fish. She notes that economic reform is the best predictor of democratization. By logical extension, the causal chain leads from the initial elections, as described by Fish, via the economic reforms to the political regime form. To quote: '[. . .] just as the best predictor of democratization is economic reform, so the best predictor of economic reform (to return to an earlier point) is the outcome of the first competitive election' (1999: 782).

It should be noted that Fish himself indicates that the causal chain touches upon the attribute of democratization, albeit not as the ultimate effect but rather as an intervening link. Thus, his (1998a: 59) illustration of the causal chain includes the 'Openness of the Political System' which, whatever else it may imply, definitely has the connotations of democracy (that is, if the political system is open).[10]

Nevertheless, as I will demonstrate, Bunce's extension is somewhat problematic due to the way Fish operationalizes the 'initial election-variable'. Before we can make that point, it is important to note that Bunce broadens the chain, too. It is not elections per se, but rather the political competition taking place during and in the immediate aftermath of the communist breakdown that is perceived as most important. To quote (1999: 787):

> The key factor that emerged in this study was the balance of the power between the liberal opposition and the communists – a balance that determined the outcome of the first competitive election and that shaped in turn the political struggles, institutional innovations, and the public policies that followed.

As indicated in the last sentence of the quotation from Fish's article, he would find this conclusion congenial. One thing needs to be stressed, however. Bunce is actually promoting a 'legacies-approach' to post-communism. Instead of stressing the voluntaristic character of the events (i.e. the wide scope for action), she (1999: 772) emphasizes that '[. . .] the socialist past, not proximate policy choices, emerges as critical'.

However, Bunce (1999: 785) leaves the legacies as a general premise and, on the concrete level, only harks back to '[. . .] the patterns and content of public protests during the socialist period', i.e. the initial level of political competition. As such, her actual elaboration can be accommodated within the actor-centre logic even though her theoretical point of departure cannot. More to the point, that the interesting variable is actually political competition, rather than the first election in itself, has found broad backing in the literature on post-communism ever since (see in particular McFaul 2002 and Vachudova 2005).

What emerges from this overview of the literature is thus an independent variable centred on the attribute of political competition, and in particular the sub-component of whether the opposition won the initial election. Depending on the existence or non-existence of such competition, a causal chain is set in motion which ultimately results in either democracy or autocracy as the outcome on the dependent variable of the political regime form.

To capture this variable, I will only zoom in on the sub-component of the outcome of the initial elections, however. Why is that? First, this outcome – in essence whether the communist incumbents were displaced or not – is the most salient step in the causal chain of Fish, Bunce, McFaul and Vachudova, whatever else they add. Second, and more critically, Fish's quite 'thick' operationalization of the initial election-variable touches upon a number of other properties that are much too closely linked to the dependent variable to be causally meaningful (or, at least, causally interesting).[11] Quoting Fish (1998a: 48) once more:

> Countries were scored along the following four questions in the manner indicated: 1) Who won the initial elections? (2=clear victory by reformers/noncommunists; 1=equivocal outcome; 0=clear victory by communists/custodians of the old regime); 2) Were the results of the elections quickly annulled by illegitimate means – namely, by the use or the threat of use of force? (no=1; yes=0); 3) Were the elections freely contested, meaning that they were open and multiple candidates competed for the office to be filled? (yes=1; no=0); 4) Were the elections complete or partial, meaning did they involve elections for all important offices on the national level or for only a portion of them? (complete=1; partial=0). Thus, the first question assesses 'who won' the elections; the second, third, and fourth questions capture whether the elections 'stuck'; whether they were 'open' (competitive); and whether they were 'complete'.

Note that properties 2, 3 and 4 are actually indicators of the level of democracy (at the very least on the electoral attribute) at the time of these elections. That the consequent measurement correlates with the level of democracy in the subsequent years is not exactly surprising. This is not much of a problem for Fish since his general dependent variable in this piece is economic reform.

But it is certainly a problem of tautology for Bunce, even if she does not reflect on it. It can, however, be overcome by focusing on property 1 only, which does not in and of itself connote democracy.[12]

With this qualification noted, the theoretical expectation is thus that the presence of a displacement of incumbent communists at the first elections (i.e. an oppositional win) favours democracy, whereas its absence (i.e. an oppositional defeat) favours autocracy. Time as a dimension of variation does not present much of a problem here. As the adjective indicates, the initial elections took place right after the breakdown of communism. Hence, as an independent variable, it stands prior to the dependent variable of the political regime form, which, in this chapter, is not measured until 1997 due to priority. On the highlighted property, Fish (1998a: 50–1, emphasis in original) scores the countries in the following manner:

> On the first question, most receive a 0 or a 2. In most countries, the custodians of the old regime either enjoyed clear victories or suffered clear defeats. The question is not whether genuine 'liberals' won or lost the first elections but, rather, whether *oppositionists* – be they liberals, nationalists, or some combination of the two – defeated or were defeated by custodians of the old regime [. . .] The ambiguous cases – the ones that do not merit a score of 0 or 2 – are Macedonia, Moldova, and Slovenia. Each of these cases is scored as a 1.

This scoring is very easily converted into a dichotomous classification. The residual category is the absence of displacement (score = 0), whereas both of the scores of 1 and 2 indicate some sort of presence of displacement. This leads me to the following operational definition of the variable: a post-communist country experienced a displacement of communist incumbents – i.e. has the attribute 'displacement' – if it obtained a score of 1 or 2 as reported by M. Steven Fish in 'The Determinants of Economic Reform'.

The economic reforming variable (reform)

When communism fell in 1989–91, a twofold transition was needed if the societies emerging from the debris were to embrace the Western model. Politically, the one-party dictatorship was to be replaced by liberal democracy. Economically, the planned economy was to be replaced by a market economy. Such a context made the transitions *sui generis*; and this was the context in which the renowned debate between shock therapy and gradualism was fought out.

Those subscribing to the former view recommended comprehensive and immediate price liberalization, a thorough privatization of state-owned enterprises and a forceful macroeconomic stabilization programme – better today than tomorrow. High speed was seen as key to the economic success of these reforms because it provided the best device for substituting state control with the market (i.e. price) mechanism, the prerequisite for harvesting the economic benefits associated with the Western model.

Interestingly, however, the political virtues of such an approach were seen as even more important than the economic equivalents. The principal political problem of post-communism was to be found in the combination of a virtual absence of groups supporting democracy and the presence of a large homogenous opposition to any reforming. Only by taking advantage of the transitional window of opportunity (i.e. only by going quickly) was it possible to overcome this resistance as the potential opposition would not find time to organize. Also, the reforms would economically empower the liberal-minded strata, thus ensuring the future sustainability of democracy (and capitalism). Among the scholars promoting this position, we find economists such as Anders Åslund (1992), Jeffrey Sachs (1993), Maxim Boycko, Andrei Shleifer and Robert Vishny (1995).

The gradualists begged to differ. According to their understanding of political and economic change, market making was as much about state building as about the transfer of property rights from the state to private actors. A state with the capacity to uphold economic freedoms and prevent the corruption of the market was seen as the prerequisite for successful economic reforms. In particular, the gradualists held that it was necessary to create effective institutions, such as the rule of law and the public ability to regulate the economy, before letting go with regard to liberalizations and privatizations.[13] This equals saying that gradual reforms spanning the political, judicial and economic realms were needed.

The gradualists also claimed that the bottom-up strategy associated with this approach was superior to the top-down strategy of shock therapy as it allowed a coupling of economic and democratic reforms. Rather than asking experts to design and carry out the reforms, they should come about from below, i.e. through the democratic process. This would diminish the dangers of a populist reaction in particular and support for non-democratic forces in general. Among the scholars adopting this perspective, Peter Murrell (1993), Joseph Stiglitz (1999) and Gerard Roland (2000) deserve mention.

The debate between shock therapy and gradualism has never ended as such, but following the fierce trench warfare of the 1990s, it has been much more low-key in the new millennium. However, in a recent contribution M. Steven Fish and Omar Choudhry (2007) have revisited the debate. Fish and Choudhry descend the ladder of abstraction and construe the former approach as 'the Washington Consensus' and the latter approach as 'the Social-Democratic Consensus'. Their descriptions of these twin paradigms are very simple: the 'Washington Consensus' favours swift economic reforms, whereas the 'Social-Democratic Consensus' favours slow or no economic reforms.

Economic reforms are measured using the single indicator of 'economic liberalization' (borrowed from De Melo et al. 1996). Regarding causality, the claim is also straightforward. In brief, the Social-Democratic Consensus posits 'the incompatibility of economic liberalization and democratization' (273). Contrastingly, the Washington Consensus posits that economic liberalization spurs democratization. Using a sophisticated statistical model, Fish and Choudhry demonstrate that whereas economic liberalization had neither a positive nor a negative effect on democratization (measured using the FH-ratings) in the short term, it has had a positive effect in the longer term, moving the countries toward the expected equilibrium. On this basis, they vindicate the Washington Consensus in the context of post-communist economic and political change and reject the Social-Democratic Consensus.

I would like to briefly mention that Fish and Choudhry's conceptual, theoretical and empirical claims are somewhat problematical. They do not even attempt to prove that causality really flows from the economic to the political variables. Hellman (1998) famously claimed that the reverse relationship characterized post-communism. More importantly, Fish and Choudhry arguably misrepresent the gradualist argument when construing it as the Social-Democratic Consensus. Basically, they argue that gradualism can be operationalized as a low degree of economic liberalization. (Contrariwise, shock therapy and, by extension, the Washington Consensus can be operationalized as a high degree of economic liberalization.) But as already described, gradualism proper consists of a particular sequencing of reforms – not the absence thereof – in which state building or strengthening the regulatory apparatus is seen as a stepping stone for creating successful privatizations/liberalizations. Otherwise said, gradualism favours liberalization, too, but as a particular sequence in a chain. The absence of any liberalization is rather the logic of an approach of no reforms. When only measuring economic liberalization, we cannot tell whether there has been any sequencing.

Likewise, shock therapy is better construed as privileging economic liberalization and privatization at the expense of the said regulatory reforms than as simply a high degree of liberalization. According to Fish, the Washington Consensus merely implies 'marketization', but that is much too simplistic (and also favoured by the gradual approach). In a nutshell, what separates the two perspectives is not the goal of a functioning market economy, but the means (sequencing or not) and the meta-theoretical assumptions about passions and constraints.

I will not get lost in the actual content of the debate, however. The objective is simply to use Fish and Choudry's contribution to operationalize and measure the proximate explanation promoted under the banner of shock therapy. As already mentioned, the numbers that Fish and Choudhry use to measure economic liberalization are derived from De Melo et al. (1996), who calculate an annual liberalization index (ranging from 0 to 1, with higher scores denoting higher degrees of liberalization) for 26 post-communist countries for each year between 1989 and 1994. The index aggregates three sub-components, viz. 'Internal markets' (weight 0.3), 'External markets' (weight 0.3) and 'Private sector entry' (weight 0.4).[14] On this basis, De Melo et al. calculate a cumulative liberalization index (CLI) which equals the sum of the yearly scores. They use this index to distinguish between advanced reformers (CLI > 3), high-intermediate reformers (2 < CLI < 3), low-intermediate reformers (1.3 < CLI < 2) and slow reformers (CLI < 1.3).

I use the distinction between the former two classes and the latter two classes to dichotomize the variable that I name 'reform'. Notice that priority is observed as the measurement ends in 1994, well before the first measurement on the dependent variable in 1997. Hence, we define: a post-communist country is grouped as 'reformer' – i.e. has the attribute 'reform' – if it obtained the predicate advanced reformer or high-intermediate reformer as reported by De Melo et al. (1996).

The constitutional engineering variable (legislature)

The issue of constitution-making has received much attention in recent decades. Two reasons seem to lie behind this interest. One reason is emphasized by Juan J. Linz and Alfred Stepan (1996) in their tour de force through the issues of transition and consolidation: the process of constitution-making leaves behind a discursive legacy that may either be conciliatory or catalyzing for future conflicts.

Yet a more institutional explanation is also present in the literature: the new constitutional arrangements put in place by actors become institutions that constrain much of the subsequent political life. Many scholars have used the latter insight to emphasize that the new constitutions played a major role in shaping the outcome of the politico-economic transitions in East-Central Europe. Employing a 'Madisonian' perspective, László Bruszt (2002: 58) thus asserts '[. . .] that what really mattered from the viewpoint of the characteristics of the state, was not the specific institutional arrangements or the actual distribution of powers among the specific institutions but the general principles shaping the structure of representation'.

Generally speaking, a structure of representation that allows a small, legitimately elected group to gather the reins of power can be perceived as detrimental both politically and economically. This is because rent-seekers or would-be autocrats will only need to capture one level of the political system (i.e. the top executive) in such a situation. Once doing so, no other checks will hinder consequent power abuse and transgression of rights. With respect to the post-communist setting, it has, *a fortiori*, been argued that presidentialism disfavours democracy generically. Bunce (1999: 778) phrases it succinctly:

> Presidentialism is a problem for democracy in general, because it undermines political routines, encourages willful politicians, and, in the extreme, tolerates, if not encourages democratic breakdown. At the same time, it is a problem for the postsocialist democracies in particular, because presidentialism augments the power of the communists (by helping ensure their continuation in political office) while reinforcing the

procedural irregularities and the leadership interventions so characteristic of the past.

The matching 'constitutional engineering explanation' has received much attention in the literature on post-communism. Both Timothy Frye (1997) and, subsequently, M. Steven Fish (2006) have obtained some remarkable results by focusing on this attribute. In what follows, I concentrate on Fish because he deliberately targets the distinction between parliaments and presidencies (whereas Frye distinguishes between a 'power-concentrating' and a 'power-dispersing' constitution).

Fish and a colleague have created a Parliamentary Power Index, according to which a country receives a relatively high score if a relatively high amount of constitutional power is vested in the parliament and a relatively low score if the opposite is the case. In the article 'Stronger Legislatures, Stronger Democracies', he employs this index in the context of 25 post-communist countries.

Fish's theoretical expectation is that a high degree of parliamentary power (and hence a weak presidency) should make for democracy, whereas a low degree of parliamentary power (and hence a strong presidency) should make for autocracy. This is exactly what he finds. To quote his (2006: 5) uncompromising claim: 'The evidence shows that the presence of a powerful legislature is an unmixed blessing for democratization'. One thing needs to be added. According to Fish (2006: 11–12), the post-communist countries have chosen constitutional systems in a more or less voluntaristic way and the institutional constraints have kicked in over the latest decades. This is thus very much an actor-oriented explanation of democratization.

Fish makes an interesting case for his claim concerning the blessings of parliamentarism. The post-communist or, more precisely, the post-Soviet experience is notorious for its reliance on outright presidential or, at the very least, semi-presidential systems. By extension, when formal power has been monopolized, it has often, if not always, been in the hands of the incumbent president. The flipside of this coin is that the post-communist legislatures have often been very weak. I will cling to this fact. The expectation derived is thus that the presence of a strong legislature to balance the president will favour democracy, whereas its absence will favour autocracy.[15]

How do we move into the operational arena from here? Bearing the dichotomous logic guiding this investigation in mind, I advocate that we simply establish a threshold of parliamentary power above which a given country can be said to have a strong legislature. That is we employ a general threshold making it possible to provide an overall separation between the presence and absence of this attribute. Fish's index measures the constitutional power of parliament on a scale from 0 to 1, with higher scores indicating stronger legislatures. He (2006: 18) emphasizes that a country that opted for a strong legislature is one that scored above 0.60 in the Parliamentary Power Index. To avoid accusations of tailoring the thresholds to suit my expectations, I will let this cut-off point denote the presence of the theoretical property. Any country that receives a score over 0.60 can be considered to have a strong legislature. Conversely, a score equal to or lower than 0.60 denotes the absence of a strong legislature.[16] Notice that this ensures that the dichotomization is embedded in theory.

Time as a dimension of variation is a bit of a problem here since the constitutions scrutinized by the Parliamentary Power Index were inaugurated in different years, during the respective 'constitutional moments', to use Fish's term. Still, none of them date from later than 1996 and only one of them (Ukraine) is in fact measured at this relatively late point in time. Since I do not zoom in on my dependent variable until 1997, the criteria of priority is observed.

One further problem needs to be tackled. Turkmenistan is not included in the survey. However, as already indicated, Fish's Parliamentary Power Index is very much of the same ilk as the so-called 'Presidential Power Index', following Timothy Frye (1997). This fact makes it possible to fill in the gap. Frye's index measures the presidential powers stipulated in the constitution of the post-communist countries in the first decade after the breakdown of communism. Twenty-seven different 'powers' are taken into consideration by the index. A country scores either 0 (the president does not hold the power in question), 0.5 (the president is sharing a power with another body) or 1 (the president exclusively holds a given power) on each of these 27 subcomponents.

Since a strong parliament equals a weak president and vice versa, it is not surprising that turning the issue upside-down does not make much of a difference. More to the point, it means that we can borrow the position of Turkmenistan in the Presidential Power Index. Upon inspection, it turns out that Turkmenistan receives an even higher score of presidential power than the four other Central Asian countries, therefore it is even more 'presidential' than its brethren. As all of these are, by a large margin, situated below 0.60 in Fish's index of parliamentary power, it is fair to situate Turkmenistan in this area, too.

This leads us to the following operational definition of the variable: a country has a constitutionally strong legislature – i.e. has the attribute 'legislature' – if it obtains a general score over 0.60 in the Parliamentary Power Index as reported by M. Steven Fish in 'Stronger Legislatures, Stronger Democracies'.

An overview of the scoring on the 'proximate' variables

Table 3.1 illustrates the actual empirical outcomes on the two independent variables. Plus (+) indicates the presence of the particular attribute covering the variable; minus (–) indicates its absence.

Table 3.1 An overview of the scoring on the proximate variables

	Displacement	Legislature	Reform
Albania	–	+	+
Armenia	+	–	–
Azerbaijan	–	–	–
Belarus	–	–	–
Bulgaria	–	+	+
Croatia	+	+	+
Czech Republic	+	+	+
Estonia	+	+	+
Georgia	+	–	–
Hungary	+	+	+
Kazakhstan	–	–	–
Kyrgyzstan	+	–	–
Latvia	+	+	+
Lithuania	+	+	+
Macedonia	+	+	+
Moldova	+	+	–
Mongolia	–	+	+
Poland	+	+	+
Romania	–	+	+
Russia	+	–	–
Slovakia	+	+	+
Slovenia	+	+	+
Tajikistan	–	–	–
Turkmenistan	–	–	–
Ukraine	–	–	–
Uzbekistan	–	–	–

A preliminary methodological discussion

Having identified, conceptualized, operationalized and measured the dependent variable in the preceding chapter and, in this chapter, the three actor-centred independent variables deemed relevant for the purpose at hand, it is time to engage in an actual analysis of the political pathways traversed by the post-communist countries. Such a quest is not an easy one and before attacking the empirical relationships some methodological guidelines are needed.

In the pitched methodological battle that characterizes the social sciences, what is often termed the 'variable-oriented' (aka quantitative, statistical or large-N) approach has incumbent status. By extension, what is often termed the 'case-oriented' (aka qualitative, comparative or small-N) approach is, at best, a possible challenger. (For the distinction between variable-oriented and case-oriented see Ragin 1987.) Tellingly, in his influential article from 1971, Lijphart went so far as to assert that the statistical method is always preferable to the comparative equivalent. Only when it is not possible to employ the former should the latter be adopted. King, Keohane and Verba's (1994) widely read *Designing Social Inquiry* has recently echoed Lijphart's claim.

The book is tacitly based on the same two-sided assumption that Lijphart frankly spells out: quantitative and qualitative methods share the same underlying logic of inference, but the former is superior as a methodological tool.

This proposition is not uniformly accepted, though. In recent decades, a number of scholars have praised the merits of the qualitative alternative (see in particular Ragin 1987, 2000; Brady and Collier 2004; and George and Bennett 2005), emphasizing its competitive edge in matters of conceptualization, understanding of the intricacies on the ground and the application of non-regression logics of inference, such as process tracing.

This disagreement testifies to the heterogeneity of the market place of methodological ideas. Where does this leave us with the present research project in mind? The simple answer is that it is flawed to state that there is one best way to compare across space or time. Choosing a method of comparison is exactly that: a choice between equally valid alternatives that cannot be solved on a meta-level (or as an exercise in scholastics), but only with a view to the problem and the empirical context (cf. also Collier et al. 2004: 224).

Recall in this connection the point of departure for the explanatory quest of this book: Kitschelt's ontological critique of proximate explanations. That Kitschelt's critique has not been assessed more systematically empirically probably owes much to the methodological issues implied by his ontological propositions. As described in the Introduction, his recommendations are based on the premise that proximate explanations are too close to the outcome, temporally speaking. But there is more to it than that. He also makes the case for a path-dependent account of political change in the former communist bloc. To a large extent, structural conditions determined whether open or closed politics characterized the transition, the argument goes, and these characteristics then paved the way for a number of proximate mechanisms of transmission. From a democratic perspective, the post-communist reality has therefore been one of either virtuous or vicious circles, a set of positive and negative spirals unleashed by the deep constraints and then reproduced by the proximate choices. To elaborate, an auspicious structural point of departure has made for auspicious proximate actor-choices, ultimately locking in an auspicious political regime form (*in casu* democracy) and likewise with an inauspicious structural point of departure.

These arguments have salient methodological consequences. Basically, they undermine, or at least question, the use of what Kitschelt terms a 'tournament of variables', i.e. conventional, multiple regression techniques. The more proximate actor-centred variables will wash out the deeper structural variables merely because they are more closely linked to the outcome on the dimension of time. But this tells us preciously little about the causal chain *in toto*.

Also, the general tendency of the variables to overlap in the post-communist setting means that we are presented with massive problems of multi-collinearity (cf. also Pop-Eleches 2007: 917). In this situation, multiple regression analysis only allows us to pinpoint the joint importance of packages of variables, not their individual effects nor their relative importance.

Kitschelt deserves much praise for having brought these issues into play. Yet, to some extent at least, he does not follow through his own methodological arguments. He seems to favour the use of sophisticated statistical techniques, such as time-series analysis, to scrutinize post-communist pathways for the simple reason that they make up what may be termed the 'industry standard'.[17] However, as argued above, the statistical techniques are not very helpful when it comes to disentangling the causal mishmash of post-communism, the helter-skelter of bivariate relationships. If it is possible to find a comparative method better suited for testing Kitschelt's proposition, one should therefore do so.

Three criteria for such a method must be observed. First, tools that pave the way for identifying causal pathways by the systematic use of simple logical arguments concerning the dimension of time are direly needed. Second, the striking empirical regularities on the dependent variable, the existence of the post-communist tripartition, suggest that manifest co-variations, which call for explicit methodological treatment, are present. Third, the logic underpinning the notion of virtuous and vicious circles implies that methodological tools capable of handling conjunctural causation, given a medium number of cases, are needed.

Bearing this in mind, qualitative comparative tools – emphasizing differences in kind – appear to be more suitable for the task at hand than standard quantitative techniques. Thus we have reached the justification for the particular comparative method that I wish to try on for size: typological theory. This qualitative tool is virtually tailored to identifying manifest causal pathways in the face of equifinality whilst embedding the temporal dimension, thereby appreciating all the said points in the context of analysing a relatively low number of cases.

That is not all. This choice of method is particularly well suited given the wish to analyse and subsequently juxtapose deep and proximate explanations. As George and Bennett (2005: 245) have pointed out,

> [a]n important advantage of typological theorizing is that it can move beyond earlier debates between structural and agent-centered theories by including, within a single typological framework, hypotheses on mechanisms leading from agents to structures and those leading from structures to agents.

Typologies and typological theory

I have already described the typological logic in Chapter 1. A typology is, to reiterate, a multidimensional and conceptual classification, i.e. an ordering on a compound of attributes (see Bailey 1994 for an excellent overview of the possible taxonomical exercises). Yet the pure ordering in a multi-dimensional property space is merely the descriptive face of typologies; indeed typologies are often construed as providing descriptive inference only (cf. Bailey 1994: 15 and George and Bennett 2005). Needless to say, providing descriptive inference is no small feat. As was demonstrated in Chapter 1, not only can a well-crafted typology bring order into an otherwise complex universe, it can also be used to check postulates about empirical phenomena, *in casu* the existence of a gap between the electoral and liberal component of democracy. Having said that, typologies make for more than descriptive inference: they offer an anchorage for causal inference as well (cf. also Elman 2005).

This should not come as a surprise. The one-dimensional classifications – the respective orderings, or serial operations, on attributes of which the compound is made up – normally capture a theoretically relevant distinction between the presence and absence of a given factor.[18] Indeed, the respective attributes are, as has been the case in this chapter, oftentimes derived straight from the theoretical literature. In other words, the classes tend to exhaust, in a mutually exclusive way, the possible outcomes on either a dependent or an independent variable. This means that a typology, or at least a typology formed in this way, necessarily posits something about theoretical relationships within the property space at hand. This is the very point of departure for the configurational method that is aptly termed 'typological theory'.[19] Quoting George and Bennett (2005: 235):

> We define a typological theory as a theory that specifies independent variables, delineates them into the categories for which the researcher will measure the cases and their outcomes, and provides not only hypotheses on how these variables operate individually, but also contingent generalizations on how and under what conditions they behave in specified conjunctions or configurations to produce effects on specified dependent variables. We call specified conjunctions or configurations of the variables 'types'.

In other words, typological theory must delineate the expected pathways within the compound of attributes. The capacity to do so is in fact the ultimate merit of typological theory. Such a design accommodates equifinality, without the need to rely on assumptions about deterministic causation. This is what George and Bennett (2005: 146) emphasize when they write that, '[. . .] typological theorizing allows for this kind of interaction, as it can incorporate causal mechanisms that offset one another in some contexts and complement one another in others'.

I will use the typological logic to analyse the post-communist pathways. As already pointed out, the analysis will be theory-driven as all of the independent attributes employed in this book are (when present) expected to strongly favour a specific outcome on the dependent variable, namely democracy. Contrariwise, when absent, they are expected to favour a very different outcome on the dependent variable, namely autocracy.

Guidelines for typological analysis

There are basically two possible ways of using typological theory. Either one identifies an empirical type and – by working backwards to the underlying property space or compound of attributes – forms the full typology. Alternatively, one first spells out the theoretical dimensions (i.e. respective attributes), and then forms the property space accordingly. Whereas the first strategy is inductive, the second is deductive (see George and Bennett 2005; Elman 2005). It will come as no surprise that the latter approach is that employed below. After all, the treatment of independent variables carried out in this chapter is as deductive as things can possibly get.

On the basis of these preliminary serial operations, it is easy to form the consequent typology by unfolding the complete property space of the dependent and the independent variables. Recall that the dependent variable was conceptualized as a trichotomy of political regime forms, a classification entailing a tripartition. Combined with the three dichotomous classifications exhausting the independent variables, a typology containing 24 types can be constructed.

I have already adopted George and Bennett's definition of typological theory, which basically represents it as a multidimensional conceptual classification specifying the expected relationship among the independent variables and between the independent variables and their dependent equivalent. As a first step, the theoretical expectations must therefore be clarified. In gist, I must provide hypotheses on the expected political pathways. The foundation of this work has already been laid in the discussion of the three independent variables. Recall that the justifications for including each of the independent variables were that when the attribute used to separate the dichotomous classes was present, the variable would theoretically make for democracy; when the attribute was absent, the variable would theoretically make for autocracy.

Furthermore, my preliminary expectation is that the independent variables will interact strongly; to vulgarize, my expectation is that good things will go together and vice versa. Mirroring the choices made by the actors of a particular domestic setting, the three orderings on the three variables should respond to each other. A displacement of communist incumbents will, for instance, probably facilitate the introduction of constitutional safeguards against a strong presidency as well as the economic reform process. By implication, the effects of the actor-choices should quickly create either a virtuous or a vicious circle with regard to the dynamics on the dependent variable of the political regime form.

Taken together, this leads me to two expectations concerning space and one concerning time. First, considering the path-dependent logic underlying the hypotheses, it is natural to expect that democracy will only be present when all three attributes are present and, contrariwise, that autocracy will only be present when all three attributes are absent. By implication, I expect very many of the cases to clump in the two polar types of cell 1 and 24, i.e. the types where: i) democracy is combined with the presence of displacement, legislature and reform; and ii) autocracy is combined with the absence of displacement, legislature and reform. I will refer to the former polar type as 'actor-induced democracy', as it connotes an actor-based expectation of democracy, and the latter polar type as 'actor-induced autocracy', as it connotes an actor-based expectation of autocracy. Second, the hybrid regimes should logically inhabit the intermediate types close to the diagonal as some attributes will be present (otherwise autocracy is the expected outcome), but some will also be absent (otherwise democracy is the expected outcome). Third, recall that I am unable to analyse the initial years of post-communism due to temporal limitations. Bearing this in mind, I expect this picture to be visible from the first analysed year (1997) because the increased returns of the actor choices should have kicked in by then.

In what way does the typological schema allow us to either confirm or disconfirm these expectations? The two most elaborate elucidations of typological theory – that of George and Bennett (2005) and that of Elman (2005) – are not very helpful on this essential question as they devote little attention to assessing the general empirical configurations. Elman basically pays no heed to the actual inferential techniques which can be used under the auspices of typological theory, instead emphasizing various strategies of compression and expansion. George and Bennett propose four research designs, but these basically consist of contrasting individual types with each other. To quote: 'These include comparing similar or differing cases in the same type; comparing most similar cases in adjacent types with differing outcomes; studying most-likely, least-likely, and crucial cases; comparing least similar cases' (2005: 251–2).

In Chapter 5, I will explicitly use one of Elman's strategies of reduction and in Chapter 4 I will sporadically touch upon some of George and Bennett's 'typewise' inferential techniques. But my overall objective is much more general: to establish the goodness of fit between the theoretical expectations and the empirical ordering within the property space *tout court*.

To do so, I turn to two other techniques. First, building on Bailey (1994), I will take note of the extent to which the ordering on the variables co-vary. As he explains it in the context of a typology consisting of four dichotomized variables (and therefore of 16 cells),

> [t]he more correlation exists among the four variables, the more grouping into a few cells we can expect. If all four variables are found to be very highly intercorrelated, all cases might clump along the main diagonal, perhaps into only two cells, the polar cells of 1 and 16 (p. 29).

To restate this with respect to the actor-centred typology with its 24 types, if all the variables are highly correlated, then over time the empirical referents will come to clump along the diagonal (types 1, 10–15 and 24) and in the two polar types (type 1 and 24) in particular.

Second, as Mahoney (2004) points out, typological theory presents a device for assessing independent variables in terms of necessary and sufficient causation.[20] I will use this configurative logic to establish the respective explanatory merits of the independent variables (given the three possible outcomes).

A typological analysis of post-communist political pathways

It is time to assess the combination of dependent and independent variables at three of the four points in time announced in Chapter 2: 1997, 2002 and 2007. (As already argued, 1992 precedes the empirical measurement on several of the independent variables. Therefore, it cannot be included.)

A preliminary note on the missing short-term picture of 1992

If it were possible to carry out this typological analysis in the early 1990s (recall that it is not, because of priority), we would find that most of the then 26 countries did not behave as expected. Such is the case because of the very modest variation on the dependent variable until the mid-1990s, i.e. the fact that most countries were then hybrid regimes (cf. Figure 4.1).

To be more precise, very many countries would inhabit the types adjacent to the two polar types because they would either have both or none of the actor-centred attributes, but would still be hybrid regimes (cf. Figure 2.1). These adjacent types can thus be construed as waiting rooms for countries traversing the respective paths to democracy and autocracy. Accordingly, I will name them 'democracy waiting room' and 'autocracy waiting room', respectively. Next, recall that by 1997 the pattern had already begun to settle down on the dependent variable. Consequently, we should expect that the types adjacent to the polar types are emptying out. Is this indeed the case?

The medium-term picture of 1997

Figure 3.1 illustrates the ordering of the post-communist countries on the compound of attributes in 1997.[21] The now 26 countries (owing to the fact that Czechoslovakia was divided into its two constituent parts in the early 1990s) are situated in eight different types, five of which inhabit the lands of the hybrid regimes.

Does this ordering match the theoretical expectation? To a large extent, the answer is in the affirmative. The typological picture of 1997 contains few surprises. All of the three proximate variables seem to push the countries in the expected direction. Seven of the eight democracies that were in existence in

		+ Leg		− Leg	
		+ Displacement	− Displacement	+ Displacement	− Displacement
Democracy	+ Ref	CZE EST HUN LTU LTV POL SVN	ROM		
	− Ref				
Hybrid regime	+ Ref	HRV MKD SVK	ALB BUL MNG		
	− Ref	MDA		ARM GEO KGZ RUS	AZE UKR
Autocracy	+ Ref				
	− Ref				BLR KAZ TJK TKM UZB

Figure 3.1 The full typology with empirical referents, 1997.

Note
'Displacement' is shorthand for the property of 'Displacement of communists in the first election', 'Ref' is shorthand for the property of an 'Economic reform process' and 'Leg' is shorthand for the property of 'Strong legislatures in the post-communist setting'.

1997 belong in the polar type of 'actor-induced democracy'; Romania constitutes the lone exception as it lacks the attribute of displacement. Likewise, all six autocracies that were in existence in 1997 belong in the opposite polar type of 'actor-induced autocracy'. In other words, if we take the ordering on the dependent variable as the point of departure, only one of the 13 non-hybrid regimes defies the theoretical expectations.

The picture does not totally conform to the expectations, however. If we focus on the orderings on the independent variables, five countries which should be democracies or autocracies are actually hybrid regimes. Thus, three countries have crossed the threshold on all three attributes but are not democracies. Conversely, two countries fall short on all three attributes but are not autocracies. These two groups of countries consequently inhabit types adjacent to the polar types – the respective 'waiting rooms' which I have indicated using a grey shade – that should not be empirical realities according to the theoretical expectations.

Other than that, notice that the identity of the democracies and autocracies presents few surprises. Only East-Central European countries are found in the polar type of actor-induced democracy. Conversely, four of the five Central Asian republics plus Belarus are situated in the polar type of actor-induced autocracy – no major surprises there, either. The four countries that are hybrid regimes in spite of the presence of all three attributes are Croatia, Macedonia and Slovakia. Azerbaijan and Ukraine have none of the three attributes but are, nevertheless, not autocracies. Finally, the remaining hybrid regimes have the expected mixed combination of the presence of one attribute with the absence of the other. Taken together, the empirics thus both confirm and contradict the expectations. First, with the exception of Romania, they confirm the expectations with regard to democracies, autocracies and most of the hybrid regimes. Second, however, a good handful of countries that should belong in the polar types actually inhabit the adjacent types. How can we interpret these inconsistencies?

One possibility is, of course, that the pattern is less clear-cut than expected because causal determinism is not to be found in the post-communist setting. Otherwise said, the variables may not explain the entire variation, even in the longer run. This is probably part of the answer, and it will come out when scrutinizing the years of 2002 and 2007, respectively. Still, another possibility is that the actor-based – and institutional – dynamics have not kicked in as yet or have not sufficiently kicked in. If this is indeed the nub of the matter, then some of the hybrid regimes may have embarked on a course that, in due time, will lead them to the polar types. In sum, we would expect even more movement toward the extremes of democracy and autocracy on the dependent variable to arise over time. Let us move one step down the temporal road to check out if such a development does indeed take place.

The medium-term picture of 2002

The 2002 distribution of countries within the compound of attributes is illustrated in Figure 3.2. The 26 countries inhabit nine different types. We now encounter even more variation on the dependent variable. This is first and foremost because an additional four countries (Croatia, Bulgaria, Mongolia

		+ Leg		− Leg	
		+ Displacement	− Displacement	+ Displacement	− Displacement
Democracy	+ Ref	CZE EST HRV HUN LTU LTV POL SVK SVN	BGR MNG ROM		
	− Ref				
Hybrid regime	+ Ref	MKD	ALB		
	− Ref	MDA		ARM GEO RUS	UKR
Autocracy	+ Ref				
	− Ref			KGZ	AZE BLR KAZ TJK TKM UZB

Figure 3.2 The full typology with empirical referents, 2002.

and Slovakia) have become democracies and one more country (Kyrgyzstan) has become an autocracy. Accordingly, the types adjacent to the polar types only contain two, rather than six countries. How may we interpret these dynamics?

The picture is still very much in line with the theoretical expectations. In 2002, 15 out of 19 non-hybrid regimes are to be found in the respective polar types. Notice, however, that three countries have become democracies while lacking one actor-centred attribute (displacement). Likewise, one country has become an autocracy without having one of the attributes (discplacement). A bit less disturbing, but still surprising considering the expectations, is that two countries that should belong in the polar types still linger in either the democracy waiting room or the autocracy waiting room.

When scrutinizing the proper names of the various referents, few surprises meet the eye. Regarding the polar types, the Czech Republic, Croatia, Estonia, Hungary, Latvia, Lithuania, Poland, Slovakia and Slovenia constitute the actor-induced democracies. In other words, Macedonia is the only country which combines the presence of all attributes but is not a democracy. Likewise, the seven actor-induced autocracies turn out to be Azerbaijan, Belarus, Kazakhstan, Tajikistan, Turkmenistan and Uzbekistan. There is not much of a puzzle there, either. Ukraine still belongs in the adjacent autocracy waiting room.

What about the countries that have crossed the threshold to either democracy or autocracy without having a clean sheet on the actor-centred attribute? These are Bulgaria, Mongolia and Romania (democracies) and Kyrgyzstan (autocracy). Interestingly, and as mentioned, all of these exceptions fall short on one and the same variable: the displacement of communist incumbents at the first elections. Bulgaria, Mongolia and Romania did not have such initial displacement, whereas Kyrgyzstan did. In the early 1990s, they conformed to this: Bulgaria and Romania did worse in East-Central Europe, whereas Kyrgyzstan was the lone star of Central Asia. But it seems that the effect was only of high importance in the shorter term, whereas the importance of having the presence or the absence of a strong legislature and the presence or absence of a reform process still holds up in 2002.

The long-term picture of 2007

Let us, finally, move to the long-term picture (2007). Figure 3.3 shows that nine types are once again in existence, but that the two polar types still claim the membership of no less than 15 out of 26 countries. How does the general picture square with the expectations?

As in 2002, only two observations are to be found in a type adjacent to the polar types in the so-called 'waiting rooms'. Out of the 17 countries that have a clean score (i.e. a full presence or a full absence) on the attributes covering the three independent variables, only two thus defy the theoretical expectations by not belonging in the polar types. That does not mean that the classes of democracy and autocracy reveal no surprises, however. No less than four observations are either democracies (three) or autocracies (one) despite either lacking or having one attribute. Let us take a closer look at the referents in the various types.

With the polar types, it is business as usual. The Czech Republic, Croatia, Estonia, Hungary, Latvia, Lithuania, Poland, Slovakia and Slovenia belong in the type of actor-induced democracy, whereas Azerbaijan, Belarus,

		+ Leg		− Leg	
		+ Displacement	− Displacement	+ Displacement	− Displacement
Democracy	+ Ref	CZE EST HRV HUN LTU LTV POL SVK SVN	BGR MNG ROM		
	− Ref				
Hybrid regime	+ Ref	MKD	ALB		
	− Ref	MDA		ARM GEO KGZ	UKR
Autocracy	+ Ref				
	− Ref			RUS	AZE BLR KAZ TJK TKM UZB

Figure 3.3 The full typology with empirical referents, 2007.

Kazakhstan, Tajikistan, Turkmenistan and Uzbekistan belong in the opposite type of actor-induced autocracy. This would probably also be the guess of most students of post-communism beforehand if they only knew the numbers and not the identity of the countries. The two countries that are still situated in a waiting room are Macedonia and Ukraine. By now, we may conclude that they diverge from the expected pattern; either there have been errors of measurement or other constraints not revealed by the present actor-analysis lie behind these relatively unexpected outcomes on the political regime form.

Much more interesting are the countries that have crossed the threshold to democracy or autocracy despite lacking or having one of the attributes covering the independent variables. Bulgaria, Mongolia and Romania have all become democracies despite lacking the attribute of displacement. Conversely, Russia has now replaced Kyrgyzstan as the autocracy lacking the attribute of displacement. Where does this leave us?

In general, the theoretical expectations have been met to a very large degree. The polar types now house more than half of all countries, confirming the existence of a virtuous and a vicious circle, respectively. Also, the waiting rooms have, taking the missing picture of the early 1990s as a frame of reference, more or less emptied out, indicating that the countries were in fact traversing the expected pathways over the period. But a more particular conclusion is also noteworthy. It turns out that the variables measuring a strong legislature and an economic reform process are more causally important than the variable measuring a displacement of communist incumbents. Hence, all of the four said exceptions fall short on the latter, whereas no democracy or autocracy fall short on the two former. This equals using a most dissimilar system design to partially disconfirm the explanatory value of displacement. Still, it should be noted that the 15 countries inhabiting the polar types fit the expectations connected with this variable. Likewise, a number of hybrid regimes fit the expectations, which is why I stress that the disconfirmation is, at most, a relative one. (To elaborate, we can question the explanatory value vis-à-vis the variables legislature and reform, not absolutely speaking.)

This also comes out in a robustness check I have undertaken by treating the differences on each variable as differences of degree only, viz. using the raw scores rather than the dichotomous scores. Using a statistical K-means analysis of the two independent structural variables and the dependent variable of political regime forms in 1997, 2002 and 2007 (specifying a three-cluster solution), an F-test allows us to see which variables are significant in accounting for differences between the clusters.[22] The three-cluster solution is meant to reflect the findings of the typological analysis, viz. that the countries mostly clump in the two polar types and in the centre area along the diagonal. While all three variables are significant at the level of 0.01, it turns out that displacement falls at the level of 0.001 and does so during the entire period. It does not fall much short, however, and these minor differences in level of significance do not justify eliminating the variable (see Appendix 3.1). Let us get back to the general level in order to sum up the analysis, cross-temporally as well as cross-spatially.

Conclusions

Viewed from the higher ground, the analysis confirms the relevance of understanding the post-communist political pathways through the prism of a proximate, actor-centred analysis. Over time, the countries have very much come to cluster in the two polar types of actor-induced democracy and actor-induced autocracy. If the analysis could have been carried out in 1992, few countries would be found here. Yet as early as 1997, 12 out of 26 countries were situated in the polar types. In 2002 and 2007, the number had risen to 15. Otherwise said, in the long term, close to 60 per cent of the countries end up in the polar types, thus confirming the existence of actor-induced virtuous or vicious political circles. Interestingly, the two adjacent types of the democracy waiting room and the autocracy waiting room practically empty out over the period. In 1992, many countries would have been situated in these types. However, from the mid-1990s onwards, we only find a small handful of specimens of this unexpected phenomenon, and in the 2000s just two are left standing. Cross-temporally, countries with either a full presence or a full absence of actor-centred properties simply leave the sphere of the hybrid regimes.

More surprisingly, the analysis shows that some countries have in fact become democracies or autocracies without a clean sheet on the attributes covering the independent variables (which means that they were 'supposed' to be hybrid regimes). Both Kyrgyzstan (in 2002) and Russia (in 2007) have visited the class of autocracy in spite of the presence of one of the three attributes, namely displacement. Conversely, Romania (in 1997, 2002 and 2007), Bulgaria (in 2002 and 2007) and Mongolia (in 2002 and 2007) were democracies in spite of the absence of the very same attribute. This last cluster, in particular, indicates that at least one other pathway to democracy than that of the polar type is empirically viable. (The same can possibly be said about Kyrgyzstan and Russia's paths to autocracy.) Let us use these observations to shift the attention from the empirical types to the relative causal importance of the independent variables.

Two pathways lead to the respective destinations of democracy and autocracy, which is the focal point here. With regard to the former terminus, either i) the combined presence of displacement, legislature and reform or ii) the sole presence of legislature and reform may bring about democracy. With regard to the latter destination, either i) the combined absence of displacement, legislature and reform or ii) the sole absence of legislature and reform may lead to autocracy.

These pathways may be easier comprehended using the language of necessary and sufficient causation.[23] The presence of the attributes of legislature and reform are necessary conditions of democracy, but the same cannot be said of the presence of displacement, which is only a facilitating cause. Likewise, the absence of the attributes of legislature and reform are necessary conditions of autocracy, whereas the absence of displacement is once again only a facilitating cause. Notice, finally, that neither the presence nor absence of any attributes (nor any combination of attributes) is a sufficient condition of the respective outcomes of democracy and autocracy due to the existence of the two full-scale aberrations of Macedonia (exhibiting a full presence of attributes) and Ukraine (exhibiting a full absence of attributes).

This indicates that a strong legislature and an economic reform process are the most essential proximate variables and, by extension, that a displacement of communist incumbents is the least essential proximate variable, at least in the longer run. But this is an aside.

The more important question is whether we may simply conclude that the actor-based explanations within the literature, and in particular the constitutional engineering hypothesis, can account for the identified variation on the dependent variable of the political regime form, at least from the mid-1990s onwards? This would be as premature as it is tempting. The actor-based explanations are encumbered with one very important logical problem. Recall that the explanations discussed in this chapter all assume that the room for action is quite wide; they are, so to speak, wearing a voluntaristic dressing, and with good reason, too. If the choices of the actors merely reflect anterior (i.e. deeper) factors, then, at the end of the day, they are spurious or only intervening. This is exactly where we encounter the one great challenge to the analysis of this chapter. The empirical referents of the various types, and in particular the polar types, seem to be very systematically dispersed across space.

Thus, mirroring a point made in Chapter 2, throughout the period, the type of actor-induced democracy solely houses East-Central European countries. Likewise, the type of actor-induced autocracy solely houses countries situated in the Eastern part of the setting (with the lone exception of Belarus). This indicates that i) the pathways of the actors may have been sealed beforehand and ii) the status on both the three independent variables and the dependent variable merely reflects that. This critique provides the basis for considering a structural corrective to the actor-explanations discussed and tested so far. This is the very subject of Chapter 4.

Appendix 3.1

Using a statistical cluster analysis as a robustness test

In the statistical cluster analyses below, I have repeated the typological analyses of this chapter. This time, I construe the differences within the setting as differences of degree only, rather than differences of kind, as was the case in the typological analyses. The objective is to see if the typological mappings are reconfirmed using more sophisticated methods. The variables employed are i) displacement, legislature and reform and ii) the Freedom House ratings for the respective years of 1997, 2002 and 2007. The procedure is twofold: first, an open-ended hierarchical cluster analysis is used to identify the number of empirical clusters in the data; second, a K-means analysis is used to identify the properties of the clusters as well as the actual cluster membership.

The hierarchical cluster analysis

In the hierarchical cluster analysis, z scores for all variables subject to cluster analysis are computed in order to standardize the data. Next, a distance measure – the squared Euclidean distance – is used as measure for similarity. Based on the resulting distance matrix, the units of observations are then combined (i.e. fused) into clusters in an iterative process until all cases have been assigned to a particular cluster. The logic of fusion is determined by a clustering algorithm. The clustering algorithm in this case is the Ward method, which determines cluster membership on the basis of the total sum of squared deviations from the mean of a cluster. The final results are then depicted in dendrograms covering the years 1997, 2002 and 2007, respectively, on the dependent variable on the political regime form. The dendrograms are too space-consuming to be illustrated here, but their results are unequivocal. Viewed from the higher ground, they all lend support to the notion that separate (geographical) clusters exist, to wit i) East-Central European democracies, ii) post-Soviet and Balkan hybrid regimes and iii) post-Soviet autocracies.

A K-means analysis

The open-ended information from the hierarchical cluster analysis provides a suitable point of departure for running a K-means analysis specifying a three-cluster solution. The three quick cluster tables illustrate the cluster centres by variables for the final cluster solution. Otherwise said, we get the characteristics of the three clusters on each of the variables. The F-test statistics indicated by asterisks tells us which variables are significant in accounting for differences between the clusters: *** = below .001; ** = below 0.01; and * = below 0.05. Notice, however, that the F-tests are best suited for descriptive purposes because the clusters have been chosen to maximize the differences among

Table 3.2a K-means analysis for 1997

	Final cluster centres 1997		
	Cluster 1	*Cluster 2*	*Cluster 3*
Displacement**	1	1	0
Legislature***	0.75	0.56	0.35
Reform ***	3.30	1.60	1.02
FH-ratings 1997***	2.15	3.79	6.0
	Bulgaria, Croatia, Czech Republic, Estonia, Hungary, Latvia, Lithuania, Macedonia, Mongolia, Poland, Romania, Slovakia, Slovenia	Albania, Armenia, Georgia, Kyrgyzstan, Moldova, Russia, Ukraine	Azerbaijan, Belarus, Kazakhstan, Tajikistan, Turkmenistan, Uzbekistan

Table 3.2b K-means analysis for 2002

	Final cluster centres 2002		
	Cluster 1	*Cluster 2*	*Cluster 3*
Displacement**	1	1	0
Legislature***	0.75	0.56	0.35
Reform ***	3.30	1.60	1.02
FH-ratings 1997***	1.69	4.14	6.0
	Bulgaria, Croatia, Czech Republic, Estonia, Hungary, Latvia, Lithuania, Macedonia, Mongolia, Poland, Romania, Slovakia, Slovenia	Albania, Armenia, Georgia, Kyrgyzstan, Moldova, Russia, Ukraine	Azerbaijan, Belarus, Kazakhstan, Tajikistan, Turkmenistan, Uzbekistan

Table 3.2c K-means analysis for 2007

	Final cluster centres 2007		
	Cluster 1	*Cluster 2*	*Cluster 3*
Displacement**	2	1	0
Legislature***	0.75	0.63	0.36
Reform ***	3.49	1.73	1.15
FH-ratings 1997***	1.36	3.25	6.07
	Bulgaria, Croatia, Czech Republic, Estonia, Hungary, Latvia, Lithuania, Macedonia, Poland, Romania, Slovakia, Slovenia	Albania, Armenia, Georgia, Kyrgyzstan, Moldova, Mongolia, Ukraine	Azerbaijan, Belarus, Kazakhstan, Russia, Tajikistan, Turkmenistan, Uzbekistan

cases in different clusters. The observed significance levels are not corrected for this and thus cannot be interpreted as tests of the hypothesis that the cluster means are equal.

Basically, the cluster analyses reconfirm the empirical patterns identified in Chapter 3 proper. The membership of the three statistical clusters does not completely mirror the tripartition identified in the typological analysis – most notably Macedonia and Mongolia behave somewhat erratic vis-à-vis the prior orderings – but at the end of the day, the fit is quite good. Also notice that Russia moves between the intermediate and the extreme clusters between 2002 and 2007, just as was the case in the categorical (i.e. typological) schema.

4   A structural analysis of post-communist political pathways

One of the often voiced criticisms of the actor-centred approach normally termed 'Transitology' is that the sustainability of democracy is very much linked to the structural constraints (see, for example, Acemoglu and Robinson 2006: 77). Even if the actors have a lot of proximate influence during upheavals, the longer-term prospects are therefore likely to be shaped by the structures. This is a valid point, but to some extent it misses the mark. O'Donnell and Schmitter (1986), in particular, were primarily preoccupied with the transitional 'black box', hence the name Transitology. Their aim was to probe into this 'window of opportunity' surrounding the breakdown of an authoritarian regime. Here, they stressed, the choices of the actors were of vital importance. The future outcome of this transition, on the contrary, was perceived as nebulous.[1]

More generally, the true test of any actor-centred perspective is a different one: whether or not the proximate actions can create what historical institutionalists term a 'critical juncture'. Basically, if the actors cannot break an antecedent structural pattern, thus sending their community off on a relatively more auspicious (or more inauspicious) political or economic track, then the transitional upheavals only reproduce the structural point of departure, which means that the perspective cannot stand alone. This goes for Transitology, too, in spite of the professed concern about the upheavals only.[2] And it is even more the case for the three actor-centred perspectives discussed and analysed in Chapter 3. After all, the explanations based on the initial elections, constitutional engineering and economic reform process all include claims concerning long-term political effects.

But has the scope for action really been wide in the post-communist setting? As already touched upon, the three operationalized regime forms seem to be systematically dispersed across the setting, at least from the mid-1990s onwards. With the sole exception of Mongolia, democracy has not made inroads outside of East-Central Europe, which means that it is reasonable to doubt whether this outcome has really been actor-induced. Conversely, the fact that autocracy is, with the partial exception of Kyrgyzstan, the common coin in all of Central Asia implies that this outcome, too, has to some extent been given in advance willy-nilly.

These geographical observations may seem trivial, and, to be sure, the lesson they hold is a simple one. But simple lessons are oftentimes important. Basically, the relatively open political highway of the early 1990s soon divided itself into three distinct paths. From the mid-1990s onwards, it seems difficult – or at least counter-intuitive – to attribute this systematic geographical variation to the contingent choices of actors during political upheavals.

The alternative explanation that comes to mind is that the structural constraints are to blame. If we assume – and it would be very heroic not to do so – that the commonalities between the structural factors are larger within each of the three geographical clusters (i.e. within what I have termed the 'subregions of post-communism') than between them, then this structural variation coincides with that on the dependent variable of the political regime form. By extension, it seems reasonable to expect that structural factors lie behind at least the longer-term empirical trichotomy of political regime forms that I identified in Chapter 2. In an actor-centred analysis of post-communist political diversity, Michael McFaul (2002: 238) has (almost) conceded as much. To quote:

> The strong correlation between geography and regime type suggests that deeper structural variables might explain the regime variances without the need for a careful accounting of balances of power and ideologies at the time of transition. Geography, as well as economic development, history, culture, prior regime type, and the ideological orientation of enemies most certainly influenced the particular balances of power and ideologies that produced democracy and dictatorship in the postcommunist world. Future research must seek to explain these transitional balances of power.

This book deliberately seeks to provide such future research on the structural roots of the actor-choices during the transition. With this in mind, I will only consider the structural independent variables found within the explanatory field in this chapter. Paraphrasing Lipset's (1959a) famous article, it is the 'structural requisites of democracy' that interest me here.

Identifying structural factors in the literature on post-communism

As should be clear from the theoretical and methodological discussion of the Introduction and Chapter 3, the aim of this book is not to find the 'smoking gun', *the* explanatory variable, of post-communist democratizations. In fact, the posited existence of virtuous and vicious circles – and, more technically, of massive multicollinearity problems – implies that chasing such mono-causality is not worthwhile. The aim of the analyses is much more general, viz. to juxtapose and possibly integrate deep and proximate explanations within the literature, thereby testing the merits of Kitschelt's influential critique.

Notice in this connection that I employ a somewhat broader understanding of deep explanations than Kitschelt does; they are thus taken to cover stable factors outside the manipulative reach of the domestic actors. This is in contrast to the proximate factors of Chapter 3, which can change significantly within short periods of time and are easier to alter besides being closer to the outcome in question on the dimension of time.

A thorough reading of the literature on post-communism has identified a number of deep explanations. This reading is based, in particular, on the overviews presented by Kitschelt (1999) and Pop-Eleches (2007). But tellingly it also, to a large extent, mirrors the explanatory field identified by Linz and Stepan (1996) in their global tour de force through matters of transition and consolidation, which indicates that the framework is relatively encompassing. In particular, three[3] structural factors have been deemed worth including.

First is the structural factor that I will term the 'political legacies explanation', associated in particular with Herbert Kitschelt himself. Building on his call for an integration between 'deep' and 'proximate' causes, Kitschelt (1999) traces the present political variation to the two pre-communist attributes of bureaucratic state legacies and the balance of power between communists and their challengers at the introduction of communist rule. The argument holds that a certain status on these attributes made for a democratic transition in 1989–91 due to the strength of the opposition (the proximate link in the causal chain), whereas a distinct status made for autocratic continuity because the communist incumbents only faced weak opposition.

Second is the structural factor that I will term the 'vicinity to Western Europe explanation', touched upon by virtually anyone writing on the subject (even pessimists such as Przeworski 1991 and Jowitt 1992), but promoted in particular by scholars such as Jeffrey S. Kopstein and David A. Reilly, Anna Milada Vachudova and Steven Levitsky and Lucan A. Way. The argument appears in many guises, some stressing neighbour effects in general, others the particular consequences of EU enlargement. But the overall empirical claim is very much of the same ilk: the post-communist countries adjacent to Western Europe have had much better democratic prospects than the countries further to the east. Or, to express it using differences of kind, that vicinity to Western Europe made for democracy, whereas its absence made for autocracy.

Third is the structural factor that I will term the 'modernization explanation'. This perspective obviously harks back to Seymour Martin Lipset's seminal article from 1959 and has more recently been revisited by Adam Przeworski and Fernando Limongi. In the context of post-communism, the perspective has been used by, for example, Marcus J. Kurtz and Andrew Barnes. In essence, the explanation posits that a relatively high level of socio-economic development made for democracy after the breakdown of communism, whereas a relatively low level of socio-economic development made for autocracy.

The political legacies variable (legacies)

In a very interesting attempt to carry out his own recommendation about integrating deep and proximate explanations of post-communist regime change, Herbert Kitschelt (1999) unfolds the deep factor that he terms 'communist legacies'. His empirical ordering is this:

> After the demise of the German Democratic Republic, the only surviving polity with a clearly bureaucratic-authoritarian legacy is the Czech Republic (score = 3). Polities with a background of national-accommodative communism are more numerous: Hungary, Poland, Slovenia, and the three Baltic states (score = 2). Patrimonial communist regimes yielding less favorable conditions for democracy prevailed in Southeastern Europe and the core areas of the former Soviet Union, Albania, Belarus, Bulgaria, Georgia, Macedonia, Romania, Russia, and the Ukraine (score = 1). The remaining fission products of the Former Soviet Union belonged to a colonial periphery with next to no articulation of civil society before the advent of communism and fully patrimonial administrative relations that jointly produce the dimmest opportunities for democratic regime entrenchment.
>
> (1999: 32)

The distinctions between the respective legacies of i) bureaucratic-authoritarian, ii) national-accommodative, iii) patrimonial communism and iv) colonial periphery build upon the two distinctive properties of, first, bureaucratic state legacies and, second, the balance of power between communists and their challengers. Both of these properties can be traced to the pre-communist era, but Kitschelt zealously emphasizes that they have been reproduced during communism, hence the tag 'communist legacies'. When present, the former legacy paved the way for a pattern of bureaucratic professionalization during communism which proved valuable by impeding rent-seeking after the breakdowns of communism in 1989–91. When present, the latter legacy made for a lingering oppositional civil society which came into its own after 1989–91, thus ensuring immediate political opposition to the communist incumbents.

In particular, both bureaucratic-authoritarian and national-accommodative communism made for either a virtual breakdown or a negotiated transition in 1989–91 because of the strength of the opposition. Contrariwise, patrimonial communism and colonial periphery made for either pre-emptive reforms or mere continuity because the communist incumbents faced such weak opposition. To phrase it more generally, the structural point of departure reproduced itself via proximate mechanisms, or actor-choices, during the transition. Kitschelt's explanatory logic is thus one of path dependency, which is further underlined by the fact that, to a large extent, the two properties of bureaucratic state legacies and the balance of power between communists and their challengers go hand in hand. Kitschelt adds them up precisely because of their collinearity and it seems reasonable to construe these two attributes as one dimension. Hence, I will use Kitschelt's ordering as a pivot for the subsequent classification.

But how do we make a distinction between two classes in this case? Theoretically, the dividing line is that which separates beneficial political legacies or, even more particularly, a beneficial communist legacy from its opposite. In other words, the expectation is that the presence of a beneficial communist legacy will facilitate democracy, whereas its absence will facilitate autocracy. A beneficial legacy describes a situation in which the bureaucratic apparatus and the societal opposition to the communist party ensured that democrats had a base to mobilize after the breakdown of communism.

As explained above, according to Kitschelt, the corresponding cut-off point is that between bureaucratic-authoritarian or national-accommodative, on the one hand, and patrimonial communism or colonial periphery on the other. Both of the two former inheritances theoretically favour democracy, whereas both of the two latter inheritances favour autocracy. As the analysis is to be theory-driven, I will cling to this. Notice also that the legacy of the former regime form by definition predates the events of post-communism, i.e. as cause it predates the effect. This is thus the threshold that separates the two classes, bringing us to the following operational definition of the variable: a post-communist country has a beneficial communist legacy – i.e. has the attribute 'legacies' – if it achieves a score of 2 or 3 as reported by Herbert Kitschelt in 'Accounting for Outcomes of Post-Communist Regime Change' (1999).

The vicinity to Western Europe variable (West)

That international influences are truly important for regime change is, somewhat surprisingly, to a certain extent a novel idea. Or, to be more precise, it was purposely placed in the shadow of the internal influences by what I have termed 'Transitology'. In 1978 Linz stressed this in regards to the breakdown of democracy; O'Donnell and Schmitter (1986) later aired the same opinion concerning transitions from authoritarian rule. To quote their (1986: 19) famous and uncompromising claim: 'More precisely, we assert that there is no transition whose beginning is not a consequence – direct or indirect – of important divisions within the authoritarian regime itself, principally along the fluctuating cleavage between hard-liners and soft-liners'.

That understanding was altered (for an illustration of this change in perception see, for example, Schmitter 1996: 5) when communism collapsed in 1989–91. First and foremost, the removal of the external Soviet pressure was something that could not be ignored as an (negative[4]) explanatory factor. Second, once democratization began, it spread like wildfire.

So, what is the prevailing claim of the theoretical literature after this sharp turn? The most general argument in the literature basically identifies a form of liberal discursive hegemony as the focal point (e.g. Levitsky and Way 2002: 61). In effect, the claim most often stated is a two-sided one. On the one hand, liberal hegemony means that virtually no country in today's world can completely ignore the pressure for democratization. On the other hand, it is underlined that responses often take the form of lip service to democratization, rather than genuine reform (cf. Gryzmala-Busse and Luong 2002: 536).

Another explanation, which also operates at a quite general level, is centred on distance to Western Europe and promoted by scholars such as Kopstein and Reilly (2000).[5] Here the very simple point is that countries adjacent to the West are more likely to become democracies than those situated further afield. More particular elaborations of this perspective emphasize notions such as the degree of leverage and linkage to the West (Levitsky and Way 2005).

Finally, even more prominent, and with an even more specific focus, is the explanation which emphasizes the EU's conditionality, associated in particular with Vachudova (2005). Needless to say, this point is especially relevant for the post-communist experience. Instead of assuming that liberal hegemony will have consequences for all post-communist countries, the claim of scholars such as Vachudova is that this is only so if a given country has the prospect of becoming an EU member.

As I will return to in the Conclusions, Vachudova's analysis is very convincing. However, some difficulties pertaining to time as a dimension of variation present themselves if we wish to include her operationalization into the deep edifice. Recall that the structural variables are to be measured at a point in time predating the occurrences of 1992 and onwards. As Vachudova (2005) has emphasized, the EU's leverage over East-Central Europe was passive until the actual membership negotiations came to the fore in the mid-1990s or, in fact, even later, as in the twin cases of Bulgaria and Romania. From then on the EU's leverage became active. Passive leverage refers to the general attraction of potential EU membership, whereas active leverage refers to the deliberate conditionality exercised in the EU's pre-accession process. Passive leverage is thus a kind of contextual variable, or a scope condition. On the one hand, it is based on the political and economic benefits of membership; on the other hand, it is based on the cost of exclusion. Active leverage's premise is based upon these incentives. In the 1990s, the political elites in the candidate countries were thus willing to accept very significant direct conditionality because the fruits of membership were so very overwhelming. Yet such direct leverage only became possible after the EU committed itself to actual accession negotiations.

Because of priority, active leverage cannot be captured in the typological analysis of this chapter. For this reason I will simply use Kopstein and Reilly's operationalization of the distance to Western Europe. Notice in this connection that the orderings that emerge from all of the explanations mentioned above correlate overwhelmingly. Bearing this in mind, such a simple operationalization will do.

Kopstein and Reilly use the distance of a post-communist country's capital to the twin capitals of Berlin and Vienna – whichever is closer – to measure the variable that I term 'West'.[6] It can be dichotomized using an overview presented by Kopstein and Reilly in which they distinguish between the three distances of 500, 1000 and 1,500 miles. I collapse the two former of these categories expected to make for democracy (0–499 and 500–999) and the two latter categories expected to make for autocracy (1,000–1,499 and 1,500–). Hence we operationalize: a country has vicinity to Western Europe – i.e. has the attribute 'West' – if its capital city is situated within a distance of 1,000 miles from either Berlin or Vienna, as reported by Kopstein and Reilly (2000).

The modernization variable (modern)

The modernization perspective on post-communism is but the contemporary acknowledgement of Lipset's (1959a, 1959b: 48–50) seminal assertion that '[t]he more well-to-do a nation, the greater the chances that it will sustain democracy'. Lipset's thesis has been at the receiving end of a lot of criticism since its conception in the late 1950s, not least because many of those borrowing his perspective attempted to transform it into a rule valid across time and space. The current version of the argument has returned to the probabilistic gestation. Termed 'neo-modernization theory' and associated with Przeworski and Limongi (1997), it holds that a country may initiate a transition to democracy at any income level. However, once democracy is initiated, the country's future prospects are very much dependent upon the level of economic development.[7] To paraphrase, a positive economic development does not create democracy, but it sustains democracy.

The mechanism most often used to underpin this relationship is that socio-economic development fosters education which, in turn, brings about political tolerance. Be that as it may, it is also possible to coin the relationship between socio-economic development and democratization in terms of naked self-interest. As Przeworski (2004: 137) notes '[a]bove some income level, in turn, losers accept an electoral defeat even when they have no chance to win in the future, simply because even permanent losers have too much to risk in turning against democracy'. Lipset (1959b: 66) himself touched upon this understanding in his famous work when he wrote that:

> If there is enough wealth in the country so that it does not make too much difference whether some redistribution takes place, it is easier to accept the idea that it does not matter greatly which side is in power. But if loss of office means serious losses for major power groups, they will seek to retain or secure office by any means available.

This latter understanding (which is also emphasized by Przeworski and Limongi 1997: 165–6) is a compelling one with respect to the post-communist experience. In many of the post-communist countries politics is first and foremost about power and the spoils of power. Hence, rather than focusing on human development characteristics such as education, I will simply look at the level of economic wealth.

More to the point, neo-modernization theory emphasizes two attributes: the absolute level of development and relative economic trends. The argument is, in a nutshell, that the presence of both a high absolute level of development and a positive economic trend bolsters democracy, whereas the absence of both of these facilitates a breakdown of democracy.

At first sight, it seems compelling to include both attributes in the classification of this variable. But the post-communist experience is remarkably out of sync with global dynamics on this point. In the early 1990s virtually all post-communist countries were burdened by economic declines of truly outstanding proportions. To quote Bela Greskovits (1998: 5):

> Against the background of a transformational recession [. . .] deeper and longer than the Great Depression had been in Western Europe, and in the context of sweeping neoliberal reforms, none of the predicted catastrophic political outcomes have so far materialized in the East. Protest against the dire economic conditions has been mostly sporadic, nonviolent, or insignificant.

Not only did the citizens of East-Central Europe remain sanguine during this precipitous economic decline, but democracy, in fact, made significant headway in many of these countries during the economic hardships. The post-communist experience simply seems to be idiosyncratic on this point, at least when placing one's faith in Przeworski and Limongi's general conclusions. To phrase it in comparative terms, negative economic trends were a constant throughout the first half of the 1990s and did not facilitate a breakdown as expected. It is thus fair to exclude this attribute from the investigation.

The same can be said about the presently popular focus on economic equality as a condition of successful democratization.[8] The post-communist experience is very hard to reconcile with this emphasis on the pernicious political effects of rising inequality. Under communism, the East-Central European countries reached very high levels of economic equality; after the advent of democracy, inequality has risen dramatically. A few examples should suffice: in Estonia, the Gini-coefficient (measured as the distribution of income) rose from a level of 28 in 1989 to 39 in 2000; in Latvia, from 26 to 33; in Lithuania, from 26 to 36; in Poland, from 28 to 35; in the Czech Republic, from 20 to 24; in Hungary, from 23 to 26; and in Romania from 24 to 31 (see Møller 2006). These very uniform trends have occurred in spite of the impressive democratic credentials of the said countries.

The absolute level of economic development is, on the contrary, a variable across the setting. Also, since political upheavals were ubiquitous in 1989–91, the absolute level would, according to the theory, impact directly upon the likelihood of locking in a democratic path. Also, the aggregate level of economic development has in fact been included in an interesting analysis of post-communism by Marcus J. Kurtz and Andrew Barnes (2002). This is, therefore, what the socio-economic variable connotes here. (This equals saying that it is not really a socio-economic variable, but only an economic variable.)

My expectation is that the presence of a (relatively) high level of economic development right after the political upheavals of 1989–91 facilitated democracy, whereas its absence facilitates breakdown of democracy and a movement towards autocracy. Due to considerations of priority, the 1991 numbers have been used. We find rather complete data series. I use 'rather' to indicate three minor qualifications. In one case (Azerbaijan) I have had to use a 1993 number due to lack of data; in two cases (the Czech Republic and Uzbekistan) I have had to use the 1992 number for the very same reason. However, as these three countries are situated far from the threshold that I propose below, this should be unproblematic

With regard to the denotative side of the coin, to make the variable comparable to that used by Przeworski and Limongi (1997: 159) it must capture the actual level of economic wealth of the average inhabitant, i.e. GDP per capita measured at 'constant U.S. dollars computed at purchasing-power parities'. But which threshold logically separates the classes of the 'haves' and the 'have-nots'? Here, I once again adhere to the analysis of Przeworski and Limongi. They (1997: 165) conclude that '[t]he probability that a democracy will die during any particular year in a country with an income above $4,000 is practically zero'. Basically, above this threshold a democracy that has been established will not break down due to economic crisis. Thus, and in order not to be accused of tampering with the cut-off points, I will employ this threshold to separate a relatively high level of economic development from a relatively low level of economic development.

Figures for GDP per capita at constant prices at purchasing-power parities (PPP) can be found in the World Bank's *World Development Indicators 2005*. Przeworski and Limongi's threshold of $4,000 is based on 1985 PPP USD. I have recalculated the figure using the World Development Indicators, which use 2000 PPP USD, and thus arrive at the number $6,236. This brings us to the following operational definition: a country has a high level of economic development – i.e. has the attribute 'modern' – if its GDP per capita (measured at constant PPP prices) in 1991 exceeds that indicated by Przeworski and Limongi (i.e. $6,236) in 'Modernization' (1997), as reported by the World Bank's *World Development Indicators 2005*.

An overview of the scoring on the 'deep' variables

As in Chapter 3 with the actor-centred variables, Table 4.1 shows the actual empirical outcomes on the three independent variables. Plus (+) indicates the presence of the attribute covering the variable, minus (–) indicates its absence.

Table 4.1 An overview of the scoring on the 'deep' variables

	Legacies	*West*	*Modern*
Albania	−	+	−
Armenia	−	−	−
Azerbaijan	−	−	−
Belarus	−	+	−
Bulgaria	−	+	+
Croatia	+	+	+
Czech Republic	+	+	+
Estonia	+	+	+
Georgia	−	−	−
Hungary	+	+	+
Kazakhstan	−	−	−
Kyrgyzstan	−	−	−
Latvia	+	+	+
Lithuania	+	+	+
Macedonia	−	+	+
Moldova	−	+	−
Mongolia	−	−	−
Poland	+	+	+
Romania	−	+	−
Russia	−	−	+
Slovakia	+	+	+
Slovenia	+	+	+
Tajikistan	−	−	−
Turkmenistan	−	−	−
Ukraine	−	+	+
Uzbekistan	−	−	−

A typological analysis of post-communist political pathways

Once again, I will employ typological theory to analyse the political pathways of post-communism, only this time from a structure-centred point of view. I intend to unfold the combination of the dependent and independent variables at the familiar four points in time (i.e. 1992, 1997, 2002 and 2007). Before doing so, the theoretical expectations must be clarified. The foundation of this work has already been laid out in the discussion of the independent variables. Recall that the justifications for including each of the three independent variables was that when the attribute used to separate the dichotomous classes was present, the variable would theoretically make for democracy and when it was absent, the variable would theoretically make for autocracy.

Again, my preliminary expectation is that good things tend to go together and vice versa. Needless to say, structural factors do not shape each other over night. Consequently, the bold virtuous and vicious circles actor-centred expectations do not have a theoretical place in this analysis. However, one would still expect, for instance, political legacies and modernization to have interacted over past generations.

To reiterate a point made in Chapter 3, the path-dependent logic infusing the general hypotheses indicates that only the full presence or full absence of the attributes legacies, West and modern are expected to pave the way for the respective outcomes of democracy and autocracy. By implication, in the longer term I expect the cases to clump along the diagonal and in particular in the two polar types of cell 1 and 24, i.e. the types where i) democracy is combined with the presence of all attributes and ii) autocracy is combined with the absence of all attributes. I will refer to the former polar type as 'structural democracy' as it connotes a structural expectation of democracy and the latter polar type as 'structural autocracy' as it connotes a structural expectation of democracy. The hybrid regimes should logically inhabit the intermediate types close to the diagonal as some attributes will be present (otherwise autocracy is the expected outcome) and some will be absent (otherwise democracy is the expected outcome).

One note needs to be added. This structurally-induced development is only expected to come to pass some time after upheavals of 1989–91 as the variation on the dependent variable is only likely to conform to that on the independent variables with a time lag. This means that the types adjacent to the polar types are even more deliberately construed as 'waiting rooms' in this analysis than was the case in the actor-centred analysis of Chapter 3 (in which the year 1992 was not included into the analysis). How does the reality of post-communism conform to these expectations?

The full typology with empirical referents, 1992–2007

Figure 4.1 illustrates the full typology with empirical referents that comes into existence when combining the ordering of the post-communist countries on the attribute covering the dependent variable of political regime forms in 1992 (the short-term) with the orderings on the attributes covering the three independent variables. The numbers in each of the cells indicate how many cases fall in that particular type.

The 25 countries in existence at the time occupy seven different types. We see that the pattern is somewhat fuzzy, confirming that the structural effects carried a time lag. To be sure, the two polar types of structural democracy and structural autocracy house all democracies and all autocracies. In other words, no country that is not a hybrid regime falls outside these two polar types. But the lands of the hybrid regimes are much more confusing. Most noteworthy, six countries that were expected to be autocracies (as all attributes are absent) are found in the autocracy waiting room, which I have once again indicated using a grey shade. Likewise, four countries expected to be democracies (as all attributes are present) are found in the democracy waiting room. Let us see what happens when we move five years down the road.

The 26 countries now in existence (due to the velvet divorce of Czechoslovakia) inhabit nine types. Figure 4.2 shows that the expected dynamics have only partly come to pass by 1997 (the medium term). First,

		+ Modern		− Modern	
		+ Leg	− Leg	+ Leg	− Leg
Democracy	+ West	CZS HUN POL SVN			
	− West				
Hybrid regime	+ West	HRV EST LTV LTU	BUL MKD UKR		ALB BLR MDA ROM
	− West		RUS		ARM AZE GEO KAZ KGZ MNG
Autocracy	+ West				
	− West				TJK TKM UZB

Figure 4.1 The full typology with empirical referents, 1992.

seven countries that either exhibit the presence or the absence of all attributes still belong in the realm of hybrid regimes, or waiting rooms. Second, one country (Romania) has moved into the class of democracy despite the absence of both of the attributes legacies and modern. Accordingly, one country with the presence of the attribute West belongs to the class of autocracy. The structural logic seems to be kicking in. What happens when we move to 2002?

| | | + Modern | | − Modern | |
		+ Leg	− Leg	+ Leg	− Leg
Democracy	+ West	CZS EST HUN LTV LTU POL SVN			ROM
	− West				
Hybrid regime	+ West	HRV SVK	BUL MKD UKR		ALB MDA
	− West		RUS		ARM AZE GEO KGZ MNG
Autocracy	+ West				BLR
	− West				KAZ TJK TKM UZB

Figure 4.2 The full typology with empirical referents, 1997.

By 2002, the 26 countries fall into no less than ten different types. Notice, however, that the pattern is now more in line with the theoretical expectations. Only two countries still belong in one of the waiting rooms, viz. that adjacent to structural autocracy. Mirroring this, the two polar types now

		+ Modern		− Modern	
		+ Leg	− Leg	+ Leg	− Leg
Democracy	+ West	CZS	BUL		ROM
		EST			
		HRV			
		HUN			
		LTV			
		LTU			
		POL			
		SVK			
		SVN			
	− West				MNG
Hybrid regime	+ West		MKD		ALB
			UKR		MDA
	− West		RUS		ARM
					GEO
Autocracy	+ West				BLR
	− West				AZE
					KAZ
					KGZ
					TJK
					TKM
					UZB

Figure 4.3 The full typology with empirical referents, 2002.

account for no less than 15 out of 26 countries. Notice, however, that three countries (Bulgaria, Mongolia and Romania) have become democracies despite lacking one or more attributes; in fact, Mongolia has become a democracy despite lacking all three attributes. Also, Belarus is still an autoc-

		+ Modern		− Modern	
		+ Leg	− Leg	+ Leg	− Leg
Democracy	+ West	CZS EST HRV HUN LTV LTU POL SVK SVN	BUL		ROM
	− West				MNG
Hybrid regime	+ West		MKD UKR		ALB MDA
	− West				ARM GEO KGZ
Autocracy	+ West				BLR
	− West		RUS		AZE KAZ TJK TKM UZB

Figure 4.4 The full typology with empirical referents, 2007.

racy despite having the attribute West. Let us finally see what happens when moving to the long-term picture of 2007.

Ten types are once again in existence. Generally speaking, the ordering confirms the structural expectations as no less than 14 of the 26 countries are situated in the respective polar types of structural democracy and structural autocracy. Notice, however, that the empirical pattern is somewhat more messy than was the case in 2002. First, three countries reside in the so-called 'autocracy waiting room', which therefore does not seem on the verge of drying out. Second, three countries (Bulgaria, Moldova and Romania) are still democracies despite lacking one or more attributes, whereas two countries (Russia and Belarus) are autocracies despite having one attribute. What can be concluded on this basis?

Conclusions

The structural analysis gives rise to another set of stark conclusions. It turns out that the deep variables have more or less sealed the longer-term fates of the post-communist countries on the dependent variable of this study: the political regime form. As expected, the structural logic is not so salient in the early 1990s. Here, a very large number of countries that were expected to be democracies (as all attributes are present) or autocracies (as all attributes are absent) were in fact hybrid regimes. However, the structural constraints seemingly kicked in over the decade.

To connect this to the ordering on the compound of attributes, the countries have very much come to cluster within the two polar types of structural democracy and structural autocracy, respectively. The pattern is somewhat more confusing with regard to the third class of hybrid regime, but – being an intermediate political phenomenon – this was only to be expected. Also, since the mid-1990s only a few hybrid regimes exhibit a clean slate (with all attributes either present or absent) on the independent variables. Countries that should in fact belong within the two polar types are outliers that more or less died out during the 1990s. Otherwise said, they do in fact move into the two polar types.

Let us try to scrutinize the relative importance of the independent variables. In the long-term, four pathways to democracy exist. The most important is, of course, that of polar type 1, which houses the eight countries that gained EU membership in 2004. However, Bulgaria and Romania testify to the existence of another pathway that does not include the presence of legacies. Bulgaria and Romania do not share the attribute modern, but this is only because Bulgaria just makes it above the threshold while Romania falls just short; they are therefore very close to following the same path. Finally, Mongolia is a complete outlier, having none of the attributes but still being a democracy. Concerning autocracy, the picture is simpler. All autocracies (save Belarus and Russia) have, in the long term, traversed one and only pathway: that of polar type 24.

Using the configurational language of necessary and sufficient causation, we thus have no necessary conditions of democracy, whereas only the absence of legacies is a necessary condition of autocracy. Notice, however, that the presence of legacies is a sufficient cause of democracy, as is the combined presence of all the three attributes. Taken together, this yields some evidence in favour of the conclusion that legacies is the most important independent variable.

But that is by the way. The basic conclusion of the analysis is that, when piecing the typological property space together, we achieve some very strong ammunition against a pure actor perspective. Clustering within the two polar types of structural democracy and structural autocracy, the countries in which the attributes were all either present or all absent conformed to the expectations in 2007 (with the sole exceptions of Armenia, Georgia and Kyrgyzstan). Likewise, most of the countries that had some but not all attributes went into the class of hybrid regime. Basically, the scope for action may not have been very large after all. This indicates that the structural perspective is inescapable for those interested in the general political tripartition of the post-communist setting. Or, to relate the findings to the Kitscheltian point of departure, it goes to show that the deep and the proximate explanations need to be integrated into a common explanatory framework. In Chapter 5, I will try to elaborate this by juxtaposing the actor-based independent variables and the structural independent variables in a final attempt to explain the variation on the dependent variable of political regime change.

5 Contrasting structures, actors and diffusion

The two preceding analyses of post-communist political pathways both exposed some striking empirical regularities. Not only was it possible to draw a very coherent picture of the causal pathways, it was possible to do so from both from an actor-centred and a structural point of view. In a nutshell, the most salient feature of post-communism seems to be the combination of intra-subregional similarities and inter-subregional differences incarnated by the respective polar types of Chapters 3 and 4. The question therefore becomes this: How do the actor-centred and structural variables relate to each other as wholes?

Piecing the general picture together

To juxtapose the actor-centred and structural variables, it is first necessary to reduce the total property space, otherwise the complexity of the joint typological schema, consisting of no less than 192 types ($2^6 \times 3$), becomes staggering. Paul Lazarsfeld (1937, and Barton 1951), to whom we owe the introduction of the typological logic into social research, identified a number of reduction strategies which have recently been revisited by Colin Elman (2005).[1]

Elman proposes five different ways to reduce – or 'compress', as he terms it – a property space: rescaling (reducing the level of measurement); indexing (weighting different variables to combine them into a composite index where the same aggregate scores are treated as being equivalent); logical compression (eliminating cells produced by impossible or highly improbable combinations of variables); empirical compression (eliminating empty cells); and pragmatic compression (collapsing contiguous cells if their division serves no useful theoretical purpose). To use Lazarsfeld vocabulary, logical and empirical compression maintains the monotheticism (i.e. the unique combination of variables captured by each cell) of the original typology, whereas rescaling, indexing and pragmatic compression result in polythetic types (i.e. collapsed cells).

Until now, I have only tacitly applied empirical compression. I have done so by solely focusing on the types which did indeed have empirical referents, therefore effectively disregarding the remaining types (the null cells). Here I will, in a much more self-conscious way, use another strategy of reduction, namely Elman's formula of indexing, thereby creating polythetic types out of the potential unreduced property space.

To elaborate, it makes sense to transform both the deep and proximate cluster of variables into what I will term a 'package' (i.e. a whole or a composite index, to use more technical terms). As already noted, the focal point here is the striking regularities discovered in the preceding chapters. To capture these regularities, I construe each of the clusters of variables as one dimension on which we may either encounter the presence of all attributes, the presence of some but not all attributes or the presence of no attributes. This equals saying that we may either encounter the absence of no attributes, the absence of some but not all attributes or the absence of all attributes. The typological technique employed here is thus, in the words of Elman, to treat 'equal totals of additive causal variables as equivalent' (2005: 300).

Embedding the reduction in theory, a 'full presence' connotes that the country in question is expected to be a democracy, a 'mixed sheet'[2] connotes that it is expected to be a hybrid regime and a 'full absence' connotes that it is expected to be an autocracy.[3]

The matching operational definitions can be stated as follows:

1   A post-communist country has a full presence of attributes with regard to the actor-based and the structure-based package, respectively, if all attributes are present as reported in the analyses of Chapters 3 and 4.
2   A post-communist country has a mixed sheet of attributes with regard to the actor-based and the structure-based package, respectively, if some but not all attributes are present (or absent) as reported in the analyses of Chapters 3 and 4.
3   A post-communist country has a full absence of attributes with regard to the actor-based and the structure-based package, respectively, if all attributes are absent as reported in the analyses of Chapters 3 and 4.

If we combine the two consequent classifications – yet again creating an ordering on a compound of attributes – the typology illustrated in Figure 5.1 comes into existence. This typology exhausts the possible logical combinations of statuses on the two dimensions.

One thing is immediately clear: the respective orderings on the two dimensions correlate strongly.[4] No less than 14 of 26 countries are found within the two polar types and an additional five fall into the mixed/mixed type. So, only seven of 26 countries do not clump along the diagonal of the typology. Notice, furthermore, that all of these seven aberrations fall into types adjacent to the two polar types. In other words, there is no country which falls into the theoretically illogical types that combine a full presence on one package with a full absence on the other package.

		Actor-based package		
		Full presence	Mixed	Full absence
Structure-based package	Full presence	CZS EST HRV HUN LTV LTU POL SVK SVN		
	Mixed	MKD	ALB BUL MDA ROM RUS	BLR UKR
	Full absence		ARM GEO KGZ MNG ·	AZE KAZ TJK TKM UZB

Figure 5.1 A typology of the possible combinations on the actor-centred package and the structure-based package.

Regarding the identity of the various referents, we recognize the now familiar, nay, expected pattern. Polar type 1 houses Croatia, the Czech Republic, Estonia, Hungary, Latvia, Lithuania, Poland, Slovakia and Slovenia (i.e.

most of East-Central Europe). Conversely, polar type 9 houses Azerbaijan, Kazakhstan, Tajikistan, Turkmenistan and Uzbekistan (i.e. the Central Asian countries – minus Kyrgyzstan – and their Azerbaijanian kindred spirit).

Recall the theoretical expectations connected to the operationalized variables: that good things go together and vice versa – up to a point, at least. This path-dependent expectation was deliberately downplayed in the deep analysis as it is somewhat difficult to establish the extent to which the structural factors have moulded each other. Contrastingly, the logic of virtuous and vicious circles was deliberately emphasized in the proximate analysis as the actor choices of the transition were likely to impact on each other. But the most important aspect of this logic is surely that describing the interplay between deep and proximate factors – an interplay that, according to Kitschelt, is likely to create a set of positive and negative trajectories unleashed by the deep constraints and then reproduced by the proximate choices. To elaborate, an auspicious structural point of departure has made for auspicious proximate actor choices, ultimately locking in an auspicious political regime form (*in casu* democracy) with a likewise inauspicious structural point of departure.

Reflecting on the multicollinearity among explanatory factors of post-communist political and economic developments, Gregorz Ekiert (2003: 116) has phrased the methodological consequences of this succinctly:

> Thus, most of the attempts to determine a limited set of specific causes and to establish simple linear relationships to outcomes are likely to be questionable. The metaphor of vicious and virtuous circles captures much better the relationship among these factors. They interact together in a complex fashion, producing the 'increasing returns' that characterize path-dependent development.

Bearing this in mind, polar type 1 can be construed as 'democracy guaranteed', whereas polar type 9 can be construed as 'autocracy guaranteed'. The rest of Figure 5.1's types predict, theoretically at least, the presence of hybrid regimes. But these predictions are much weaker than those connected with the polar types as the virtuous and vicious circles imply overdetermination – or, to put it differently, equilibrium points – at the extremes, but more randomness in the intermediate area. Let us add the dependent variable to the picture, and thus also reintroduce the dimension of time, to check whether the empirical reality conforms to these expectations, cross-spatially as well as cross-synchronically. I will go straight to a full functional reduction, only depicting the types that have referents. As in Chapter 3, I am unable to include 1992 because of priority; Table 5.1 thus shows the empirical distribution in 1997.

By 1997, the post-communist tripartition has already come into existence. As a consequence, the theoretical expectations connected to the polar types of Figure 5.1 are very close to being fulfilled. Only two of the eight countries that were found in the polar type of democracy guaranteed are still hybrid regimes and therefore do not belong within the new polar type 1.

Table 5.1 The types that have empirical referents, 1997

	Status on actor-based package	*Status on structure-based package*	*Political regime form*
Czech Republic Estonia Hungary Latvia Lithuania Poland Slovenia	Presence	Presence	Democracy
Romania	Mixed	Mixed	Democracy
Croatia Slovakia	Presence	Presence	Hybrid regime
Macedonia	Presence	Mixed	Hybrid regime
Albania Bulgaria Moldova Russia	Mixed	Mixed	Hybrid regime
Armenia Georgia Kyrgyzstan Mongolia	Mixed	Absence	Hybrid regime
Ukraine	Absence	Mixed	Hybrid regime
Azerbaijan	Absence	Absence	Hybrid regime
Belarus	Absence	Mixed	Autocracy
Kazakhstan Tajikistan Turkmenistan Uzbekistan	Absence	Absence	Autocracy

Likewise, four of the five countries situated within the polar type of autocracy guaranteed are actually autocracies in 1997. Thirteen of the remaining 15 countries are all hybrid regimes, meaning that only five of 26 countries were misclassified in 1997, theoretically. What happens five years down the road?

By 2002, all of the nine countries that were situated within the polar type of democracy guaranteed in Figure 5.1 have become democracies. Likewise, all of the five countries that were situated within the opposite polar type of autocracy guaranteed in Figure 5.1 are autocracies. However, no less than four countries not situated within these two polar types defy the expectation of being hybrid regimes (Bulgaria and Romania by being democracies and Belarus and Kyrgyzstan by being autocracies). This implies, however, that in 2002 only four of the 26 observations are not classified correctly on the dependent variable (given the theoretical expectations). Let us, finally, finish the excursion by moving to 2007.

Table 5.2 The types that have empirical referents, 2002

	Status on actor-based package	Status on structure-based package	Political regime form
Croatia Czech Republic Estonia Hungary Latvia Lithuania Poland Slovakia Slovenia	Presence	Presence	Democracy
Bulgaria Romania	Mixed	Mixed	Democracy
Mongolia	Mixed	Absence	Democracy
Macedonia	Presence	Mixed	Hybrid regime
Albania Moldova Russia	Mixed	Mixed	Hybrid regime
Armenia Georgia	Mixed	Absence	Hybrid regime
Ukraine	Absence	Mixed	Hybrid regime
Kyrgyzstan	Mixed	Absence	Autocracy
Belarus	Absence	Mixed	Autocracy
Azerbaijan Kazakhstan Tajikistan Turkmenistan Uzbekistan	Absence	Absence	Autocracy

At this temporal endpoint of the analysis, the theoretical expectations are, again, completely fulfilled with regard to both the polar type democracy guaranteed and its opposite autocracy guaranteed. Thus, Croatia, the Czech Republic, Estonia, Hungary, Latvia, Lithuania, Poland, Slovakia and Slovenia have all reached the promised land of democracy. Likewise, Azerbaijan, Kazakhstan, Tajikistan, Turkmenistan and Uzbekistan have all become autocracies.

However, with regard to the remaining types of Figure 5.1, the expectations are now more violated than what was the case in both 1997 and 2002. Bulgaria, Mongolia and Romania have become democracies despite lacking attributes on both the actor-centred package and the structural package. Likewise, Belarus and Russia has become autocracies from a quite similar point of departure. Consequently, five of 24 observations now defy the expectations.

What about the hybrid regimes in the period in question? Recall once more the logic of a classification: classes are separated by differences in kind

Table 5.3 The types that have empirical referents, 2007

	Status on actor-based package	Status on structure-based package	Political regime form
Croatia Czech Republic Estonia Hungary Latvia Lithuania Poland Slovakia Slovenia	Presence	Presence	Democracy
Bulgaria Romania	Mixed	Mixed	Democracy
Mongolia	Mixed	Absence	Democracy
Macedonia	Presence	Mixed	Hybrid regime
Albania Moldova	Mixed	Mixed	Hybrid regime
Armenia Georgia Kyrgyzstan	Mixed	Absence	Hybrid regime
Ukraine	Absence	Mixed	Hybrid regime
Russia	Mixed	Mixed	Autocracy
Belarus	Absence	Mixed	Autocracy
Azerbaijan Kazakhstan Tajikistan Turkmenistan Uzbekistan	Absence	Absence	Autocracy

(whether the attribute is present), whereas the differences within a class are measured in degree (to what extent the attribute is present).[5] Reaching back to the original trichotomy of political regime forms, we can elucidate the differences in the degree of hybrid regime-ness by scrutinizing the Freedom House scores for the empirical referents in this class. Two things are noteworthy. Throughout the period in question (1997–2007) the countries that that have a relatively large number of attributes and the countries that lack a relatively large number of attributes were situated at opposite ends of the continuum, covered by the class of hybrid regime.

Bulgaria, Croatia, Romania and Slovakia, which all have several or all attributes present, were very close to the threshold of democracy throughout their careers as hybrid regimes. Contrastingly, countries with few attributes present, such as Kyrgyzstan, Armenia and Georgia, were close to the threshold of autocracy for most of the period. Some countries – notably Russia (with relatively many attributes present) and Mongolia (with relatively few attributes present) – behaved more erratic, especially diachronically. Still, in general, the countries also mirror the classificatory logic when we shift focus from differences in kind to differences of degree – although, the pattern is less clear-cut than when analysing differences (in kind) across the classes on the dependent variable.

The stability of the tripartition confirms the merits of employing a typological mapping. As I stated with the assistance of Giovanni Sartori in Chapter 3, a classificatory schema requires a certain amount of stability on behalf of the empirical referents. To quote once more: 'The very act of assigning something to a type imposes upon it a definiteness, a fixity, a form. Therefore, with respect to a state of flux, classes and types can be more deceptive than informative' (Sartori 1976: 255–6). If it were not for the longevity and boundedness of the tripartition[6] – characteristics that also extend to the explanans – continuous measures would arguably have a competitive edge. The lack of cross-temporal variation after the mid-1990s should thus be seen as an advantage, considering the chosen approach. Moving to the higher ground, it is more interesting to identify the differences in kind within the post-communist setting than the differences in degree for one very simple reason: this macro-region is indeed characterized by systematic, not random, diversity.[7]

Integrating the packages

The preceding analysis demonstrated that the clear majority of the post-communist countries move in sync on the actor-centred and structural dimensions (the respective packages). Both packages accurately predict the status on the dependent variable for most of the countries, most of the time. Also, the mutual correspondence is striking, which comes out clearly when using the notions of necessary and sufficient causation. Notice that neither the full presence of the deep or proximate package is a necessary condition of democracy, nor is a full absence of either package a necessary condition of autocracy. Such is the case because of the identity of the configurations housing the few exceptions to the otherwise manifest patterns (i.e. Belarus, Bulgaria, Mongolia, Romania and Russia). However, a simultaneous full presence of the two packages is a sufficient condition for democracy in both 2002 and 2007, whereas a simultaneous full absence is a sufficient condition for autocracy in both 2002 and 2007. Finally, a full presence of the deep package is a sufficient condition for democracy in both years. Only two other empirical pathways lead to the democratic terminus, namely the mixed/mixed combination of Romania and Bulgaria and the idiosyncratic pathway of Mongolia,[8] which includes a full absence on the structural package. This underscores that the two packages are intimately wedded.

What does this mean with regard to juxtaposing the two alternative approaches? Over time, both packages generally do the job, particularly with regard to democracies and autocracies, respectively. That is not the end of the discussion, however. As already mentioned, establishing causality implies at least four requirements: first, the presence of a theoretical link between cause and effect; second, the establishment of a matching empirical link; third, that the cause predates the effect; and fourth, that other factors are held constant. As causes, both the structural and the actor-centred variables more or less fulfil each of these criteria. Recall that the respective variables were, first, selected due to their theoretical relationship with the outcome in question, second, turned out to stand in the expected empirical relationship to the dependent variable, third, measured at a point in time antedating the measurement on the dependent variable, and, fourth, chosen from a plethora of theoretical propositions based on their explanatory power in relation to their alternatives in other studies.

But notice that much the same can be said about the relationship between the structural variables (as causes) and their actor-centred equivalents (as effects). The structural attributes all predate the actor-centred attributes. Legacies, West and modern were all measured at a point in time prior to those at which displacement, reform and legislature were measured. More to the point, the structural attributes were meant to capture phenomena that can be traced almost centuries back in time, whereas the actor-centred attributes were meant to capture contemporary choices. This is important because temporal concerns often override correlations when seeking to establish spuriousness. Quoting Gerring (2001: 142):

> The further away we can get from the outcome in question, the better (ceteris paribus) our explanation will be. This explains some of the excitement when social scientists find 'structural' variables that seem to affect public policy or political behavior. It is not that they offer fuller (deeper) explanations; indeed, the correlations between X and Y are likely to be much weaker than with cultural or leadership theories. It is not that they are more relevant; indeed, they are less relevant for most policy purposes, since they are least amenable to manipulation (usually). And it is not that they offer more accurate explanations; as we move away from the outcome of interests to causes that have greater priority, our explanation is likely to become more difficult to prove. Thus, priority often imposes costs on other criterial dimensions.
>
> (See also Gerring 2001: 126.)

Also, the analysis of this chapter has demonstrated that the two packages stand in a very systematic empirical relationship. Most stunningly, a full presence of attributes on the structural package fully predicts a full presence of attributes on the actor-centred package. The relationship is weaker with regard to a mixed sheet and a full absence, yet only seven of 26 countries do not show complete correspondence. Can we, finally, establish a theoretical link between the two packages? Clearly we cannot establish a causal chain leading from the choices of the actors to the structural attributes because of their respective position on the dimension of time. We humans cannot alter the circumstances of the past. But what about a causal chain leading from the structural attributes to the choices of the actors? I will argue that it is very much possible to make the case for such a chain.

Recall that the actor-centred variables such as initial elections and constitutional choice largely capture various aspects of 'open politics' and societal mobilization. It is to be expected that the structural point of departure should impact this. If, on the one hand, a modernized society with a partial liberal inheritance and links to Western Europe is in existence – as was the case in East-Central Europe after the breakdown of communism – then competitive politics, including the formation of viable oppositional parties, is very much to be expected. If, on the other hand, no liberal inheritance, no significant modernization and virtual isolation from the Western world is a fact of life – as was the case in Central Asia and, albeit to a lesser extent, the Caucasian countries – then competitive politics, including the formation of viable oppositional parties, is not to be expected.[9]

In a nutshell, the actors do not act in a vacuum and the structural package is likely to significantly shape their room for action. As Kitschelt and Malesky (2000: 16) phrase it, the actor-centred variables may be '[. . .] endogenous to the political power configuration at the point of communist collapse, but reflecting a variety of deeper layers of political-economic power structures'.[10] Otherwise said, even though the causal chain may very well work through the actor-centred variables, they will be spurious as root causes or ulterior independent variables. This is what Herbert Kitschelt points to when he terms the 'proximate' (i.e. actor-centred or institutional) explanations 'shallow' in contrast to the 'deeper' structural explanations. To quote him (2003: 64), a relationship as the one found in the preceding analysis '[. . .] may reveal interaction effects between deeper causes ("structural conditions") affecting shallower causes ("triggers")'.

In an insightful methodological critique of actor-centred explanations in general and Transitology in particular, Michael Coppedge (1999: 474–5) phrases it in a way that is worth quoting at length:

> The insistence on bridging levels of analysis is not mere methodological prudery. Empirical questions of great theoretical, even paradigmatic, import, such as whether individuals affect democratization, depend on it. Rational choice theory assumes that they do; Linz and Stepan and O'Donnell, Schmitter and Whitehead asserted they do. Yet, despite all the eloquent theorizing that led to 'tentative conclusions about uncertain transitions', all the cases covered by *Transitions from Authoritarian Rule* underwent successful transitions that have lasted remarkably long. There are many possible explanations for this genuinely surprising outcome but one that is plausible enough to require disconfirmation is the idea that these transitions were driven by structural conditions. Even if it is true that elites and groups had choices and made consequential decisions at key moments, their goals, perceptions, and choices may have been decisively shaped by the context in which they were acting. If so, they may

have had a lot of proximate influence but very little independent influence after controlling for context.

In sum, then, the present claim holds that the structural point of departure constrains the very choices of the actors and these two dynamics then, taken together, shape the political pathways. *A fortiori*, the deep and proximate factors need to be integrated into a coherent framework if we wish to obtain an encompassing understanding of the political variation in the post-communist world. We should not get carried away by the merits of this explanatory edifice, however. As Kitschelt (2003: 75) has (correctly) pointed out, the actor-centred choices may be completely spurious. To quote:

> Either the deeper causes x 'work through' the shallower cause y to bring about the final outcome z (x → y → z); or the cause x bring about both what appears as the shallower cause y as well as the outcome z (x → y; x → z). Because of collinearity, we cannot statistically distinguish between these alternatives.

This objection goes for my analysis, too. As a result of the high collinearity, it is very difficult to distinguish between these alternatives. The ultimate test requires actual process-tracing of the post-communist cases (cf. George and Bennett 2005), but that exercise lies beyond the scope of this book. Notice, however, that the convincing theoretical links between the identified actor-centred attributes and the outcome on the dependent variable indicate that the causal chain does indeed pass through these choices. Also, the ability to construct theoretical links between the structural constraints and the actor-choices further underpin the notion of one coherent chain. Figure 5.2 illustrates this by letting the full-drawn arrows pass through 'the choices of actors', whereas the hypothetically possible causal link leading from the 'structural constraints' directly to the 'political regime form' is represented by a dotted arrow.

Notice also that this theoretical edifice, when including 'the choices of the actors' as the intervening link, ties the structural attributes to the political outcome via the choices of the actors. Otherwise said, the explanation of post-communist democratization (and 'autocratization') does more than

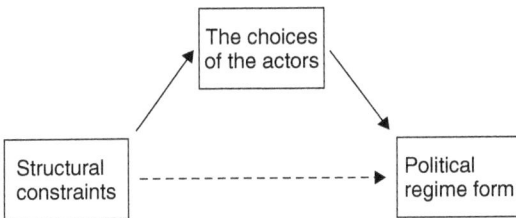

Figure 5.2 The general causal chain emerging from the typological analyses.

demonstrate correlations, it elucidates the causal chain[11] as well. Finally, notice that this explanation can account for the most striking aspect of the variation on the dependent variable of the political regime form, to wit the systematic combination of intra-subregional similarities and inter-subregional differences. To reiterate a now somewhat tedious observation, the notion of voluntaristic action (i.e. the very premise of the actor-centred approaches) does not fit with the facts that i) most of the East-Central European countries have travelled one particular path, ii) the same can pretty much be said about the five Central Asian countries and iii) the paths of the countries situated between these two extremes, albeit to a lesser extent, also show mutual kinship.[12] The structural approach, on the other hand, elucidates this pattern quite nicely because each region would logically have a relatively equal structural point of departure.

One other possibility exists, however, and we need to discuss this as well. Maybe it is neither the independent choices of the actors nor the structurally contingent choices of the actors that explain the described pattern on the dependent variable? Maybe it is regional effects as such? To elaborate, is it possible that the choices of the actors have been subregionally interdependent not due to the structural point of departure but due to diffusion? This is the issue to which we now turn.

Enter diffusion

The question that I am posing is once again this: Why is it that the independent deep and proximate variables correlate so very systematically with the dependent variable of political regime forms (and with each other as well, for that matter)? The structural point of departure provides one possible answer. But let us try to further scrutinize the question by revisiting the particular actor-centred variable of 'constitutional engineering'. What I will do in the subsequent sections is to – via the variation on this variable – build a strong case for diffusion before using the preceding typological analyses to criticize the logic of regional effects.

M. Steven Fish on the unmixed blessing of stronger legislatures in the post-communist world

Recall that M. Steven Fish (2006) has, with a colleague, created a Parliamentary Power Index, according to which a country receives a relatively high score if a high degree constitutional power is vested in the parliament and a relatively low score if the opposite is true. Fish's hypothesis is that parliamentarism will favour democracy. In the article 'Stronger Legislatures, Stronger Democracies', he tests this claim in the context of 25 post-communist countries. The expectations are very much confirmed by the data. The statistical correlation between the Parliamentary Power Index (measured in the early 1990s) and the average Freedom House ratings (measured in

2003–5), which is a proxy of democracy, finds expression in a Pearson's r of no less than –0.92. The independent variable thus accounts for an astonishing 85 per cent of the variation on the dependent variable.

Furthermore, Fish quickly checks if the general relationship is spurious. Perhaps, he speculates, the Parliamentary Power Index reflects the democratic achievements at the time of the inauguration of the respective constitutions ('the constitutional moment') (2006: 9). The answer turns out not to be in the affirmative. Or, better, the constitutional moment explanation only accounts for a very modest part of the variation. This leaves Fish (2006: 11) free to conclude that '[...] the power of legislatures, as established in constitutions adopted between the late 1980s and mid-1990s, predicts political openness in the mid-2000s more accurately than political openness at the time of the adoption of constitutions predict the power of legislatures'.

Spuriousness and regional effects

Fish acknowledges that spuriousness could stem from other sources than initial open (or closed) politics. He also checks for structural variables such as economic development and consequently points out that, '[w]hat is more, the effect of the PPI score on change in FH scores holds up well in statistical analyses that control for other variables that might affect democratization, such as economic development' (2006: 12). In other words, he considers whether the institutional choices are endogenous to prior structural constraints, and then rejects this potential objection.

The argument of this book, build on the premise that it is necessary to make explicit temporal distinctions between causal factors, is, of course, that it does not make much sense to contrast deep and proximate factors directly in such a 'tournament of variables'. This is because the actor-centred variables will wash out the structural simply because they are situated closer to the outcome.

That said, it is laudable that Fish checks for spuriousness. Yet even if we accept this method of controlling for deeper factors one very noteworthy speculation does not enter into his account: that regional effects may be relevant. This is somewhat surprising. The fact of the matter is that the values on both his independent and dependent variables are very systematically dispersed across the space of the former communist world. A simple illustration should suffice to make this point. Table 5.4 turns Fish's indexes covering the independent variable and the dependent variable[13] into two classifications each yielding three respective classes.

Notice that the classification on both the dependent and the independent variables differs from those I crafted in Chapter 3. The reason is twofold. First, I am merely performing this exercise to illustrate some shortcomings in Fish's analysis. Second, and related to this, I use new thresholds to avoid producing a critique that is biased by my previous conceptualization. On

Table 5.4 The tripartite orderings on Fish's independent and dependent variable

Parliamentary Power Index	Parliamentary systems	Hybrid systems	Presidential systems
	Albania, Bulgaria, Croatia, Czech Republic, Estonia, Hungary, Latvia, Lithuania, Macedonia, Moldova, Mongolia, Poland, Romania, Slovakia, Slovenia	Armenia, Georgia, Ukraine	Azerbaijan, Belarus, Kazakhstan, Kyrgyzstan, Russia, Tajikistan, Uzbekistan
Freedom House Ratings 2004	Free	Partly free	Unfree
	Bulgaria, Croatia, Czech Republic, Estonia, Hungary, Latvia, Lithuania, Mongolia, Poland, Romania, Slovakia, Slovenia	Albania, Armenia, Georgia, Macedonia, Moldova, Russia, Ukraine	Azerbaijan, Belarus, Kazakhstan, Kyrgyzstan, Tajikistan, Uzbekistan

the dependent variable of the political regime form, I have relied on the Freedom House's tripartition between 'free', 'partly free' and 'not free' states covering the year of 2003 (i.e. the 2004 ratings). On the independent variable, matters are somewhat more complicated. In the article, Fish indicates that a score below 0.5 is a sufficient condition for remaining authoritarian. Hence, I have employed this threshold to capture the seemingly pernicious class of 'presidential systems'. To delimit its opposite number (i.e. 'parliamentary systems') I have chosen the threshold of 0.65 simply to achieve some kind of a trichotomy; everything in between falls into the class 'hybrid systems'.

These orderings are not so much meant to demonstrate that the variations on the two variables correlate; Fish's statistical coefficient has already been quoted to that effect. Rather, my objective here is to demonstrate that the combination of intra-subregional similarities (within subregional clusters) and intra-subregional differences (between subregional clusters) is strikingly clear-cut on both the independent and the dependent variable. In East-Central Europe, we encounter all free countries and all parliamentary systems (save Mongolia). In Caucasus and Central Asia, we encounter all not free countries and all presidential systems (save Belarus and Russia). In between, we find most of the intermediary cases (i.e. the 'partly free' countries and hybrid constitutional systems).

In a nutshell, out of no less than 25 countries only Mongolia and, to a lesser extent, Belarus and Russia are genuinely able to break the subregional logic. Otherwise said, we find the very same pattern as the one revealed by the preceding typological analyses. This is interesting. When we meet geographical differences such as these, the explanation may simply be geographical. This leads us to the doorstep of regional effects.

Diffusion and post-communism

According to Fish, the post-communist countries have chosen constitutional systems in a more or less voluntaristic way and the institutional constraints have then kicked in over the latest decade. But why is it, one cannot help wonder, that Mongolia was the only country outside of East-Central Europe that opted for parliamentarism after the breakdown of communism? And, conversely, why is it that no country in East-Central Europe opted for pure and simple presidentialism?

Regional effects such as diffusion present a possible answer to this riddle. Let me try to underpin this assertion with two qualitative examples from the post-communist setting. In the early 1990s, Vladimir Meciar was the pre-eminent political actor in the newly-born republic of Slovakia. Backed by the strongest and most well-organized political force in the country, Meciar had emerged from the so-called 'velvet divorce' of 1992 as a peerless power-claimant. Most scholars and commentators have, ever since, keenly emphasized Meciar's semi-autocratic instincts and desire for centralized power – with good reasons, too. Whereas other Visegrad countries, such as the Czech Republic, Hungary and Poland, quickly went into the class of democracy as operationalized in this book, Slovakia lingered as a hybrid regime for years and years. This is why Slovakia has been a partial outlier throughout the empirical analyses of Chapters 2 through 4. Equally interesting, scholars have emphasized that Meciar was, ultimately, responsible for crafting the new constitutional framework. As Karen Henderson (2002: 55) notes,

> Slovakia's constitution was controversial from its inception. It was largely the product of only one part of the political spectrum – the supporters of the second Meciar government elected in June 1992 [. . .] The constitution was passed in haste, and never legitimated by a popular referendum [. . .].

With this in mind, it seems somewhat paradoxical that Slovakia ended up with a parliamentary system and, by extension, with a very weak presidency. Why did Meciar not simply gather the (constitutional) reins of power as president? Why did he opt for the parliamentary complexity that led to his first stay on the oppositional benches shortly after the inauguration of the new constitution? One possible answer is, of course, that Meciar and his supporters perceived the parliamentary battleground as one in which they would triumph – which, to a large extent, they did, at least during the 1990s. But it seems equally plausible that regional effects tied their hands. Notice how all East-Central European countries, according to Fish's index, chose a parliamentary form of government after the breakdown of communism. With a strong presidency, Slovakia would have constituted a very evident exception, the odd man out. I do not mean to say that the choice of a strong presidency was impossible. However, the path leading to it was, arguably, strewn with obstacles for the simple reason that Slovakia is situated in the heart of Europe.

The situation was strikingly different at the other extreme of the post-communist setting: Central Asia. This brings me to my second example – Kyrgyzstan. In the early 1990s, this small Central Asian republic was hailed as an 'island of democracy' (Anderson 1999) in an otherwise autocratic sea. Its president, Askar Akayev, in particular, was perceived as a genuine democrat through and through. Relatively untainted by communism, he was, or so it seemed, both willing and able to fight off the autocratic fashions of his neighbourhood. In 1992, Kyrgyzstan had an average Freedom House score of 3.0, and for the better part of its post-communist history, the country has been a hybrid regime according to my definition and operationalization. This was why the small country constituted a regional exception in at least some of the analyses of Chapters 2 through 4. In the early 2000s, however, it turned out that the optimism that surrounded Akayev was misplaced. Kyrgyzstan (still ruled by Akayev) became an autocracy. But notice one more thing. Even in the heyday of the optimism (the early 1990s), Kyrgyzstan opted for a presidency no less centralized than that of Tajikistan (and very close to those of Kazakhstan and Uzbekistan with regard to the degree of centralization), according to Fish's index. If Akayev was in fact a convinced democrat back then – and he may very well have been just that – then on this point he did not break the subregional logic either.

All that I have said here can, at a more general level, be reduced to a statement about diffusion. Very crudely put, maybe the political elites of Kazakhstan opted for a strong president (and hence a weak parliament) in January 1993 because the political elites in neighbouring Uzbekistan had done so the month before? And maybe the political elites of Kyrgyzstan and Tajikistan simply followed suit when they chose their constitutional arrangement within the subsequent 12 months? Likewise, maybe the political elites in Lithuania opted for a strong parliament (and hence a weak president) in October 1992 because their Estonian counterparts had just done so in June of the same year? And so on and so forth with Central Europe, South-Eastern Europe, Russia, Ukraine and Belarus and the Caucasian countries.[14] Maybe we have a situation of spatial autocorrelation?

This is an intriguing notion. Once put in place, constitutional systems become (more or less) lasting constraints on actions. In the language of 'new institutionalism', the arrangements 'freeze' (i.e. they become institutions) and shape the arena in which the actors operate. But if the initial constitutional choice is merely the result of diffusion, then it is this factor – and not the institutional choice per se – that accounts for the variation on the dependent variable of the political regime form. Also, regional effects mean that the assumption of causal homogeneity, which the use of OLS-regressions requires, is violated. If diffusion is important within subregional clusters, then we have a situation of causal heterogeneity, i.e. the status on the independent variable will have different consequences with respect to the dependent variable depending on the locality. Only within (sub)regions do we, in such cases, have the required causal homogeneity (cf. Mainwaring and Perez-Linan 2005).

And that is not all. Quoting John Gerring (2001: 179, emphasis in original):

> Moving to the social science ground: suppose, in our study of government growth, that certain countries were influenced *by each other* (rather than deciding taxing and spending issues independently of one another). This could occur through the influence of an international agency like the World Bank, the IMF, or the EU, or through a simple process of diffusion. What, one might inquire, is the logic of counting each as a separate case? Indeed, N is equal to precisely 1 if country policies are entirely the product of diffusion. Of course diffusion, and the criterion of independence more generally, is usually a matter of degrees. (*All* cross-national studies suffer from some violation of the independence criterion.)

To relate this assertion to the setting under investigation, if we take the diffusion argument to the extreme, we do not even have a medium-sized population of post-communist cases; we only have one case of post-communist diffusion. More realistically, given the regional dividing lines identified by the typological analyses, we may have only three cases, to wit the three identified subregional clusters.

Interestingly, the diffusion argument is very seldom voiced in the institutionalist literature on post-communism and it is virtually never tested.[15] In Timothy Frye's (1997) aforementioned attempt to account for the rise of presidential systems in the post-communist setting, a large number of competing economic, political and societal approaches are discussed. But Frye does not even mention diffusion in his overview of theories of constitutional choice. This is all the more strange as the diffusion argument seems plausible enough to require disconfirmation, at least with regard to the constitutional explanation of democracy in the post-communist setting. How else can we, in the absence of antecedent structural factors, explain that Fish's constitutional variable – and Frye's for that matter – varies so very systematically from a geographical point of view? As a proximate cause, the constitutional variable definitely holds its own. But the puzzle here is why the members of each geographical cluster move in a uniform direction at the outset of the period; diffusion may indeed have been the ulterior cause. Either way, the proponents of the proximate explanations need to refute this objection.

The logical problem burdening the diffusion argument

I also need to refute this objection if I wish to confirm the explanatory value of the deep or structural approach in explaining political regime forms in the post-communist setting. If diffusion holds the key to the empirical regularities then this equals saying that the structural regularities do not hold the key.[16] Let me, then, try to argue against diffusion as the root cause of the post-communist political pathways.

As I have just demonstrated, much can be said to support the relevance of regional effects. Still, I resist accepting the argument sketched above with regard to the post-communist setting. My rejection has to do with a quite salient logical problem. The empirical analyses of this book have, to reiterate a pivotal point, clearly demonstrated that a combination of intra-subregional similarities and inter-subregional differences exists within the post-communist setting – and that this combination extends to the orderings on both the independent variables and their dependent counterparts. This is exactly why regional diffusion offers a tempting explanation.

But recall, first, that regional effects create causal heterogeneity. To elaborate, a given causal mechanism will hold in some (sub)regions but not in others. This does, however, not seem to have been the case in the post-communist setting as the prime findings of the analyses have been the striking (but theoretically expected) regularities across the entire realm, not only within subregional clusters. As such, the analyses support the presence of causal homogeneity, not causal heterogeneity.[17] Second, recall the point about the dimension of time that I made when contrasting the structural and actor-centred approaches in the first part of this chapter. The argument that the structural attributes predate the actor-centred attributes applies equally well to the diffusion variable. Any potential post-communist diffusion comes on top of the structural point of departure, so to speak. Therefore, it seems likely that diffusion, if relevant, only worked as yet another link in the causal chain through which the structural similarities and differences kicked in throughout the 1990s. In short, diffusion may simply mirror (and reinforce) the fact that neighbouring countries share many structural features.

As a final note, let me try to elaborate this point by revisiting a particular and important contribution on diffusion in the context of post-communism: Jeffrey S. Kopstein and David A. Reilly's influential article on 'Geographic Diffusion and the Transformation of the Postcommunist World' from 2000. In the analysis of Chapter 3, I included Kopstein and Reilly's most simple proxy for diffusion from the West, namely the distance to the twin capitals of Berlin and Vienna, as a deep variable. However, they also operate with a more fine-grained measurement of diffusion and their analysis is worth a visit because it is, on the one hand, very incisive, yet, on the other hand, still does not pay heed to the structural counter-argument described above.

In the article, Kopstein and Reilly demonstrate that geographical locations hold up very well in a statistical analysis of post-communist political[18] diversity which pits this factor against Fish's 'initial election variable' and Kitschelt's 'bureaucratic rectitude variable'. The latter is (one property of) the variable I have used to cover the attribute of the 'political legacies', but Kopstein and

Reilly use the present level of corruption as a proxy for it rather than Kitshelt's own, historically-based ordering.

Departing from this somewhat trivial exercise, they attempt to unfold the logic of diffusion. Building on the existing sociological literature, diffusion is construed as having two dimensions: stock and flows. To quote, '[i]n a diffusion model the stock of a country can be represented by its external environment, whereas flows represent the movement of information and resources between countries' (2000: 13). Moving to a lower level of generality, the two attributes are conceptualized and measured as follows:

- Stock: 'For the purpose of this study we posit a given country's spatial stock to be who its neighbors are. This is best indicated by the Polity IV democracy scores and the Economic Reform scores of the countries geographically contiguous with it' (2000: 13).
- Flows: 'Our measure of openness is a composite score based on indicators that are conceptually linked to the exchange of ideas and associated in prior research studies to processes of diffusion. The set of six indicators gathered from the World Development Indicators, 1998, includes the number of televisions per thousand households; newspaper circulation per thousand people; outgoing international telecommunications, measured in minutes per subscriber; international inbound tourists; total foreign direct investment as a percentage of GDP; and international trade (sum of exports and imports) as a share of GDP, using purchasing power parity conversion factors' (2000: 14–15).

Notice that these definitions and, particularly, these operationalizations overlap with conventional structural factors to a very large extent. First, keeping in mind that the post-communist countries most often share the structural properties of their immediate neighbours, stock can be said to measure the political attributes of countries that virtually mirror the country in question structurally. Second, and even more problematic, with the possible exception of 'international inbound tourists', flows basically measure the level of modernization of the country in question (for this criticism, see also Kitschelt 2003).

All this goes to show that it is very hard to empirically disentangle diffusion from structural factors. In this connection, note also that diffusion must logically start somewhere. If we accept that the presidential model was disseminated throughout Central Asia – and the parliamentary model through East-Central Europe – then this only begs the following question: What determined the earliest choice of model within these particular settings? And this once more leads us back to the structural constraints.[19]

To reiterate, then, diffusion is best construed as, first, a mechanism through which the structures affect the actor choices and as, second, and less interestingly for our purposes, a process that makes the structures conform to the general makeup of their particular subregion over time – not as an independent variable of post-communist diversity. The second argument merely equals saying that the structural constraints have themselves been created by actor choices and diffusion at some ulterior point. That fact is an obvious one as the social world of man is, by definition, a constructed one. However, such antecedent creation is situated so far back in time that it is not relevant for the present analysis. In short, I feel confident enough to disregard diffusion as an independent variable in its own right – at least in the context of post-communism.

Conclusions

In this chapter, I have contrasted the deep and the proximate approaches to post-communist political change. The point of departure for this exercise is a simple one: both approaches do the job, at least in the longer run, when it comes to accounting for the striking empirical regularities on the dependent variable. It cannot come as a surprise, then, that the orderings on each of these two packages – i.e. the respective clusters of independent variables construed one-dimensionally – also co-vary systematically (not to mention overwhelmingly). The notion of virtuous and vicious circles, respectively, thus captures the entire triangle of actor-centred and structural causes and their political effects. Gazing upon the two regional extremes, everything seems to have favoured the East-Central European countries, whereas virtually nothing seems to have favoured their Central Asian counterparts – and in between we find most of the remaining countries. The post-communist tripartition is, it seems, created by both the choices of the actors and the structural constraints.

However, this is where the dimension of time enters the picture. The structural attributes all predate their actor-centred equivalents. This may seem a simple point, but it is also an important one, for it is possible to link the two packages theoretically. To elaborate, one can argue, as I have in fact argued, that the structural point of departure is likely to have shaped the arena within which the actors mobilized politically and in which they made their choices concerning the constitutional framework and the economic reform process of the early 1990s.

Such an argument can be understood as an attempt to lay bare the causal chain through which the structures shaped the political regime form. It should be kept in mind that structures do not create democracies or autocracies – actors do.[20] However, it is possible to establish a link between structures and actors. Otherwise said, the actor-centred attributes are too close to the attributes on the dependent variable to form genuinely independent variables (see also Kitschelt 2003). They are better construed as the structurally-induced causal mechanisms which brought about the outcomes on the dependent variable.

Much the same can be said with respect to a third causal alternative: diffusion. The systematic combination of intra-subregional similarities and inter-subregional differences makes the notion of regional effects a tempting one.

But within the post-communist setting, the diffusion of the 1990s seems to have mirrored the systematic structural similarities between neighbouring countries. Furthermore, theoretically it is only possible to connect the impact of diffusion to the choices of the actors, not to the structural attributes. The reason is once again a very simple one: the structural set-up predates the diffusion of post-communism. As such, diffusion, too, is best construed as a causal mechanism through which the structural logic comes to the fore. This is, then, the conclusion of the empirical analyses: deep, structural attributes seem to have sealed the fate of most post-communist countries most of the time, but we can only grasp the causal chain by embedding the proximate, actor-centred attributes into the explanatory edifice.

Conclusions

The breakdown of communism took an entire generation of scholars by surprise. To be sure, many had observed how state socialism had petrified from the 1970s onwards. But, literally speaking, petrifaction (aka 'freezing' or 'institutionalization') has a lot of intrinsic stability. Few anticipated the grand historical turnaround of 1989–91.[1] Maybe it was the extreme character and surprising speed of these events that paved the way for the subsequent tendency to expect a post-communist future of either doom or deliverance. Thus, one camp – which I termed 'the optimists' in the Introduction – saw liberal democracy beckoning beyond the ruins of communism. Another camp – which I termed 'the pessimists' – foresaw an unenviable future of populism or outright autocracy.

How do these two competing sets of *ex ante* predictions square with the *ex post* descriptive findings of this book (i.e. with Part I's analysis of the cross-sectional and cross-temporal outcomes) on the dependent variable of the political regime form? The answer is simple as neither turn out to be very accurate. Rather than travelling uniformly – or randomly but with a general trend – toward success or failure, the post-communist countries have gone their separate ways on two significant accounts. First, the setting came to exhibit a trichotomy or tripartition of democracies, hybrid regimes and autocracies as early as the mid-1990s. Since then this division has showed a remarkable stability, although some dynamics seem to have re-entered the picture in the 2000s. Second, the tripartition has been subregionally fixed. The East-Central European countries have become democracies, the Central Asian countries (together with Azerbaijan and Belarus) have become autocracies and most of the countries situated in between geographically have lingered in a hybrid state.

The descriptive analysis of Part I, which elucidated this tripartition, also paved the way for rejecting the empirical value of the conceptual or theoretical distinction between the electoral and the liberal components of democracy, which Larry Diamond and Fareed Zakaria have advocated that scholars keep in mind. When the electoral and liberal components are conceptualized as independent attributes and when these two attributes are measured using the Freedom House ratings, no significant gap – and definitely not a growing gap – between the two is in evidence, neither on the global level nor with regard to the post-communist sub-set. Generally speaking, a country that scores high on one attribute also scores high on the other; the empirical demarcation lines between democracies, hybrid regimes and autocracies are therefore operating on both dimensions.

This initial exercise in descriptive inference thus laid the problem bare. How is it possible to explain the identified tripartition between post-communist political regime forms? In particular, how do we account for the systematic cross-spatial combination of intra-subregional similarities and inter-subregional differences? And finally, how are we to understand the way in which the countries move along these political pathways over time? These questions can only be answered by moving into the realm of causal inference.

The theoretical literature that has evolved since the breakdown of communism contains a great number of potential answers. Concerning the study of post-communism, proximate actor-centred explanations such as those promoted by M. Steven Fish presently dominate the field. In Chapter 3 I identified, discussed, operationalized and measured three such actor-centred variables: displacement (the political competition variable), reform (the economic reform variable) and legislature (the constitutional engineering variable). Each of these variables was conceptualized as one-dimensional attributes, i.e. they were dichotomized to capture either the presence or the absence of the matching attribute.

It turned out that the consequent ordering on a compound of attributes could adequately account for the described tripartition on the dependent variable of the political regime form in the period 1997–2007. Otherwise said, the typological analysis demonstrated that, in the longer run, only the countries with the combined presence of displacement, reform and legislature were able to cross the threshold to democracy (with the sole exceptions of Romania and Bulgaria in a large part of the period and Mongolia since 2002). Conversely, in the longer term only the countries that fell short on all three attributes have crossed the threshold to autocracy (with the sole exceptions of Kyrgyzstan in the early 2000s and Russia in the most recent years). The two corresponding polar types – which I termed 'actor-induced democracy' and 'actor-induced autocracy', respectively – thus housed no less than 15 of 26 countries by 2007, pointing to the existence of virtuous and vicious circles of political change.

So, the actor-centred explanations are the right place to look for those who wish to understand the post-communist political pathways? Unfortunately, it is not as simple as that. The typological analysis of Chapter 4 demonstrated that the structural explanations found on the theoretical market place did the job, too. This time around, I identified, discussed, operationalized and measured another three independent variables: legacies (the political legacies variable), West (the vicinity to Western Europe variable) and modern (the modernization variable). All three were dichotomized depending on the presence or absence of the matching (i.e. underpinning) attribute.

When analysing the political pathways of the period 1992–2007, it quickly became clear that the three structural variables predicted the political pathways nicely, once again confirming the existence of virtuous and vicious circles. It turned out that only countries exhibiting the combined presence of legacies, West and modern have been able to cross the threshold to democracy (with the sole exceptions of Romania, Bulgaria and Mongolia). Conversely, only countries exhibiting the absence of all three attributes have been able to cross the threshold to autocracy (with the sole exception of Belarus through most of the period and Russia in 2007). The two corresponding polar types – which I termed 'structural democracy' and 'structural autocracy', respectively – held no less than 14 of 26 countries by 2004. The situation was vastly different at the outset of the period (i.e. in 1992[2]), but over the subsequent decade the countries moved into the polar types as expected. In sum, the cross-temporal variation conforms to the structural predictions, as does the cross-spatial variation after the initial upheavals ebbed away.

The most salient fact about the post-communist pathways hence seems to be the striking regularities we encounter, both from an actor-centred and a structural point of view. This is relevant when considering the use of typological theory. Needless to say, dichotomizing (or trichotomizing, in the case of the explanandum) variables entails a significant loss of information vis-à-vis continuous measures. At first glance, this is a clear limitation of the analyses carried out in this book. But looks may be deceiving. First and foremost, the massive problems of multicollinearity present in analysing post-communist political change means that configurational methods, such as typological theory, arguably have a competitive edge compared to regression analysis when it comes to assessing both deep and proximate factors in a common explanatory framework.

Second, the fact that the empirical relationships identified are so clear-cut also carries implications for the choice of method. As Giovanni Sartori has zealously pointed out, classificatory and typological schemas rest on an assumption of empirical boundedness. That is, we must have a large degree of stability within the ordering on the compound of attributes for the method to be convincing. Otherwise, measuring differences in degree – using continuous measurements – often makes more sense than measuring differences in kind (as classifications do).

Yet the flipside of the coin is that striking regularities on the ground warrant the use of typological theory. And, to reiterate, the post-communist setting is indeed characterized by such regularities. In fact, the tripartition between the three geographical subregions extends to the explanans as well as the explanandum, especially when the former is construed as actor-centred and structural 'packages' (i.e. as composite indices). This equals saying that the former communist bloc is, at the end of the day, best described by differences in kind rather than differences in degree. And this is why using the classificatory logic (and, by extension, the typological schemas) is merited, and not just as a heuristic device, when compared to standard statistical procedures.

But, harking back to the theoretical discussion, the fact that the regularities characterize both of the competing sets of independent variables means that we are left with a Gordian knot. Which set of factors should we pin our faith on: the deep or the proximate? How do we cut the knot? The claim staked in the preceding analyses rests on three premises. First, it makes sense to relate the actor-centred and structural approaches to see if an integrated explanatory framework can be established. As demonstrated in Chapter 5, the two are indeed strongly interlinked; a full presence of attributes on one package accurately predicts a full presence on the other. Likewise, a full absence of attributes on one package mostly entails a full absence on the other. Combined into a unified property space, we thus end up with two polar types – which I termed 'democracy guaranteed' and 'autocracy guaranteed' – under which the lion's share of the empirical referents can be subsumed. These polar types capture the most general dividing lines of post-communism and underline the value of explaining classes of events rather than differences in degree. Second, and critically, the deep attributes predate the proximate attributes temporally. Third, we can establish a theoretical link between the two that posits that the actor-centred attributes were (at least to a large extent) shaped by their structural counterparts. To elaborate, the extent to which a post-communist country was characterized by competitive politics at the time (and during the immediate aftermath) of the transition very much seems to depend upon the structural point of departure.

In sum, the theoretical logic underpinning these premises is that 'increasing returns' characterize not only the relationship among the actor-centred and structural variables, respectively, but between them as well – what I attempted to illustrate with the metaphors of 'virtuous' and 'vicious' circles. But the circles rotate in a certain direction, in turn reflecting the three premises. In a nutshell, the actor-centred attributes should be construed as intervening links in a causal chain that leads from the structural attributes to the political outcome.

To phrase this slightly differently, structures do not create democracy (or autocracy, for that matter); actors do. But the systematic combination of intra-subregional similarities and inter-subregional differences found within the post-communist setting – on the dependent variable, the actor-centred package and the structural package, respectively – can only be explained with reference to the deeper attributes as these are the ulterior attributes of the edifice. As such, the structural factors are the only genuinely independent variables, but they kick in via the causal mechanisms that are laid bare by the proximate actor-centred variables.

Notice how this explanatory edifice represents a criticism of actor-centred approaches, such as those of M. Steven Fish (and, albeit more implicitly, the current of Transitology), even though it incorporates and relies on the findings of these approaches. None of the scholars associated with the bold actor-centred explanations construe their highlighted factors as intervening in nature; rather they see them as the interesting independent variables and emphasize the possibility of choice (i.e. the high degree of voluntarism) that the actors have. This book has argued otherwise and, on this point, the analysis is very much indebted to Kitschelt's ontological distinction between deep (structural) and shallow (proximate) causes.

Notwithstanding the emphasis on the structural point of departure, the argument promoted is not deterministic. The described patterns only hold on the general level, not with respect to all particular cases. Most strikingly, the Mongolian pathway completely contradicts the expectations. Mongolia's 'democratic miracle' is just that – a miracle – in so far as it cannot be explained by either the actor-centred approaches or their structural counterparts. Something idiosyncratic has happened in this isolated corner of the setting. And that is not all. To a lesser extent, the same can be said of Bulgaria and Romania. Both of these countries have been able to sustain democracy despite lacking a full presence of attributes on both the proximate and deep packages. The surprising merits of Bulgaria and Romania can probably, at least in part, be explained by a factor not considered in this analysis: the causal importance of EU enlargement. As Milada Anna Vachudova (2005) has convincingly argued, Bulgaria and Romania only really made the democratic turn after the initiation of what she terms the 'active' leverage of the EU, i.e. after the initiation of actual membership negotiations. In the early 1990s, by contrast, the lack of political competition allowed the communist incumbents to pursue an 'illiberal' course of action – something the then 'passive' leverage of the EU could not hinder.

Translated into my explanatory edifice, the structural constraints – in particular those associated with the political legacies described by Kitschelt – were unfavourable to political competition and hence to democracy. Only the ascendancy of the EU made it possible to break with these constraints. This goes to show that more attention could be paid to the ability of variables to trump each other, at least when descending the ladder of abstraction and scrutinizing particular countries. Finally, a number of other countries do not match the expectations perfectly, albeit the overall fit is rather satisfactory. In short, the analysis has identified general causes (or probabilistic causation) and equifinality, not deterministic causation.

By now, we are dressed to answer the problems raised in the Introduction. It turns out that the presence in East-Central Europe, for example, of deep, structural factors such as legacies, West and modern accounts for the presence of democracies in the post-communist setting. These factors kicked in via the mobilization of the opposition to communism on the eve of the transition of 1989–91 and the consequent actor-choices concerning the constitutional institutions and economic reforms. Conversely, the absence in, for example, Central Asia of these structural factors paved the way for autocracy by virtually ruling out the benign actor-choices just sketched. Finally, the hybrid regimes, which are geographically situated in the middle, owe their existence to a mixed sheet on the structural package, one that also facilitated ambivalence on the actor-centred counterpart.

Notice, however, that the structural point of departure only kicked in with a time lag. As such, while explaining the cross-temporal variation encountered in the setting (i.e. the political pathways leading to the described tripartition), the identified factors are only able to explain the cross-spatial variation after the mid-1990s (i.e. after the tripartition came into its own).

This brings us to the more general puzzle that was also raised in the Introduction, to wit that the tripartition is systematically dispersed geographically, despite a common window of opportunity in 1989–91. According to this book, the combination of intra-subregional political similarities and inter-subregional political differences that has locked in since the early 1990s is a consequence of (and therefore mirrors) the very salient dividing lines separating the post-communist countries on the eve of the transitions. These dividing lines were created by i) the inheritance from pre-communist regimes (political as well as economical) which lingered on during communism and ii) vicinity to Western Europe. Critically, these dividing lines were reproduced by the opposition to communism of the late 1980s and the constitutional engineering of the early 1990s.

The very answer to the puzzle thus arrived at brings us to the first limitation of the present study. At the end of the day, a deep approach, such as that of Kitschelt, begs the following question: To which ulterior attributes should we trace the dividing lines of pre-communism? More generally, how do we explain the origins of the (systematically dispersed) structural diversity characterizing post-communism? Kitschelt (1999) emphasizes that even 'deeper' factors, such as 'religious doctrines' and historical 'zones of administrative-political control', do not make for viable explanations as no causal mechanism explains their cross-temporal impact. But, logically, it must be possible to deliver an explanatory account of diverging patterns of state capacity that allows us to explain Kitschelt's point of departure, i.e. an account that (successfully) treats Kitschelt's explanans as explanandum. Doing so would merely mean extending the causal mechanism further back in time. Notice in this connection that the underpinning mechanism cannot be exclusively geographical (i.e. proximity to Western Europe) as East-Asian countries such as Japan, South Korea and Taiwan have also been able to bring about felicitous patterns of bureaucratization and state–society relations (see Doner et al. 2005). In short, if this book has answered the question 'Wherefore the post-communist tripartition?', then we need to answer the 'why of the wherefore'. (This formulation paraphrases Kopstein and Reilly 1999.)

This limitation is deeply temporal, or even historical, in that it raises the questions of origins of diversity. The second set of limitations on the present study is of a very different nature, methodologically as well as theoretically. I have not been able to expound differences in degree within the classes of democracy, hybrid regime and autocracy. This has not been a major problem due to the general aim of the book and the fact that both the democracies (in

East-Central Europe) and the autocracies (in Central Asia) were, to reiterate and elaborate a point made above, heavily overdetermined. With respect to the orderings on the independent variables, everything has favoured the former cluster, whereas nothing has favoured the latter. Consequently, they inhabit polar types within which the differences in degree are negligible, at least when viewed from the higher ground.

Another way of framing these empirical findings is to use the notion of equilibriums. In an interesting article, Scott Gates, Håvard Hegre, Mark P. Jones and Håvard Strand (2006: 893) demonstrate that '[...] purely autocratic and purely democratic regimes' are more stable than more inconsistent or compounded regimes. They use equilibrium theory to underpin this finding, arguing that a consistent mix of institutional features (i.e. an equilibrium) makes for political stability, be it democratic or autocratic, whereas inconsistent combinations make for political instability.

Although the preceding analysis does not rely on institutional theory, one and the same line of reasoning can be used to underpin the findings of this book. Gates, Hegre, Jones and Strand (2006: 896) define their three categories as follows:

> A polity that is neither an ideal Democracy nor an ideal Autocracy is an Inconsistent polity. Institutional consistency is present at all points in and on the cube aside from the regions immediately around the two respective vertices (1,1,1) and (0,0,0) defining ideal Democracies and ideal Autocracies.

Correspondingly, I have shown that the twin combinations of the presence of all (deep and proximate) theoretically relevant attributes (1,1,1...) and the absence of all theoretically relevant attributes (0,0,0...) make for stable democracy and stable autocracy, respectively. Other combinations normally make for much more unstable hybrid regimes. This empirical result reflects the presence of virtuous and vicious circles and, *ipso facto*, of two stable equilibriums and an intermediate zone of instability.

Let me elaborate a bit on this zone of instability. In the typological analyses I ventured into the issue of the differences in degree that exist within the class of hybrid regimes, albeit in a rather tentative manner. My finding was that the relatively high (or low) presence of actor-centred and structural attributes within the combinations that I termed a 'mixed sheet' did in fact seem to correlate with the Freedom House scores. Thus, the hybrid regimes with more attributes present were closer to the threshold to democracy than the hybrid regimes with fewer attributes present. But this only brings us so far. Generally speaking, the analysis of this book has been unable to account for the lively activity taking place within this class.

In fact, and to phrase it more analytically, the analyses showed that the countries not situated in the two stable lock-ins were characterized by diversity rather than uniformity. Although many of the countries showing a mixed score on both the deep and the proximate packages were hybrid regimes, there were even more exceptions to this rule – indicating that countries with a mixed score can move between the regime types. Such combinations, therefore, cannot be construed as stable equilibriums. Rather, they have an intrinsic propensity to create conjunctures, as has in fact been empirically demonstrated by the recent 'colour revolutions' in Georgia (2003), Ukraine (2004) and Kyrgyzstan (2005).

Why this is the case is a question that will not be addressed here as it would require a new research project, but one hypothesis that arises from the analysis is the following: the very fact that these countries have a mixed sheet on the explanatory factors, in particular with regard to the deep factors, means that the actors have much more room for maneuvering than what would otherwise be the case (for an example of a lucid analysis of actor-choices within such structural constraints, see Hale 2005). If correct, this lends support to Kitschelt's (2003: 75) observation that in the context of post-communism, there may 'be structural reasons for randomness'.[3] Otherwise said, is possible to argue that, even in these seemingly deviant cases, the deep constraints have set the parameters for the actors.

However, to grasp the dynamics within this zone of instability, two further steps are necessary. First, on the theoretical front, an understanding of the interplay between actors and structures, and the matching process of diachronic social learning, is required. Second, a methodological appreciation of the more particular, context-specific causal mechanisms is needed. In short, then, the work laid out in this book should be followed up by what may be termed an 'historical institutional' – and small-N – analysis of the current patterns of change afflicting the hybrid regimes, including meticulous process-tracing.

Reflecting on these limitations, one could accuse the present study of being caught up in the kind of 'paradigmatic thinking' that Albert O. Hirschman (1970) famously cautioned against.[4] However – and this is important – the somewhat crude contrasting of actor-centred and structural explanations is very much a consequence of the chosen level of abstraction. When seeking to explain the cross-spatial political variation of no less than 26 countries over one and a half decades, general categories and general contrasts of explanatory factors are necessary. The gist of the matter is that we can in fact navigate between different paradigms, as long as the test employed is an empirical one. This point should not be disguised by the (obviously true but also unhelpful) objection that the intricacies of particular cases are not easily unfolded when attacking the reality on the ground in this manner.

Endnote
Montesquieu's 'General Rule' and the rule of law in the post-communist setting

Contrasting the competing approaches to explaining post-communist political diversity, this book has reached a simple but unequivocal conclusion: the geographical tripartition between democracies, hybrid regimes and autocracies that locked in throughout the 1990s cannot have been caused by the 'voluntaristic' choices of actors alone. To paraphrase Herbert Kitschelt, we need to dig 'deeper' than that, i.e. we need to uncover the structural origins of post-communist diversity.

What has basically been done, then, is to affirm the empirical value of a 'legacies-approach' to post-communism (on 'legacies' and post-communism, see Ekiert and Hanson 2003). The variables measuring political legacies (legacies) and the initial level of modernization (modern) thus both capture antecedent legacies. Vicinity to Western Europe (West) is obviously more a matter of geography than of legacies. However, as it basically discriminates between the countries in a like manner on the spatial dimension, this makes little difference.

If we keep viewing the situation from the higher ground, then the legacies relevant to post-communism logically derive from one (or both) of two periods: communism and pre-communism.[1] Since the events of 1989–91, scholars emphasizing legacies have pinned their faith to either of these. Let us try to take a closer look at some of the approaches on offer in the literature.

Legacies: approaches to post-communism

In the early 1990s, Ken Jowitt (1992) famously warned about the pernicious political consequences of the 'Leninist legacy'. By the end of the same decade Valerie Bunce (1999) pointed out – with a deliberate emphasis on diversity rather than the uniformity that was a virtual antithesis of Jowitt's analysis – that the socialist past, and the paths of extrication it offered each country, appears to be the key factor accounting for the present economic and political variation. Finally, Grzegorz Ekiert (2003) has presented a more elaborate account of the importance of the socialist past.

Moving to pre-communist legacies, Samuel P. Huntington's *Clash of Civilizations* presents the most notorious contribution. The very notion of competing civilizations points to a distant cultural line of demarcation, a formative period in which the various civilizations crystallized and moved their separate ways. More recently, and as discussed in this book proper, Herbert Kitschelt has made a less categorical distinction between legacies of pre-communism. Also, he has extended the causal chain into the communist era, in turn arguing that this diversity has, to a very large extent, been reproduced during post-communism (see Kitschelt et al. 1999, Kitschelt and Malesky 2000 and Kitschelt 2003).

But who has more to offer here? First and foremost, it is quite obvious that any legacies dating from before communism must be traced into (and throughout) the communist period, otherwise the causal chain has a large missing link. Having said that, in which of the two periods should we, in general, seek the roots of the post-communist diversity (i.e. the ulterior process of diversification)?

Simple logical reasoning may lead us some of the way. First, Jowitt's description of the uniform legacy of the Leninist past simply does not square with the spatial variation identified in the preceding chapters. Jowitt posits that the area has what he terms a 'catholic' point of departure, a 'sameness' or even 'universalism'. The only variable creating diversity that he allows for seems to be Western influence (1992: 304–5). This general focus on uniformity does not carry with it an expectation of inter-subregional differences – although it does, of course, predict intra-subregional similarities – and can thus be disregarded or even disconfirmed on the basis of the analyses carried out in this book.

Bunce and Ekiert have more to offer in this regard. Both of them emphasize that the communist period was very much characterized by diversity, and that this diversity has been reproduced after 1989–91. In both instances, the mechanism of reproduction pointed to is Fish's 'initial election' variable. The outcomes of the elections can, the argument holds, be traced to the particular properties of the socialist path, and this outcome has then locked in the respective post-communist outcomes. To quote Ekiert (2003: 111) on the dividing lines of communism,

> The initial experience of transitions shows that the most successful East Central European countries share common historical legacies. First, all these countries had a history of major political conflicts and political reforms. As a result they were more liberal in the declining years of communism than their neighbors [. . .] Second, the extent of marketization and economic liberalization prior to the end of communist rule was larger. These countries had a relatively large private sector and many state-owned firms had cooperated with Western firms or produced foods for Western markets. Third, these countries had pragmatic communist elites and/or substantial political

and cultural opposition. Finally, these countries had stronger ties to the West.

These factors, and the corresponding causal chain leading through the initial elections, strike me as very convincing. But, and referring back to my arguments in Chapter 5, the highlighted factors still seem too proximate to constitute root causes. In brief, no account is given as to how the combination of intra-subregional similarities and inter-subregional differences that also characterize the ordering of these attributes came into existence in the first place. Bunce and Ekiert simply beg the following question: Which ulterior attributes are behind the diversity of the state-socialist past?

This is a general problem, and it naturally brings us to the legacies of pre-communism. It is not possible to refute Huntington outright. After all, the geographical distinctions between civilizations that he describes are very much reproduced politically today. However, as Kitschelt has argued, when using deep, structural factors to explain post-communist diversity, it must be possible to link these anterior factors to the posterior outcome via causal mechanisms that touch upon human actions. To phrase this slightly differently, the causal chain must not be excessively long; it must be able to work through postulates about the beliefs and experiences of the actors. Otherwise, the structural explanations are simply too deep to be convincing. This requirement represents a shield against infinite regress into the recesses of history – which is appropriate since all explanations could otherwise be construed as too 'close' to the explanandum, relatively speaking.

To illustrate this argument, Kitschelt touches upon Robert Putnam's (1993) influential study of democratic processes and performances in northern and southern Italy. Putnam's attempt to trace the present political and social properties of the Italian regions back to the division between centralized Norman rule (in southern Italy) and municipal or republican governments (in central and northern Italy) in the twelfth and thirteenth centuries is flawed, Kitschelt (2003: 64) asserts, because '[n]o mechanism translate the "long-distance" causality across eight hundred years into a more proximate chain of closer causal forces acting upon each other'.

In short, the cause is so far removed from the effect that the causal mechanism is virtually impossible to establish. One should not overextend oneself causally (and thus temporally), so to speak. What is important for our purposes is that Huntington's emphasis on religion and competing civilizations does not embed such causal mechanisms; it is, therefore, faulty. In fact, Huntington does not demonstrate how the civilizational lines of demarcation played out during communism; he does not show that they lingered until 1989–91.[2]

Kitschelt himself has more to offer in this regard. As already noted, he develops a causal chain extending from pre-communist patterns of state formation, via communist regime forms, to the scope of actor-choices after the breakdown of communism. On a more general level, I repeated (and expanded) this exercise in Chapter 5 when I linked the deep, structural factors to the political regime outcome via the proximate, actor-centred attributes. That is, I argued that, to a large extent, the structural point of departure shaped the potential for competitive politics at the breakdown of communism and, through this, favoured one regime form over another, especially in the longer run. In this brief endnote, I will further (re)test the virtues of Kitschelt's particular explanation by engaging in an exercise that is more about descriptive than causal inference.

The claim of the 'legacies' approach promoted by Kitschelt et al. (1999) is the following: the properties of the state apparatus and the properties of the state–society relations during communism shaped the political destiny of post-communism. These 'communist' regime properties, in turn, reflect pre-communist patterns of state formation. More specifically, Kitschelt shows that the presence (or absence) of a formal-rational bureaucratic state apparatus and the presence (or absence) of a vibrant civil society before the advent of communism has produced four different regime forms under communism: 'bureaucratic-authoritarian communism', 'national-accommodative communism', 'patrimonial communism' and 'colonial periphery'.

Let us try to rephrase this by moving to a higher level of abstraction. In brief, Kitschelt's argument is that the actor-choices of post-communism were, at least to a very large extent, endogenous to the dominant legacies of state formation across the setting, and in particular to patterns preceding the communist era. Otherwise said, the political outcomes depended upon inherited state capacity and the inherited strength of the civil society.

I have tested this particular explanation by ordering the countries on the attribute of legacies in Chapter 4. But Kitschelt's basic premise is that legacies are something that survives over time, even in the face of totalitarian and democratic junctures. This paves the way for a different form of test, one which requires the assistance of one of the giants of our discipline.

Montesquieu's 'General Rule' of taxation and liberty

In Book 13 of *The Spirit of the Laws*, Charles-Louis de Secondat, baron de la Brède et de Montesquieu (1989 [1748]), directs attention to the intimate relationship between the fiscal infrastructure of the state and what he terms 'liberty'. He states nothing less than a 'General Rule':

> [o]ne can levy heavier taxes in proportion to the liberty of the subjects and one is forced to moderate them insofar as servitude increases. This has always been and will always be [. . .] In moderate states, there is a compensation for heavy taxes; it is liberty. In despotic states, there is an equivalent for liberty; it is the modest taxes.

(220–1)

Whereas several of the observations of Montesquieu's formidable work, such as the virtues of a separation of powers, are known by any undergraduate student, this very clear-cut dictum receives scant attention today. To spell it out, we first need to understand Montesquieu's concept of liberty.

The definition found in *The Spirit of the Laws* is as famous as it is comprehensible: 'Liberty is the right to do everything the laws permit; and if one citizen could do what they forbid, he would no longer have liberty because the others would likewise have this same power' (155). Liberty thus consists of the absence of judicial arbitrariness and it can be said to obtain what we today term the rule of law obtains. As this requires the presence of a state-sponsored aegis against limitless power, the relationship is really between the fiscal properties of the state and constitutional liberalism. In a nutshell, Montesquieu's point is that the *quid pro quo* between revenue and sanctioned rights constitutes the inner essence of any liberal order.

Montesquieu has not been alone in making this assertion. In fact, it has figured prominently within political theory for more than 300 years. John Carteret, one of the great seventeenth-century English statesmen, explained it prosaically in his statement that '[t]he Security of our Liberties are (sic) not in the Laws but by the Purse being in the Hands of the People' (quoted in Brewer 1989). We encounter it on the Continent as well. Contemporary actors to a large extent perceived the French Revolution to be a consequence of the financial bankruptcy of the *ancien régime*. This was what Mirabeau referred to when, on the eve of the Revolution, he declared that: 'The nation's deficit is the nation's treasure' (quoted in Ash 1990: 135). Likewise, it was recognized on the other side of the Atlantic, where the telling slogan of the American independence movement was 'no taxation without representation'.

As late as in the 1920s, Guido de Ruggiero (1927: 54–5) virtually echoed Montesquieu in his *History of European Liberalism*, noting that

[a]s a general rule, heavier taxes can be raised in proportion as the subject enjoys more liberty; as liberty decreases taxes must be diminished. In free States heavy taxes are counterbalanced by liberty; in despotic States the lightness of the taxes is a compensation for the loss of liberty.

In fact, the relationship described in *The Spirit of the Laws* received zealous attention between the World Wars. Austrian scholars such as Rudolf Goldscheid (1958 [1925]) and Joseph Schumpeter (1991) attempted to carve the subdiscipline of 'Fiscal Sociology' (*Finanzsoziologie*) out of sociology proper. The intent was to unfold the fiscal logic of the state. In Goldscheid's famous formulation, which was picked up by Schumpeter (1991: 100), '[. . .] the budget is the skeleton of the state stripped of all misleading ideologies'.

But the owl of Minerva flies only at dusk and after the Second World War Montesquieu's dictum has more or less passed into oblivion. In recent decades, the fiscal–political connection has, to be sure, been partly incorporated into the two bodies of theory captured under the headlines of 'sectoral analysis' (e.g. Shafer 1994) and 'the rentier state' (e.g. Ross 2001). However, sectoral analysis targets the sectoral imbalances of the economy *in toto*, not merely the character of the tax base. And the rentier state approach is, on the contrary, preoccupied with the narrower question of the rents emanating from natural resources.

This short note will go back to basics and evaluate the relevance of Montesquieu's General Rule in the context of post-communism. But why is that an interesting place to test it? How does it link up with Kitschelt's focus on political legacies?

Post-communism and state formation revisited

First, and as a general premise, the absence of the rule of law is today recognized as the economic and political problem *par excellence* of (especially) post-Soviet transitions.[3] Second, and as a theoretical premise, surprisingly little research has been carried out on what may be termed the fiscal properties of post-communist change.[4] Third, and bringing us back to the subject matter of the book, the application of Montesquieu's General Rule promises to elaborate (or even unpack) the structural explanation of Kitschelt et al. (1999, 2003).

Recall that the basic premise of Kitschelt's explanatory edifice is that of path dependency: legacies are something that survives the hands of time. Hence, it makes sense to order the post-communist countries according to his two attributes of state capacity and state–society relations after the transitions of 1989–91 – and then see how this bears upon the political outcomes.

This brings us back to the fiscal focus. As the political philosopher and statesman Edmund Burke (1988 [1970]) noted in his famous *Reflections on the Revolution in France*, '[t]he revenue of the state is the state'. At the most general level, then, state capacity and revenue extraction are virtually synonymous. Also, based on the theoretical review above, if the state is capable of taxing its citizens, then this entails (or, better, mirrors) an auspicious pattern of state–society relations (represented by the existence of a strong civil society, the second of Kitschelt's twin properties).

Hence, if Kitschelt's liberal-bureaucratic legacies of state formation are in fact requisites of liberal constitutionalism[5] (when present), then we should expect to find a strong relationship between rights and revenue in the post-communist setting. This is tantamount to saying that we expect the rule of law and a certain legacy of state formation (the result of which is a high degree of contemporary state capacity) to go together.

The reality on the ground

Enter Montesquieu. His twin variables of taxation and liberty (i.e. the rule of law) are very much amenable to operationalization and measurement. As he makes no qualifications, Montesquieu seems to be preoccupied with the general level of taxation – an attribute that can be operationalized using the standard formula of 'taxation as a proportion of GDP'. I have obtained a dataset measuring this proportion in the post-communist setting from the World Bank's *World Development Indicators 2004*.[6]

With regard to the rule of law, I will, first, use another World Bank source: the so-called 'Aggregate Governance Indicators' created by Kaufmann et al. (2004). This database contains a composite measure of the 'Rule of Law' that brings together virtually all the offers on the marketplace. Second, I will use the Freedom House's rating on 'Civil Liberties' to carry out a robustness test. This measure is less valid. As the reader will recall from Chapter 1, it captures the civil liberties that surround standard electoral rights, e.g. the freedom of speech and the freedom of association. Yet the measure also expressly includes the rule of law and, as a proxy meant to test whether the findings are robust, these ratings should be adequate.

I will simply construe Montesquieu's General Rule as a descriptive relationship between rights and revenue, rather than assume one to be the cause of the other. The basic argument is that – like the horse and the carriage – the two go together: you cannot have one without the other. Consequently, I will zoom in on the two variables at the same point in time. More specifically, I will scrutinize the relationship in the years 1996 and 2000. These years have been chosen not for some intrinsic merits but for two pragmatic reasons. First, the World Development Indicators contain relatively[7] complete data on taxation for these two years. Second, the chosen years allow us to check whether the relationship increases over time – as one would assume, due to the transitional nature of the post-communist countries.

Concerning nomenclature, I name the two different temporal orderings on the revenue-variable 'TAX1996' and 'TAX2000' and the equivalent orderings on the rule of law variable 'RL1996' and 'RL2000'. What do the numbers show? As depicted in the scatter plot below, we find a strong statistical result in 1996.

Pearson's r is an impressive 0.62 despite the fact that the relationship is weakened substantially by two outliers (underachievers!) situated more than two standard deviations from the regression line, viz. Belarus and Croatia. If these were eliminated, Pearson's r would reach a stunning 0.85. I cannot justify doing so,[8] but one might expect these two outliers to fit the general relationship better over time. What happens when we move to 2000?

Figure 6.2 demonstrates that the strength of the association increases substantially over time. Pearson's r is thus 0.72 this time around. Notice, further, that whereas Belarus is still a very significant outlier, Croatia conforms better to the expectations this time around.

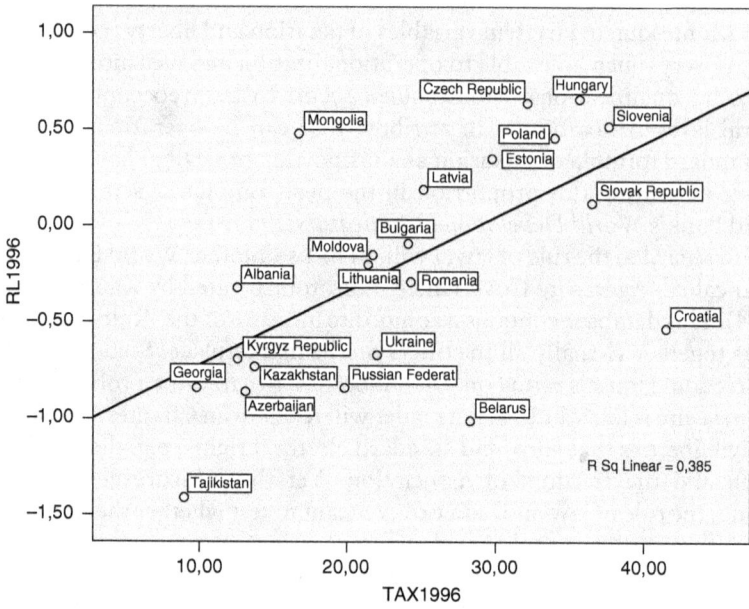

Figure 6.1 A scatter plot of the linear regression of TAX1996 and RL1996.

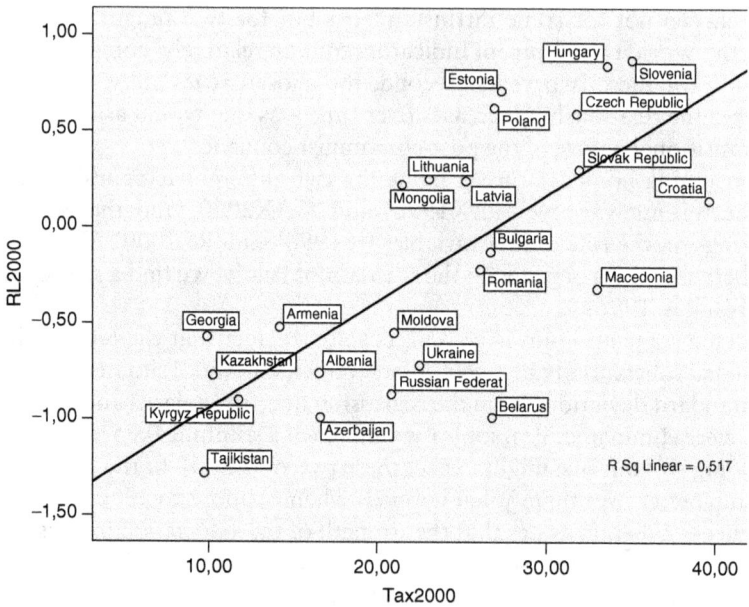

Figure 6.2 A scatter plot of the linear regression of TAX2000 and RL2000.

Table 6.1 Pearson's r for the robustness test

	TAX1996	TAX2000
CL1996	.52	—
CL2000	—	.68

Let us, finally, use Freedom House's ratings of Civil Liberties in 1996 and 2000 to carry out a robustness test. I name the twin orderings on this variable 'CL1996' and 'CL2000'. As illustrated in Table 6.1 below, the relationship turns out to be quite robust – and it yet again increases over time – with correlations of 0.52 in 1996 and 0.68 in 2000.

Concerning statistical significance, all of the four bivariate correlations are significant at the 0.05-level and only one, between TAX1996 and CL1996, falls at the 0.01-level (with a two-tailed significance of 0.013).

Conclusions

The conclusion of the statistical exercise carried out in this short note is thus very clear-cut. In sum, the more effective a post-communist state is at taxing its citizens, the more likely it is to uphold the rule of law. With a few notable exceptions (in particular, Belarus), the two simply go together. This is the case in both 1996 and in 2000, but the relationship becomes stronger over time, as one would expect due to the transitional nature of these polities.

This relationship makes up a robustness test of the influential structural explanation of Herbert Kitschelt, or so I argue here. The statistical result indicates that the pre-communist dividing lines of state formation have indeed been carried over into the post-communist era. The theoretical notion of 'legacies' thus allows us to link up with the conclusions of the typological analyses of Chapters 3 through 5. In a nutshell, the argument promoted here is that the structural point of departure can be traced to the fiscal properties.

More particularly, what this endnote indicates is that the legacies Kitschelt highlights – the character of the state bureaucracy and the character of state–society relations before the advent of communism – shape the potential for trading rights for revenue during post-communism. This is so because a 'tax state' is a state characterized by both an effective bureaucracy and relatively balanced state–society relations; these are preconditions for striking the fiscal bargain.

This is only a tentative conclusion, however, because the data material is very insufficient and I have not included any control variables. Also, one may object that the fiscal variable is in fact too proximate to the explanandum to be very interesting – i.e. that taxation mirrors the rule of law achievements as such. This is the very objection which I have raised against the actor-centred approaches. I do not think that this is the case as the state infrastructure's ability to extract revenues is likely to be very path dependent. Also, this is not so much a problem here as I only endeavoured to uncover a descriptive relationship.

Having said that, and as already noted in the Conclusions, ultimately it would be more interesting to trace the historical origins of the pre-communist dividing lines described by the legacies approach of Kitschelt. Hopefully, I will be able to do this in a future book.

Appendix 6.1

1 The data on tax revenue (% of GDP) [TAX] is derived from the World Bank's World Development Indicators 2004. Note the following qualifications due to the incompleteness of the data:

- Where the *World Development Indicators 2004* did not hold data for the years 1996 or 2000 but for an alternative year, this figure was used. In the former instance, such was the case with Georgia (1997 used instead), Kazakhstan (1997 used instead), Russia (1995 used instead), Tajikistan (1998 used instead) and Ukraine (1999 used instead). In the latter instance, such was the case with Albania (1998 used instead), Armenia (2002 used instead), Azerbaijan (1999 used instead) and Macedonia (2002 used instead).
- Where the *World Development Indicators 2004* contained no data at all, the country in question was excluded from the regression. In the former instance, such was the case with Armenia, Macedonia, Turkmenistan and Uzbekistan. In the latter instance, such was the case with Turkmenistan and Uzbekistan.

2 The data on 'Rule of Law' [RL] is derived from the World Bank's 'Aggregate Governance Indicators 2004'.

3 The data on 'Civil Liberties' [CL] is derived from Freedom House Ratings.

Notes

Introduction

1 I have borrowed both this observation and formulation from Carothers (2002: 8). For an important early contribution which expressed such optimism with regard to Eastern Europe, see Di Palma (1993).

2 As Kitschelt (2003: 49) has emphasized, the post-communist political pathways were established very quickly: 'This postcommunist diversity came about in the short window of about three years (1990–93). Since that time, new regime structures have been more or less "locked in" in almost all polities.'

3 On this, see also Bunce (1999: 761). She takes note of the tripartition, albeit with respect to a combined politico-economic dimension.

4 Throughout this book, I use the term 'East-Central Europe' to denote the area comprised by the countries Bulgaria, Croatia, Czech Republic, Estonia, Hungary, Latvia, Lithuania, Poland, Romania, Slovakia, Slovenia. These are the post-communist countries which – with the exception of the Baltic States – were not part of the Soviet Union or the Western Balkans (i.e. Albania, Bosnia-Herzegovina, Macedonia and Serbia-Montenegro). Whether Bulgaria and Romania should be excluded from 'East-Central Europe' – thus creating a more coherent residual category named 'the Balkans' – is a matter of taste; as indicated, I have chosen no to make this exclusion.

5 As we shall see, whereas the four other Central Asian republics quickly became entrenched autocracies, Kyrgyzstan has oscillated between the class of 'hybrid regime' and the class of 'autocracy' throughout the period, hence this qualification.

6 If a process of diffusion is found to explain the tripartition, actor-choices can still be said to have brought it about as actors carry out the diffusion. But then these choices are not important in their own right. They are not 'voluntaristic'; they are only a consequence of diffusion. This is basically the same argument as that used by adherents of structural approaches, only with diffusion substituted for structures as the 'root cause'. See Chapter 5 for more on the diffusion argument.

7 This is my formulation. Of course, as there are indeed exceptions to the tripartite distribution – we will see this later – it is not a genuine 'iron law'. I merely use this phrase to convey the fact that the geographical dividing lines, or regularities, are very salient.

8 To paraphrase the quotation from Jowitt above, both the optimists and the pessimists viewed the setting through 'catholic' glasses: stressing the 'sameness', or at least similarity, of the post-communist world rather than its diversity.

9 A few authors, such as Janos (1994), anticipated Kitschelt to some extent. But many more were to follow in his footsteps, including those in Ekiert and Hanson

(2003). See also Darden and Grzymala-Busse (2006), Pop-Eleches (2007) and Skaaning (2007).

10 The term 'package' is meant to capture the notion of the deep and the proximate variables taken together as wholes, or composite indices, to use more technical terms.

11 I do not intend to use the distinction between transition and consolidation (on this distinction, see in particular O'Donnell and Schmitter, 1986 and Linz and Stepan, 1996). Regarding the genus of democracies, my focus is on the institutionalized (i.e. self-reproducing) species. This may – pending the conceptual discussion of Chapters 1 and 2 – be termed 'democracy proper' or 'liberal democracy'. This instance of democracy obviously has much in common with the logic of consolidation, but I do not see the value added by using this concept which, by now, carries a lot of (conflicting) conceptual baggage of its own.

1 The gap between electoral and liberal democracy revisited

1 That is to say that I will create a classification of political regime forms. As Bailey (1994) emphasizes, the very definition of a classification is this: that at one and the same time, it maximizes within-class similarity and maximizes between-class dissimilarity.

2 The new tendency to construe some hybrid regimes as diminished subtypes of authoritarianism rather than diminished subtypes of democracy, associated in particular with Andreas Schedler's (2002) concept of 'electoral authoritarianism' and Steven Levitsky and Lucan A. Way's (2002) concept of 'competitive authoritarianism', does not change this fact. There is no doubt that this conceptual agenda has been influential lately. This influence is underscored by the following remark from Guillermo O'Donnell's (2007: 8–9) 'speech of thanks' upon receiving the first Lifetime Achievement Award of the International Political Science Association (IPSA):

> This set of countries can be distinguished in turn, albeit in some cases somewhat hazily, from a third set wherein elections, even if held, are not reasonably fair and many political freedoms are seriously curtailed. These are democracies *pour la galerie,* especially the international *galerie.* They are the 'electoral authoritarianisms' that have recently been drawing much attention in the scholarly literature.

However, what is new here is basically only the nomenclature, as the countries being ordered do not belong in the heartland of autocracy – as was the case for the countries classified by the constructs of 'totalitarianism' and 'authoritarianism' in earlier decades. More formally, the new subtypes are constituted by dividing the defining attributes of democracy between each other, rather than the defining attributes of autocracy.

3 Such is the case, at least, when using a 'thin' definition of democracy, one emphasizing only the defining Dahlian attributes of free elections and rights of speech, assembly and association, for instance. The referents thereby classified as democracies obviously all share the presence of these attributes – otherwise they would simply be cases of non-democracy. But, and to spell out the conceptual logic of a classificatory schema, they have very diverse statuses on accompanying attributes, such as the rule of law and horizontal accountability, hence the heterogeneity. This can be appreciated by the classificatory *genus et differentiam* principle, the logic of which is that each referent is defined by its *genus*, or class, and by its *differentiam*, the attributes that make it dissimilar from the other referents within

the class. When embracing a 'thicker' definition, in which all the said properties are construed as defining attributes, the membership of the class of democracy once again becomes quite homogenously and largely confined to the Western world (depending on the thresholds demarcating the presence of the attributes). But this attempt to solve the problem of empirical variation by definitional fiat is unsatisfactory, not to mention futile. For it simply means that the class of democracy borders a heavily populated zone of diminished subtypes.

4 Needless to say, other scholars have emphasized distinct dynamics – and properties – with regard to the present processes of democratization. On this conceptual diversity, see Collier and Levitsky (1997). However, what is important for this discussion is that a number of influential scholars – e.g. Diamond (1999) and Zakaria (1997, 2003) – have concluded that such a gap is globally salient.

5 The claim will be probed on the conventional three levels, with regard to: its logical structure, its theoretical relevance and its empirical meaningfulness. The empirical test will, however, function as a *primus inter pares* among these three *desiderata* as it decides the ultimate value of the conceptual constructs.

6 In their seminal article on classifications and typologies, Lazarsfeld and Barton (1951: 172) employ this terminology to denote '[. . .] "types" which are the result of serial operations on one attribute', i.e. what is normally referred to as classes. Genuine types '[. . .] refer to special compounds of attributes'.

7 In fact, Diamond explicitly emphasizes that his four-fold typology between liberal democracies, electoral democracies, pseudo-democracies and authoritarian regimes is based on differences in degree only – not differences in kind as a genuine multi-dimensional construct would necessarily dictate. This is also indicated by his use of 'midrange conceptions', i.e. regime forms situated between the respective 'types' of electoral and liberal democracy. See Diamond (1999: 13).

8 Here, I use 'connotation' in the commonsensical meaning of the associations brought to mind by the use of the term. When engaging in conceptualizations later on in this chapter, I will use it in its more technical, or narrower, meaning of indicating the properties or characteristics implied by a particular definition (of a term).

9 The term 'taxonomy' is more widely used in the biological sciences than in the social sciences (where 'typology' is normally preferred). Tellingly, its exact meaning within social science is somewhat disputed, or at the very least unclear (cf. Bailey 1994: 6). Throughout this book, I use the term – most often in its adjective form, i.e. as 'taxonomical' – in the pragmatic meaning proposed by Sartori (1976: 115), who writes that '[w]henever it is unnecessary to distinguish the classification from the typology, I shall use the term taxonomy'.

10 'Almost nothing' relative to the lower levels of the ladder only, however. Following Sartori (1970: 1042), even at the most abstract level there must be a contrary to the concept. To quote:

> The crucial distinction would thus be between 1) concepts defined by negation or *ex adverso*, i.e., by saying what they are *not*, and 2) concepts *without negation*, i.e., no-opposite concepts, conceptions without specified termination or boundaries. The logical principle involved in this distinction is *omnis determinatio est negatio*, that is, any determination involves a negation. According to this principle the former concepts are, no matter how broad, *determinate*; whereas the latter are indeterminate, literally *without termination*.

11 This is not surprising. Witness Adcock and Collier's (2001: 533) general assertion that '[. . .] the systematized concept, rather than the background concept, should be the focus in measurement validation'.

12　What I am in effect doing, then, is to disregard the more 'substantive' (i.e. thicker) definitions also found within the literature (see e.g. Held 1987 and Przeworski et al. 1995). What is interesting about these definitions – which may, in fact, be better construed as discussions – is that they are virtually never used when seeking to measure democracy across a large number of units. Rather, authors (e.g. Sørensen 1998) mention, and sometimes even recommend, the substantive definitions in the conceptual discussion and then opt for either a Schumpeterian or a Dahlian operationalization when attacking the empirical world. And with good reason; as argued in this chapter, it is not easy to travel with the heavy and multifaceted baggage of the substantial definitions.

13　I have borrowed this formulation from Schmitter and Karl (1993).

14　In fact, it is a bit more complicated than this. Dahl does not seek to capture the two components as independent entities. Rather, his point seems to be that the liberal freedoms are necessary conditions of fair elections, they stand in a causal relationship so to speak – as also emphasized by O'Donnell (2001). I come back to this issue in the first sections of Chapter 2.

15　This conceptual construction is my own but the exercise as such follows the logic of making classifications and typologies put forward by Lazarsfeld and Barton (1951: especially pages 155–65 and 169–80).

16　Using Collier and Levitsky's (1997) terminology this equals 'precising the definition'.

17　As the nomenclature shows, I have restricted the term 'democracy' to the types that denote the presence of 'free and fair elections'. This implies two things with regard to the electoral property. First, that 'free and fair elections' are construed as a necessary but not sufficient condition for the existence of democracy proper (i.e. 'liberal democracy'). Second, that 'free and fair elections' are sufficient for the existence of a 'diminished subtype' of democracy (i.e. 'electoral democracy'). The attribute of 'freedom rights and the rule of law' (the liberal property) is also a necessary but not sufficient condition for 'liberal democracy'. However, as the nomenclature shows, it is not a sufficient condition for a diminished subtype of democracy because it would not be meaningful to use the term 'democracy' to denote a country in which 'free and fair elections' do not take place. To sum up, even though the nomenclature does not – and this is both intentional and important – force us to opt for a pure 'electoral' definition of democracy (with the liberal property becoming an adjective only), it does introduce some differential conceptual treatment of the two dimensions. Although regrettable, this is necessary to appreciate the prevailing conceptualizations of democracy and thus to retest them empirically. I am indebted to an anonymous reviewer on *Acta Politica* for suggesting this clarification.

18　When referring to this quantity, viz. all the countries that have the attribute of free and fair elections, I will simply use the phrase 'all electoral democracies'.

19　I should add that, in my view and in consideration of the definitions proposed in this chapter, the disaggregated data compiled in the so-called Bertelsmann Transformation Index (BTI) clearly has a competitive edge compared with the Freedom of the World Survey. However, the BTI, covering 125 developing and transformation countries with more than two million inhabitants, is a relatively new dataset and the fact that I need scores for the entire period of 1992–2007 disqualifies it.

20　Notice that I only include 'defining properties', i.e. properties that bound the concept extensionally, in my operational definitions throughout this book; accompanying properties are deliberately ignored.

21　These countries are grouped using Freedom House's electoral democracy designation, a list of countries allegedly established on the basis of electoral criteria only (see <http://www.freedomhouse.org/template.cfm?page=35&year=2006>).

However, the important thing is that the countries on this list are not necessarily the ones scoring high marks (i.e. 1 or 2) on the political rights index; it is much more lax than that. Thus, using this list does not allow the two dimensions to vary independently of each other with the same threshold.

22 In the post-communist subset alone, this year saw the number of countries rise from eight to 24 (cf. Table 1.4).

23 I stop in 2007 because these are the numbers that were available to me during this analysis.

24 The Freedom House ratings of 'political rights' and 'civil liberties' are basically an ordinal measurement. Yet within the democratization literature there is precedence for treating the scores as being on a ratio scale. Accordingly, I have used Pearson's r rather than gamma to measure the bivariate correlations. Also, and not surprisingly, the gamma-values paint very much the same picture as that depicted in Figure 1.6.

25 This is less the case for O'Donnell as he is mostly interested in Latin America, a setting in which the gap seems to be somewhat more meaningful than on the global level. See the Freedom House scores for Latin America, 1990–2007.

26 On conceptual stretching, see Sartori (1970). As Sartori succinctly puts it, '[. . .] "conceptual stretching" [. . .] adds up to being an attempt to augment the extension without diminishing the intension: *the denotation is extended by obfuscating the connotation*' (1041). With regard to democracy, Collier and Levitsky (1997: 431) translate this into the assertion that '[. . .] conceptual stretching [. . .] arises when the concept of democracy is applied to cases for which, by relevant scholarly standards, it is not appropriate'. This is a very common understanding (see also Gerring 1999) of conceptual stretching, but I find it inadequate. Technically, stretching arises when the empirical referents are subsumed under a concept which does not cover these by own's own denotative definition – or only does so because the denotative definition is not loyal to the prior connotative definition. This is how I define 'conceptual stretching' in this book.

27 Also, some of the countries posited as being more liberal than democratic – e.g. Malaysia (Pr =4, CL = 5), Singapore (PR = 4, CL = 5) and Japan (PR = 1, CL = 2) – do in fact score lower (i.e. better) on 'political rights' than 'civil liberties' in the 1997 Survey.

28 Notice the slight change in nomenclature as compared to the typology crafted in chapter 1 proper. This time around I term the diminished subtype combining the absence of free and fair elections with the presence of constitutional liberalism (i.e. freedom rights and the rule of law) 'illiberal democracy' rather than 'electoral democracy'. This change is the consequence of following in the footsteps of Zakaria's purely electoral definition of democracy (as opposed to Diamond's more encompassing definition which embeds the liberal property).

29 Redoing Zakaria's analysis, I do not find that countries with lower 'political rights' ratings than 'civil liberties' ratings make up 35 percent of all the democratizing states in the 1992 survey (which covers 1991) as he did (cf. Zakaria 1997). Rather, I find the proportion to be 41 percent.

2 The post-communist tripartition described

1 The very same point is emphasized by Adcock and Collier (2001: 530).

2 Sartori (1987) has argued that democracy is inherently a 'contrary' to non-democracy and must thus be conceptualized using a dichotomy. However, as Collier and Adcock (1999: 543) have shown, this proposition cannot be made in a generic fashion. Instead, Collier and Adcock advocate a 'pragmatic' approach

which focuses on the problem under scrutiny and the matching empirical context. To quote (546):

> [. . .] scholars should be cautious in claiming to have come up with a definitive interpretation of a concept's meaning. It is more productive to establish an interpretation that is justified at least in part by its suitability to their immediate research goals and to the specific research tradition within which they are working.

This appreciation of the context is exactly what I have sought to achieve in this chapter. On the empirical value of including the intermediate category, see also Epstein, Bates, Goldstone, Kristensen and O'Hallran (2006).

3 The conceptual aspect of this observation is that the prior definition of 'illiberal autocracy' constituted a case of conceptual stretching, i.e. of subsuming empirical referents under a concept that does not cover these by one's own definition (the full absence of the electoral and liberal properties). This was necessary to test Diamond's claim about a gap between electoral and liberal democracies, but it is not necessary when these two dimensions are collapsed.

4 I might seem preferable to define this category as instances which fulfil i) Schumpeter's criterion of free and fair elections for political leadership *or* ii) Dahl's criterion of certain liberal rights *or* iii) O'Donnell's criterion of the rule of law but still fall short on the average of these three attributes. However, as demonstrated in Chapter 1 and the first part of this chapter, the countries do in fact move in the same direction on the separate indicators. Hence, the logical '*or*' would not really be helpful. It is – and this is important – the average scores on the separate attributes that delimit the three categories, hybrid regimes included.

5 The reason that I simply add up the scores on the respective indicators, rather than multiply or weight them, is to avoid any accusations for tampering with the data.

6 This formulation paraphrases Sartori's (1987: 264), so-called 'semantic field test', which expresses the following rules: 'Whenever the definition given to the term unsettles the semantic field to which the term belongs, then it has to be shown that (*a*) no 'field meaning' is thrown overboard; and (*b*) the overall 'field ambiguity' (fuzziness, unboundedness, disorder) is not being increased'. My corresponding argument is that I do not severely upset (Freedom House's) dominant classification of the empirical referents when using the mentioned thresholds.

7 The magnitude of 'democracies as a proportion of all non-autocracies' is used to measure the equivalent proportion as that measured by 'liberal democracies' as a proportion of all 'electoral democracies' in Chapter 1. In both cases, the proportion expresses the number of 'proper' democracies as a proportion of all non-autocratic countries.

8 As Thomas Carothers (2007) has recently described, Diamond's analyses were, more particularly, a product of the scholarly mood oscillating from the 'democratic optimism' of the early 1990s to the 'democratic pessimism' encountered at the end of the decade. This context also helps us to understand Zakaria's project.

9 Needless to say, the notions of short-term and long-term are arbitrary. In the present case, 2007 is long-term considering the time of writing, while 1992 is more genuinely short-term considering the genesis of post-communism in 1989–91.

10 It is of course worth recalling that the sheep are in fact eaten in Aesop's fable. More to the point, if Huntington's wave metaphor is more than a mere image, i.e. if it does indeed capture some intrinsic dynamic of the process of democratization, then the tide must turn at some point. And Diamond and Puddington do present one very good argument in favour of a beckoning reverse wave: significant global players, such as Russia and China, are currently doing their worst to hinder the spread of democracy, at least in their own regions. According to Puddington, what

is noteworthy about these two champions of autocracy (or at least non-democracy), is that they combine political unfreedom (i.e. non-democracy) with economic freedom (i.e. a market economy). If this combinations proves stable – and that is, to be sure, a big 'if' – then this challenge to liberal democracy might in a sense be more formidable than that of the communist dictatorships with their planned economies; and then the tide may indeed turn. But, and this is the gist of my objections, all of this is unreliable guesswork. Furthermore, the confidence in these Cassandra-like attempts to predict what is still hidden in the nebula of things to come is not exactly increased by the manifold prior cries of 'wolf'.

3 An actor-centred analysis of post-communist political pathways

1 Needless to say, the classificatory schema arrived at in Chapter 2 is itself infused by theory. Gerring (1999: 381) has phrased it as follows: 'Classificatory frameworks (which I shall consider a species of "theory") are particularly important since their effort is more explicitly *conceptual* than other sort of inferences'. Having said that, I have not been able to infer anything about causality so far; that is what I seek to underline via the distinction between descriptive and causal inference.

2 For the distinction between 'descriptive inference' and 'causal inference' see King, Keohane and Verba (1994).

3 It can also be expressed in similar, but less demanding terms, as done by Sartori (1991: 249–50): 'In order to reduce the number of conditions, to isolate them, and to specify their role, the investigator is required i) to organize the conditions into independent, intervening and dependent variables, and ii) to treat some causal conditions as *parameters*, parametric constants or givens (as when we invoke the *ceteris paribus* clause) that are assumed not to vary, while treating other conditions as *operative variables* that are instead allowed to vary in order to assess their influence upon the dependent variable(s)'. See, finally, Smelser (1976: 153–4, 161).

4 Lijphart (1971: 690) gives a piece of advice that points in the same direction as that of George and Bennett:

> *Scanning* all variables is not the same as *including* all variables, of course, as long as one is on one's guard against an unrealistic and eventually self-defeating perfectionism. Comparative politics should avoid the trap to the study of international politics fell, of specifying and calling for the analysis of an exhaustive list of all variables that have any possible influence on the decision-making process.

See also Coppedge (1999: 465–6).

5 Agresti and Finlay only spell out the first three criteria, but the fourth is tacitly implied. See also Gerring (2001).

6 As I will explain later, Valerie Bunce is a partial exception here.

7 Note that Frye (1997) is a partial exception as he construes the chosen institutions as the explanandum, not the explanans. However, his conclusion is that the choice of presidentialism depended on i) the interests of the actors and ii) the uncertainty created by the transition. Basically, the choice depended on 'the electoral bargaining approach to institutional choice', not on antecedent structural constraints. As such, his analysis is very much of the same ilk as that described in the main text.

8 Other works that can roughly be categorized within the dominant actor-centred approach on post-communism include: McFaul (2002), Vachudova (2005), Fish (2001), Bruszt (2002), Åslund (1992), Sachs (1993), Boycko, Shleifer and Vishny

(1995) and Hellman (1998). Some of these pieces seek to explain other phenomena than democratization per se (e.g. the dominant pattern of market making). Notice in particular that the latter four pieces touch upon a completely separate explanandum, viz. the economic reform process. However, the direction of causality – from actor-choices to political or economic outcomes – remains the same.

9 Once again, the ladder of abstraction is the roadmap I will use to conceptualize the variables. This time around, I will be less explicit, however, as the basic logic has already been described in Chapter 1. Still seeking to be a 'conscious thinker' (cf. Sartori 1970), I do not wish to build up a scheme of conceptualization, operationalization and measurement that is too rigid and repetitive.

10 For this version of the causal chain, see also Fish (1998b).

11 Here, 'causally meaningful' does not refer to Kitschelt's (2003) warning about proximate factors being temporally situated too close to the outcome. Rather, it refers to the danger of genuine tautology, i.e. the explanans being the same as the explanandum.

12 Although this property is, from a certain perspective, not completely independent of democracy either. One of the defining attributes of a number of conceptualizations of democracy (e.g. Huntington's (1991) so-called 'two-turnover' test) is thus that incumbents lose elections. Still, I have not treated displacement as a generic (i.e. regularly repeated) attribute of the political regime form, but rather as a singular instance. This diminishes the danger of tautology.

13 To sum up the differences between the two positions as slogans, it was "Get the prices right" (shock therapy) versus "Get the institutions right" (gradualism).

14 Returning to my critique of Fish and Choudhry, the third property, 'Private sector entry', arguably measures something other than 'liberalization' proper; a certain amount of conceptual stretching is, in my view, present here. However, and to repeat the pragmatic argument above, I merely use Fish and Choudry's analysis and De Melo et al.'s numbers to capture this explanation.

15 This distinction does not in itself bear upon the outcome (i.e. it is not tautological). Quoting Fish (2001: 67):

> Only the view that strong executive power is *itself* the very definition of authoritarianism could produce the impression of endogeneity or tautology. Such a perspective would equate a *diagnostic feature* with a *hypothetically facilitating* or *sustaining condition* – a gross error, albeit one that is sometimes encountered in social science.

16 Lowering or increasing the threshold to, say, 0.5 would make little difference. In lowering it to 0.55 no referents would be classified differently; in increasing it to 0.65 only one referent (Georgia) would be classified differently.

17 This assertion is based on a critical review by Herbert Kitschelt of my doctoral dissertation in which he advises – *verbatim* – for observing such an 'industry standard'.

18 Also, to classify is necessarily to parameterize, which, as argued at the outset of this chapter, is a required step in any method of gaining scientific knowledge. To quote Smelser (1976: 168), '[c]lassification renders phenomena comparable by asserting that they inhere in a common context. Thus classification is a species of that operation of converting possibly operative variables into parametric constants'.

19 Note that the distinction between descriptive typologies and typological theory is not a novel one. Sartori (1976: 290) touches upon this very dividing line when he contrasts what he terms the 'mapping or charting purposes' of a classificatory or typological scheme with the 'causal and predictive ambitions of a taxonomy'.

20 Although Elman disregards necessary and sufficient causation, he (2005: n. 15) stresses that typological theory is basically a simpler version of Ragin's QCA, the very premise of which is the notions of necessary and sufficient causation.

21 The respective positioning of the independent variables is coincidental. It could take many other shapes, but that would change only their position in the eye of the beholder, not the identity of the 24 types.

22 The significance levels are not that trustworthy as cluster analysis is, to reiterate, by and large a descriptive, or at least explorative, technique. Still, the general picture is telling.

23 As Mahoney (2004) has emphasized, typological theory provides a device for a systematical use of these configurational notions of causation.

4 A structural analysis of post-communist political pathways

1 To be sure, many of those following in the footsteps of O'Donnell and Schmitter did indeed hint that the actor-focus was relevant for longer-term developments as well.

2 See Kitschelt (1993) for a trenchant version of this critique of Transitology.

3 I have also, theoretically and empirically, considered a fourth variable or attribute, viz. 'ethnic-linguistic homogeneity' ('ethno'). It was thought to make for democracy when present and autocracy when absent. The variable was measured using the so-called 'Ethnic Diversity Score', published by Country Indicators for Foreign Policy. It ranged from 1 to 9 was dichotomized using a threshold of a score below 5. However, this variable only obfuscated the general typological picture as the ordering on the dichotomous attribute did not co-vary with the trichotomous ordering on the dependent variable. This result was reinforced by a statistical cluster analysis (i.e. K-means using an F-test), in which the variable, when operationalized using differences of degree only, turned out not to be significant, even at a very high p-level. Also, simple OLS-regressions show that this variable is not even strongly correlated with the outcome bivariately and is very quickly washed completely away when including other independent variables. For these reasons, I have chosen to wield Occam's razor, eliminating the variable (on the typological justification for discarding the variable, see George and Bennett 2005: 30).

4 By 'negative', I mean to imply that the Brezhnev doctrine was a hindrance to democratization and, as such, its removal was a necessary condition for regime change. Yet, its removal did not positively facilitate democracy. Otherwise said, it was a barrier that had to be removed and nothing else.

5 Kopstein and Reilly (2000) also propose that a process of diffusion is critical. In Chapter 5 I will return to 'diffusion', which is obviously also an aspect of international influences but is not really a structural variable. In this chapter, I only set out to capture 'vicinity to the West'.

6 Kopstein and Reilly also operate with a distinct neighbour-effects variable based on the average democracy score in neighbouring countries. Once again, these basically measure the same. It turns out that the two correlate overwhelmingly (Pearson's r = 0.93). To avoid awarding double weight to the geographical factor, I have therefore confined attention to the former attribute.

7 However, see Epstein, Bates, Goldstone, Kristensen and O'Hallran (2006) for a dissenting view that reconfirms the direct relationship between socio-economic development and democratization.

8 See Acemoglu and Robinson (2006) and Boix (2003) for two recent attempts to explain the global dynamics of democratization with reference to the dynamics of socio-economic distribution.

5 Contrasting structures, actors and diffusion

1 See also Bailey (1994: 26–8) for an explanation of the possible strategies of reduction.

2 As should be fairly obvious, the 'mixed sheet' category does not reflect 'equal totals of additive causal variables' in Elman's sense. Rather, it captures two different general combinations, namely the presence of either one or two attributes. Otherwise said, I use the technique of 'indexing' in a broader, more polythetic way than that described by Elman.

3 This is merely a restatement of the theoretical expectations of Chapters 3 and 4.

4 If we interpret the three values as an ordinal scale of 1 ('full presence'), 2 ('mixed sheet') and 3 ('full absence'), the statistical correlation (Kendall's Tau-b) between the two packages is an impressive 0.78.

5 As Sartori (1970: 1044) pertinently reminds us, '[. . .] it is only within the same class that we are entitled – and indeed required – to ask which object has more or less of an attribute or property'.

6 Notice, however, that Sartori (1976) works within the confines of systems theory. Hence, the required permanence also reflects '[. . .] the contention that classifications are not merely mapping devices but also seize, when felicitous, systemic properties' (148). With the possible exception of the two polar types, which are indeed construed as equilibrium points, my agenda is more humble, but the need for form rather than formlessness still applies.

7 A further argument favouring the typological schemas is that any encompassing explanatory framework combining deep and proximate explanations (i.e. one that seeks to elucidate a cross-temporal causal chain) is more preoccupied with general rather than with particular differences in the explanandum. This is what Kitschelt (1999: 24) points out when making the following assertion: 'If the object of explanation is *classes of events or persistent arrangements in polities*, however, it is more likely that structural constraints, mediated by causal mechanisms that involve intentional human action, account for the outcomes'.

8 As should be clear by now, Mongolia constitutes the outlier *par excellence* considering the general typological findings. In the process of writing the dissertation which this book is based on, I carried out a qualitative case study of the Mongolian aberration. However, it simply turned out that I was unable to expound the surprising democratic merits of the case. That conclusion did not seem interesting enough to justify including a 20-page case study. What Mongolia shows, then, is that some of the variation on the dependent variable is simply unaccounted for by the present analysis. I will briefly reflect on this in the Conclusions.

9 This point can be underpinned by a reference to cleavage theory. As Seymour Martin Lipset and Stein Rokkan once so lucidly described, the structural properties of a given society may create social cleavages that i) become politicized via actors such as parties and ii) freeze. See Bartolini and Mair (1990) for a thorough elucidation of this claim.

10 See also Kopstein and Reilly's (2000: 4) observation that,

> [t]he problem with this [institutional] literature is that, on the whole, it does not include within its theoretical ambit an explanation for why some countries could choose the right policies and institutions and why others could not. As useful as it is, therefore, it calls out for a deeper causal analysis.

11 As Kitschelt (1999: 13) has pointed out that, '[w]hat social science should explore are *chains of causation*, organized around variables at different levels of causal depth'. I fully concur.

12 This conclusion both echoes and substantiates (by scrutinizing a larger setting) that of Kitschelt et al. (1999: 394) on the so-called *tabula rasa* approach to post-communism. To quote:

> The tabula rasa view may permit the random variation of democratic experiences across the entire cohort of post-communist countries, but not the presence of systematically diverging patterns of democratic competition, as we have observed them in our four East Central European countries and, if we are correct, as they are likely to exist in many of the other post-communist polities as well.

13 Note that the dependent variable is only measured in 2004 (covering 2003) here, whereas Fish employs the average of the period 2003–5.

14 The causal mechanisms underlying the regional effects normally pointed to under the headline of 'diffusion' are, first, dissemination of norms and ideas and, second, the stance of international actors such as the EU. See Mainwaring and Perez-Linan (2005).

15 However, it is sometimes raised and tested in structural analyses. See e.g. Doorenspleet (2001).

16 Of course, a more realistic statement would be that the structural factors could explain part of the outcome and diffusion another part.

17 This is also, up to a point, Kopstein and Reilly's (2000: 36) conclusion. I write 'up to a point' because though their general assertion is that '[. . .] there is strong spatial dependence across the full set of states' they also emphasize that their statistical analyses '[. . .] indicate statistical significance for states within each of these subregions'.

18 Kopstein and Reilly (2000) also analyse economic diversity through the same lens but this does not interest me here.

19 I am indebted to Svend-Erik Skaaning for this argument.

20 To quote Huntington (1991: 107):

> General factors create conditions favorable to democratization. They do not make democratization necessary, and they are at one remove from the factors immediately responsible for democratization. A democratic regime is installed not by trends but by people. Democracies are created not by causes but by causers.

Conclusion

1 Witness McFaul's (2002: 212–13) observation that '[a]t the beginning of the 1990s Adam Przeworski pointed to the inability to predict communism's collapse as a 'dismal failure' of political science. Ten years later the paucity of plausible explanations for regime patterns in the postcommunist world stands as an even greater indictment'.

2 Recall that it was possible to initiate the structural analysis earlier than the actor-centred equivalent because of priority, i.e. because the structural attributes, reflecting legacies of the past, were measured at the breakdown of communism, whereas the actor-centred attributes, reflecting institutional choices during the transition, were by necessity measured after the breakdown of communism.

3 It should be emphasized that Kitschelt here refers to an intermediate status on the socio-economic variable only. However, the logic of the insight can easily be expanded so that it is a mixed score on the deeper (and, by extension, on the proximate) variables in general which structure or create randomness.

4 This should not be confused with the physical, paradigmatic sciences. Hirschman's point is only that strong and prespecified paradigms, which only allow confirmation or disconfirmation, make up a straightjacket by hindering more open-ended ruminations about the lessons to be drawn from the cases under study.

Endnote

1 'Pre-communism' is here construed as a residual category that captures everything that went before communism.
2 This is not his objective either as he is as such not interested in the post-communist setting in its own right. But it goes to show that we cannot uncritically adopt this particular explanatory aspect of his book.
3 Cf. e.g. Fukuyama (2004: 28).
4 Two exceptions are Easter (2002) and Møller (2007b).
5 As indicated, Kitschelt's dependent variable is comprised by differences in political regimes, not the more particular question of differences in the extent of the rule of law. But, as the electoral and liberal elements of modern or liberal democracy correlate very strongly, descending the ladder of abstraction to liberal constitutionalism (understood as the rule of law) seems unproblematic.
6 I wish to emphasize that the data on tax revenue (% of GDP) is derived from the *World Development Indicators 2004*. In the 2005 version, the World Bank has changed its methodology with regard to 'governance finance data', including taxation. The main difference between the two methods is that whereas the former is cash-based, the latter is based on accounting. Furthermore, social security taxes are considered tax revenue in the 2004-version whereas they are treated separately as social contributions in the 2005-version. Therefore, the numbers in the 2005-version are different from their 2004-equivalents for most countries; and thus different from the numbers employed in the present analysis.
7 The qualifier 'relatively' should be taken at face value as the data is somewhat incomplete (see Appendix 1 for the qualifications).
8 Notice, though, that the relationship between taxation and the rule of law is underpinned by the taxpayer being a legal entity – one that controls his private economy and therefore can trade rights for revenue with the officialdom. In other words, moving to a lower level of abstraction, the posited link is one between private taxpayers and rights. In a planned economy such as Belarus, this link makes little sense because the citizens do not fund the state as private stakeholders. Rather, the state taxes itself because it controls the economic activity directly. Hence, it may in fact be fair to eliminate Belarus from the test, although I have not done so here.

Bibliography

Åslund, A. (1992) *Post-Communist Economic Revolutions. How Big a Bang?, Creating the Post-Communist Order*, Washington, DC: The Centre for Strategic and International Studies.

Acemoglu, D. and Robinson, J.A. (2006) *Economic Origins of Dictatorship and Democracy*, Cambridge: Cambridge University Press.

Adcock, R. and Collier, D. (2001) 'Measurement Validity: A Shared Standard for Qualitative and Quantitative Research', *American Political Science Review*, Vol. 95, No. 3, 529–46.

Agresti, A. and Finlay, B. (1986) *Statistical Methods for the Social Sciences*, Englewood Cliffs, NJ: Prentice Hall.

Anderson, J. (1999) *Kyrgyzstan: Central Asia's Island of Democracy?*, London: Routledge.

Ash, T. G. (1990) *We The People. The Revolution of 89. Witnessed in Warsaw, Budapest, Berlin and Prague*, Cambridge: Granta Books.

Bailey, K.D. (1994) 'Typologies and Taxonomies. An Introduction to Classification Techniques', Series: *Quantitative Applications in the Social Sciences* 102, Thousand Oaks, CA: Sage.

Bartolini, S. (1993) 'On Time and Comparative Research', *Journal of Theoretical Politics*, Vol. 5, No. 2, 131–67.

Bartolini, S. and Mair, P. (1990) *Identity, Competition and Electoral Availability. The Stabilisation of European Electorates 1885–1985*, Cambridge: Cambridge University Press.

Bertelsmann Transformation Index 2006, <http://bti2006.bertelsmann-transformation-index.de>, accessed 15 August 2008.

Boix, C. (2003) *Democracy and Redistribution*, Cambridge: Cambridge University Press.

Boycko, M., Shleifer, A. and Vishny, R. (1995) *Privatizing Russia*, Cambridge, MA and London: The MIT Press.

Brady, H.E. and Collier, D. (eds) (2004) *Rethinking Social Inquiry. Diverse Tools, Shared Standards*, Lanham, MD, Boulder, CO, New York, Toronto and Oxford: Rowman and Littlefield Publishers, Inc.

Brewer, J. (1989) *The Sinews of Power. War, Money and the English State. 1688–1783*. London, Boston, Sydney, Wellington: Unwin Hyman.

Bruszt, L. (2002) 'Market Making as State Making: Constitutions and Economic Development in Post-communist Eastern Europe', *Constitutional Political Economy*, Vol. 13, 53–72.

Bunce, V. (1995) 'Comparing East and South', *Journal of Democracy*, Vol. 6, No. 3, 87–100.

Bunce, V. (1999) 'The Political Economy of Postsocialism', *Slavic Review*, Vol. 58, No. 4, 756–93.

Burke, E. (1988 [1790]) *Reflections on the Revolution in France*, London: Penguin Classics.

Carothers, T. (2002) 'The End of the Transition Paradigm', *Journal of Democracy*, Vol. 13, No. 1, 5–21.

Carothers, T. (2007) 'The "Sequencing" Fallacy', *Journal of Democracy*, Vol. 18, No. 1, 12–27.

CIFP, 'Ethnic Diversity Score', <http://www.carleton.ca/cifp>, accessed 7 August 2008).

Collier, D. and Adcock, R. (1999) 'Democracy and Dichotomies: A Pragmatic Approach to Choices about Concepts', *Annual Review of Political Science*, Vol. 2, 537–65.

Collier, D. and Levitsky, S. (1997) 'Democracy with Adjectives: Conceptual Innovation in Comparative Research', *World Politics*, Vol. 49, No. 3, 430–51.

Collier, D., Brady, H.E. and Seawright, J. (2004) 'Critiques, Responses, and Trade-Offs: Drawing Together the Debate', in Brady, H.E. and Collier, D. (eds), *Rethinking Social Inquiry. Diverse Tools, Shared Standards*, Lanham, MD, Boulder, CO, New York, Toronto and Oxford: Rowman and Littlefield Publishers, Inc.

Coppedge, M. (1999) 'Thickening Thin Concepts and Theories', *Comparative Politics*, Vol. 41, No. 4, 465–76.

Coppedge, M. and Reinicke, W.H. (1990), 'Measuring Polyarchy', *Studies in Comparative International Development*, Vol. 25, No. 1, 51–72.

Dahl, R.A. (1989) *Democracy and its Critics*, New Haven and London: Yale University Press.

De Melo, M., Denizer, C. and Gelb, A. (1996) 'Patterns of Transition from Plan to Market', *The World Bank Economic Review*, Vol. 10, No. 3, 397–424.

Di Palma, G. (1993) 'Why Democracy Can Work in Eastern Europe', in Diamond, L. and Plattner, M.F. (eds), *The Global Resurgence of Democracy*, Baltimore and London: The Johns Hopkins University Press.

Diamond, L. (1996) 'Is Pakistan the (Reverse) Wave of the Future?', *Journal of Democracy*, Vol. 11, No. 3, 91–106.

Diamond, L. (1999) *Developing Democracy. Toward Consolidation*, Baltimore and London: The Johns Hopkins University Press.

Diamond, L. (2002) 'Thinking About Hybrid Regimes', *Journal of Democracy*, Vol. 13, No. 2, 21–35.

Diamond, L. (2003) *Can the Whole World Become Democratic? Democracy, Development, and International Policies*, Paper 03'05, Irvine, CA: University of California, Center for the Study of Democracy.

Diamond, L. (2008) 'The Democratic Rollback', *Foreign Affairs*, March/April, 36–48.

Diamond, L. and Morlino, L. (2004) 'An Overview', *Journal of Democracy*, Vol. 15, No. 4, 20–31.

Doner, R.F., Ritchie, B.K. and Slater, D. (2005) 'Systemic Vulnerability and the Origins of Developmental States: Northeast and Southeast Asia in Comparative Perspective', *International Organization*, Vol. 59, No. 2, 327–361.

Doorenspleet, R. (2001) *The Fourth Wave of Democratization. Identification and Explanation*, PhD, Leiden: University of Leiden.

Easter, G. (2002) 'Politics of Revenue Extraction in Post-Communist States: Poland and Russia Compared', *Politics and Society*, Vol. 30, No. 4, 599–627.

Ekiert, G. (2003) 'Patterns of Postcommunist Transformation in East-Central Europe', in Ekiert, G. and Hanson, S.E. (eds), *Capitalism and Democracy in East-Central Europe. Assessing the Legacy of Communist Rule*, Cambridge: Cambridge University Press.

Ekiert, G. and Hanson, S. E. (2003) *Capitalism and Democracy in East-Central Europe. Assessing the Legacy of Communist Rule*, Cambridge: Cambridge University Press.

Elklit, J and Svensson, P. (1997) 'What Makes Elections Free and Fair', *Journal of Democracy*, Vol. 8, No. 3, 32–46.

Elman, C. (2005) 'Explanatory Typologies in Qualitative Studies of International Politics', *International Organization*, Vol. 59, No. 2, 293–326.

Elster, J. (1990) 'When Communism Dissolves, *London Review of Books*, 24 January, 3–6.

Epstein, D.L., Bates, R., Goldstone, J., Kristensen, I. and O'Hallran, S. (2006) 'Democratic Transitions', *American Journal of Political Science*, Vol. 50, No. 3, 551–69.

Fish, M.S. (1998a) 'The Determinants of Economic Reform in the Post-Communist World', *East European Politics and Societies*, Vol. 12, No. 1, 31–78.

Fish, M.S. (1998b) 'Democratization's Requisites: The Postcommunist Experience', *Post-Soviet Affairs*, Vol. 14, No. 3, 212–47.

Fish, M.S. (2001) 'The Dynamics of Democratic Erosion', in Richard D. Anderson, Jr., M. Steven Fish, Stephen E. Hanson, Philip G. Roeder (eds), *Postcommunism and the Theory of Democracy*, Princeton and Oxford: Princeton University Press.

Fish, M.S. (2006) 'Stronger Legislatures, Stronger Democracies', *Journal of Democracy*, Vol. 17, No. 1, 5–20.

Fish, M.S. and Choudhry, O. (2007) 'Democratization and Economic Liberalization in the Postcommunist World', *Comparative Political Studies*, Vol. 40, No. 3, 254–82.

Freedom House 'Freedom of the World Survey', <http://www.freedomhouse.org>, accessed 7 August 2008.

Freedom House 'Methodology', <http://www.freedomhouse.org>, accessed 7 August 2008.

Frye, T. (1997) 'A Politics of Institutional Choice: Post-Communist Presidencies', *Comparative Political Studies*, Vol. 30, No. 5, 523–52.

Fukuyama, F. (1992) *The End of History and the Last Man*, New York: Free Press.

Fukuyama, F. (2004) 'The Imperative of State-building', *Journal of Democracy*, Vol. 15, No. 2, 17–31.

Gates, S., Hegre, H., Jones, M.P. and Strand, H. (2006) 'Institutional Inconsistency and Political Instability: Polity Duration, 1800–2000', *American Journal of Political Science*, Vol. 50, No. 4, 893–908.

George, A. and Bennett, A. (2005) *Case Study and Theory Development*, Cambridge, MA: The MIT Press.

Gerring, J. (1999) 'What Makes a Concept Good? A Criterial Framework for Understanding Concept Formation in the Social Sciences', *Polity*, Vol. XXXI, No. 3, 357–93.

Gerring, J. (2001) *Social Science Methodology. A Criterial Framework*, Cambridge: Cambridge University Press.

Goldscheid, R. (1958 [1925]) 'A Sociological Approach to Problems of Public Finance', trans. Henderson, E., in Musgrave, R. A. and Peacock, A. T. (eds), *Classics in the Theory of Public Finance*, London: Macmillan Press Ltd.

Greskovits, B. (1998) *The Political Economy of Protest and Patience. East European and Latin American Transformations Compared*, Budapest: CEU Press.

Gryzmala-Busse, A. and Luong, P.J. (2002) 'Reconceptualizing the State: Lessons from Post-Communism', *Politics and Society*, Vol. 30, No. 4, 529–54.

Hale, H. E. (2005) 'Regime Cycles. Democracy, Autocracy, and Revolution in Post-Soviet Eurasia', *World Politics*, Vol. 58, 529–54.

Held, D. (1987) *Models of Democracy*, Cambridge: Polity Press.

Hellman, J.S. (1998) 'The Politics of Partial Reform in Postcommunist Transitions', *World Politics*, Vol. 50, 203–34.

Henderson, K. (2002) *Slovakia. The Escape from Invisibility*, London and New York: Routledge.

Hirschman, A.O. (1970) 'The Search for Paradigms as a Hindrance to Understanding', *World Politics*, Vol. 22, No. 3, 329–43.

Huntington, S.P. (1991) *The Third Wave. Democratization in the Late Twentieth Century*, Norman, OK and London: University of Oklahoma Press.

Huntington, S.P. (1996) *The Clash of Civilization and the Remaking of the World Order*, New York: Simon and Schuster.

Ishiyama, J. and Velten, M. (1998) 'Presidential Power and Democratic Development in Post-Communist Politics', *Communist and Post-Communist Studies*, Vol. 31, No. 3, 217–34.

Jowitt, K. (1992) *New World Disorder. The Leninist Extinction*, Berkeley, CA, Los Angeles and London: University of California Press.

Kaufmann, D., Kraay, A. and Mastruzzi, M. (2005) *Governance Matters IV: Governance Indicators for 1996–2004*, Washington, DC: The World Bank.

Karatnycky, A. (2003) 'Liberty's Advances in a Troubled World', *Journal of Democracy*, Vol. 14, No. 1, 100–13.

King, G., Keohane, R.O and Verba, S. (1994) *Designing Social Inquiry. Scientific Inference in Qualitative Research*, Princeton: Princeton University Press.

Kitschelt, H. (1988) 'Left-Libertarian Parties: Explaining Innovation in Competitive Party Systems', *World Politics*, Vol. 40, No. 2, 194–234.

Kitschelt, H. (1993) 'Comparative Historical Research and Rational Choice Theory: The Case of Transitions to Democracy', *Theory and Society*, Vol. 22, No. 3, 413–27.

Kitschelt, H. (1999) 'Accounting for Outcomes of Post-Communist Regime Change: Causal Depth or Shallowness in Rival Explanations?', Paper presented at the annual meeting of the American Political Science Association in Atlanta, GA.

Kitschelt, H. (2003) 'Accounting for Postcommunist Regime Diversity. What Counts as a Good Cause?', in Ekiert, G. and Hanson, S.E. (eds), *Capitalism and Democracy in East-Central Europe. Assessing the Legacy of Communist Rule*, Cambridge: Cambridge University Press.

Kitschelt, Herbert and Malesky, E. (2000) 'Constitutional Design and Postcommunist Economic Reform', Paper presented at the Midwest Political Science Conference in Chicago, IL.

Kitschelt, H., Mansfeldova, Z., Markowski, R and Toka, G. (1999) *Post-Communist*

Party Systems. Competition, Representation, and Inter-Party Cooperation, Cambridge: Cambridge University Press.

Kopstein, J.S. and Reilly, D.A. (1999) 'Explaining the Why of the Why: A Comment on Fish's "Determinants of Economic Reform in the Post-Communist World", *East European Politics and Society*, Vol. 13, No. 3, 613–26.

Kopstein, J.S. and Reilly, D.A. (2000) 'Geographic Diffusion and the Transformation of the Postcommunist World', *World Politics*, Vol. 53, 1–37.

Kurtz, M.J. and Barnes, A. (2002) 'The Political Foundations of Post-Communist Regimes: Marketization, Agrarian Legacies, or International Influences', *Comparative Political Studies*, Vol. 35, No. 5, 524–53.

Lazarsfeld, P.F. (1937) 'Some Remarks on the Typological Procedures in Social Research', *Zeitschrift für Sozialforschung*, Vol. 6, 119–39.

Lazarsfeld, P.F. and Barton, A.H. (1951) 'Qualitative Measurement in the Social Sciences: Classification, Typologies, and Indices', in Lerner, D. and Lasswell, H. D. (eds), *The Policy Sciences*, Palo Alto, CA: Stanford University Press.

Levitsky, S. and Way, L.A. (2002) 'The Rise of Competitive Authoritarianism', *Journal of Democracy*, Vol. 13, No. 2, 51–65.

Lijphart, A. (1971), 'Comparative Politics and the Comparative Method', *The American Political Science Review*, Vol. 65, No. 3, 682–93.

Linz, J.J. (1978) *The Breakdown of Democratic Regimes: Crisis, Breakdown and Reequilibration*, Baltimore: The Johns Hopkins University Press.

Linz, J.J. and Stepan, A. (1978) *The Breakdown of Democratic Regimes*, Baltimore and London: The Johns Hopkins University Press.

Linz, J.J. and Stepan, A. (1996) *Problems of Democratic Transition and Consolidation. Southern Europe, South America, and Post-Communist Europe*, Baltimore and London: The Johns Hopkins University Press.

Lipset, S.M. (1959a) 'Some Social Requisites of Democracy: Economic Development and Political Legitimacy', *American Political Science Review*, Vol. LII, No. 1, 69–105.

Lipset, S.M. (1959b) *Political Man. The Social Bases of Politics*, London, Melbourne and Toronto: Heinemann.

McFaul, M. (2002) 'The Fourth Wave of Democracy and Dictatorship. Noncooperative Transitions in the Postcommunist World', *World Politics*, Vol. 54, 212–44.

Mahoney, J. (2004) 'Comparative-Historical Methodology', *Annual Review of Sociology*, Vol. 30, 81–101.

Mainwaring S. and Perez-Linan, A. (2005) 'Why Regions of the World Are Important. Regional Specificities and Region-Wide Diffusion of Democracy', Paper 9, presented at the annual meeting of the American Political Science Association, Pennsylvania Convention Center, Philadelphia, PA, 31 August 2006.

Mair, P. (2005) 'Popular Democracy and the European Union Polity', *European Governance Papers*, <http://www.connex-network.org/eurogov>.

Mair, P (2008) 'Democracies', in Caramani, D. (ed.). *Comparative Politics*, Oxford: Oxford University Press.

Marshall, M.G. and Jaggers, K. (2002) *Polity IV Project. Political Regime Characteristics and Transitions, 1800–2002. Dataset Users' Manual*, Integrated Network for Societal Conflict Research (INSCR) Program, University of Maryland, College Park 20742: Center for International Development and Conflict Management (CIDCM).

Montesquieu (1989 [1748]) *The Spirit of the Laws*, Cambridge, New York, Port Chester, Melbourne, Sydney: Cambridge University Press.

Moore Jr., B. (1991 [1966]) *Social Origins of Dictatorship and Democracy. Lord and Peasant in the Making of the Modern World*, London: Penguin Books.

Møller, J. (2006) 'Equality or liberty?', Review of *Economic Origins of Dictatorship and Democracy, Journal of Democracy*, Vol. 17, No. 4, 169–72.

Møller, J. (2007a) 'The Gap between Electoral and Liberal Democracy Revisited. Some Conceptual and Empirical Clarifications', *Acta Politica*, Vol. 42, No. 4, 380–400.

Møller, J. (2007b) 'Wherefore the Liberal State? Post-Soviet Democratic Blues and Lessons from Fiscal Sociology'. *East European Politics and Society*, Vol. 21, No. 2, 294–315.

Møller, J. (2008) 'A Critical Note on "The Rise of Illiberal Democracy"', *Australian Journal of Political Science*, Vol. 43, No. 3, 555–61.

Munck, G.L. (2006) 'Drawing Boundaries: How to Craft Intermediate Regime Categories', in Schedler, A. (ed.), *Electoral Authoritarianism. The Dynamics of Unfree Competition*, Boulder, CO, London: Lynne Rienner Publishers,

Munck, G.L. and Verkuilen, J. (2002) 'Conceptualizing and Measuring Democracy. Evaluating Alternative Indices', *Comparative Political Studies*, Vol. 35, No. 1, 5–34.

Murrell, P. (1993) 'What is Shock Therapy? What Did It Do in Poland and Russia?', *Post-Soviet Affairs*, Vol. 9 No. 2, 111–40.

O'Donnell, G. (1992) *Delegative Democracy?*, Working Paper 172, University of Notre Dame, Kellogg Institute Kellogg Institute.

O'Donnell, G. (1993) *On the State, Democratization and Some Conceptual Problems*, Working Paper 192, University of Notre Dame, Kellogg Institute.

O'Donnell, G. (2001) 'Democracy, Law, and Comparative Politics', *Studies in Comparative International Development*, Vol. 36, 7–36.

O'Donnell, G. (2007) 'The Perpetual Crises of Democracy', *Journal of Democracy*, Vol. 18, No. 1, 5–11.

O'Donnell, G. and Schmitter, P.C. (1986) 'Tentative Conclusions about Uncertain Democracies', in O'Donnell, G., Schmitter, P.C. and Whitehead, L. (eds), *Transitions from Authoritarian Rule. Prospects for Democracy*, Baltimore: The Johns Hopkins University Press.

Offe, C. (1991) 'Capitalism by Democratic Design? Democratic Theory Facing the Triple Transition in East Central Europe', *Social Research*, Vol. 58, No. 4, 865–92.

Pop-Eleches, G. (2007) 'Historical Legacies and Post-Communist Regime Change', *Journal of Politics*, Vol. 69, No. 4, 908–26.

Przeworski, A. (1991) *Democracy and the Market. Political and Economic Reforms in Eastern Europe and Latin America*, Cambridge: Cambridge University Press.

Przeworski, A. (2004) 'Why Do Political Parties Obey Results of Elections?' in Maravall, J.M. and Przeworski, A. (eds), *Democracy and the Rule of Law*, Cambridge: Cambridge University Press.

Przeworski, A. with Bardhan, P., Pereira, L.C.B., Bruszt, L., Choi, J.J., Comisso, E.T., Cui, Z., di Tella, T., Hankiss, E., Kolarska-Bobi´nska, L., Laitin, D., Maravall, J.M., Migranyan, A., O'Donnell, G., Ozbudun, E., Roemer, J.E., Schmitter, P.C., Stallings, B., Stepan, A., Weffort, F., Wiatr, J.J. (1995) *Sustainable Democracy*, Cambridge: Cambridge University Press.

Przeworski, A. and Limongi, F. (1997) 'Modernization: Theories and Facts', *World Politics*, Vol. 49, No. 2, 155–83.

Przeworski, A., Alvarez, M., Cheibub, J.A. and Limongi, F. (1996) 'What Makes Democracies Endure', *Journal of Democracy*, Vol. 7, No. 1, 39–55.

Puddington, A. (2008) 'Is the Tide Turning?', *Journal of Democracy*, Vol. 19, No. 2, 61–73.

Putnam, R.D. (1993) *Making Democracy Work. Civic Traditions in Modern Italy*, Princeton, NJ: Princeton University Press.

Putnam, R.D. (2000) *Bowling Alone. The Collapse and Revival of American Community*, New York: Simon and Schuster.

Ragin, C.C. (1987) *The Comparative Method. Moving Beyond Qualitative and Quantitative Strategies*, Berkeley, CA: University of California Press.

Ragin, C.C. (2000) *Fuzzy-set Social Science*, Chicago and London: The University of Chicago Press.

Roeder, P.G. (1994) 'Varieties of Post-Soviet Authoritarian Regimes', *Post-Soviet Affairs*, Vol. 10, No. 1, 61–98.

Roland, G. (2000) *Transition and Economics: Politics, Markets, and Firms*, Cambridge, MA: The MIT Press.

Ross, M. L. (2001) 'Does Oil Hinder Democracy', *World Politics*, Vol. 53, No. 3, 325–61.

de Ruggiero, G. (1927) *The History of European Liberalism*, Boston: Beacon Press.

Sachs, J. (1993) *Poland's Jump to the Market Economy*, Cambridge, MA and London: The MIT Press.

Sartori, G. (1970) 'Concept Misformation in Comparative Politics', *The American Political Science Review*, Vol. 64, 1033–53.

Sartori, G. (1976) *Parties and Party Systems. A Framework for Analysis*, Vol. 1, Cambridge: Cambridge University Press.

Sartori, G. (1984) 'Guidelines for Concept Analysis', in Sartori, Giovanni (ed.), *Social Science Concepts. A Systematic Analysis*, London: Sage.

Sartori, G. (1987) *The Theory of Democracy Revisited*, Chatham, NJ: Chatham House Publishers, Inc.

Sartori, G. (1991) 'Comparing and Miscomparing', *Journal of Theoretical Politics*, Vol. 3, No. 3, 243–57.

Schedler, A. (2002) 'Elections Without Democracy: The Menu of Manipulation', *Journal of Democracy*, Vol. 13, No. 2, 36–50.

Schmitter, P. C. and Karl, T. L. (1991), 'What Democracy Is . . . and Is Not', *Journal of Democracy*, Vol. 2, No. 3, 75–88.

Schmitter, P.C. and Karl, T.L. (1993) 'What Democracy Is . . . And Is Not', in Diamond, L. and Plattner, M.F. *The Global Resurgence of Democracy*, Baltimore and London: The Johns Hopkins University Press.

Schmitter, P.C. and Karl, T.L. (1994) 'The Conceptual Travels of Transitologists and Consolidologists: How Far to the East Should They Attempt to Go?', *Slavic Review*, Vol. 53, No. 1, 49–62.

Schumpeter, J.A. (1974 [1943]) *Capitalism, Socialism and Democracy*, London: Unwin University Books.

Schumpeter, J. A. (1991) 'The Crisis of the Tax State', in Schumpeter, J. A., *Joseph A. Schumpeter. The Economics and Sociology of Capitalism*, Swedberg, R. (ed.), Princeton, NJ: Princeton University Press.

Shafer, M. D. (1994) *Winners and Losers. How Sectors Shape the Developmental Prospects of States*, Ithaca and London: Cornell University Press.

Skaaning, S. (2006) *Democracy besides Elections: An Inquiry into the (Dis)respect for Civil Liberty in Latin American and Post-Communist Countries after the Third Wave*, Århus: Institut for Statskundskab, Århus Universitet: unpublished Doctorate Dissertation.

Smelser, N.J. (1976) *Comparative Methods in the Social Sciences*, Englewood Cliffs, NJ: Prentice Hall.

Sørensen, G. (1998) *Democracy and Democratization*, Boulder, CO: Westview Press.

Stiglitz, J. (1999) 'Wither Reform: Ten Years of the Transition', Paper presented at The World Bank Annual Bank Conference on Development Economics, April.

Vachudova, Milada Anna (2005) *Europe Undivided. Democracy, Leverage, and Integration After Communism*, Oxford: Oxford University Press.

World Bank (2004) *World Development Indicators 2004*, CD-ROM.

World Bank (2005) *World Development Indicators 2005*, CD-ROM.

Zakaria, F. (1997) 'The Rise of Illiberal Democracy', *Foreign Affairs*, Vol. 76, No. 6, 22–43.

Zakaria, F. (2003) *The Future of Freedom: Illiberal Democracy at Home and Abroad*, New York and London: W. W. Norton and Company.

Index

actor-centred analysis 4–6, 63–92, 93–4, 134, 136–7, 137–8; constitutional engineering variable 66, 72–4, 74–5; diffusion 129–30, 131; economic reforming variable 65–6, 69–72, 74–5; integrating actor-based and structure-based packages 118–22, 130; methodology 75–81; overview of scoring 74–5; package based on 111–18, 130, 136; political competition variable 65, 66–9, 74–5; robustness test 87, 90–2; three explanations on post-communism 65–75; typological analysis of post-communist political pathways 81–9
actor-induced autocracy 80, 81–9, 134
actor-induced democracy 80, 81–9, 134
Adcock, R. 16–17, 158–9
Aggregate Governance Indicators 147
Agresti, A. 65
Akayev, A. 126
alternative information 25–7
American independence movement 145
Åslund, A. 70
associational autonomy 25–7
attitudes 21–2
autocracy 1–2, 13–14, 133–4, 137; actor-centred analysis of post-communist political pathways 81–9; guidelines for typological analysis 79–81; liberal 23–4, 25–9, 31, 32, 35, 38, 43, 44; illiberal 23–4, 25–9, 31, 32, 35, 36, 38, 43, 44, 47–8; structural analysis of post-communist political pathways 103–9; tripartite classification 48–59

autocracy guaranteed 114, 136; typological analysis of packages 114–18
autocracy waiting room: actor-centred analysis 81–8; structural analysis 103–8

background concept 17; conceptualization of democracy 18–19
Bailey, K.D. 80
Barnes, A. 101
Barton, A.H. 111
Belarus 106, 108, 109, 147, 164
beneficial legacies 97
Bennett, A. 64, 77, 78, 80
Berlin 98–9
border problem 25, 49
Bosnia-Herzegovina 7
Boycko, M. 70
Bruszt, L. 72
Bulgaria 106, 108, 109, 137
Bunce, V. 2, 6, 67–8, 69, 72–3, 141–2, 143
bureaucratic-authoritarian communism 96–7, 144
Burke, E. 146

Carteret, J. 145
causal chain 121–2, 130–1
causal heterogeneity/homogeneity 126–7, 128
causal inference, fundamental problem of 65
Central Asia 3, 55–7, 93, 126, 133, 137; actor-centred analysis 83, 85, 85–6, 89
ceteris paribus condition 63
Choudhry, O. 70–1

civil liberties 50–1, 59, 147, 149;
   fourfold typology of political
   regime forms 27–9, 33–4, 38; rise
   of electroral democracy 39–40,
   41–3
civil society 22
clash of civilizations 1–2, 142, 143
Collier, D. 16–17, 158–9
colonial periphery 96–7, 144
'colour revolutions' 140
communist legacies 141–4; *see also*
   legacies
comparative vs statistical approach
   75–7
conceptual stretching 40, 157, 158
conceptualization 15–17; of democracy
   17–29
constitutional engineering variable
   (legislature) 66, 72–4, 74–5;
   diffusion 122–6; typological analysis
   79–89, 90–2
contestation 19–20
Coppedge, M. 46, 49–50, 120–1
critical juncture 93
Croatia 7, 147
cumulative liberalization index (CLI)
   71–2

Dahl, R.A. 19–20; *see also* elaborated
   Dahlian model
De Melo, M. 71–2
deep explanations 5–6; *see also*
   structural analysis
delegative democracy 12
democracy 1, 3, 11–44, 133–4, 137;
   actor-centred analysis of post-
   communist political pathways 81–9;
   conceptualizing 17–29;
   considerations about the gap between
   electoral and liberal 12–15; gap
   between electoral and liberal 11–37;
   guidelines for typological analysis
   79–81; reappraisal of third wave
   29–36; rise of electoral democracy
   39–44; structural analysis of post-
   communist political pathways
   103–9; tripartite classification of
   political regime forms 48–59
democracy guaranteed 114, 136;
   typological analysis of packages
   114–18
democracy waiting room: actor-centred
   analysis 81–8; structural analysis
   103–8

democratization 4; reverse wave of
   52–3; third wave of 11, 29–36
dendrograms 90
descriptive inference 78
Diamond, L. 1, 12, 13–15, 18, 19, 20,
   29, 30, 45, 51, 52–3, 57, 155
diffusion 122–30, 130–1; logical
   problem burdening the diffusion
   argument 127–30; and post-
   communism 125–7
displacement *see* political competition
   variable

East-Central Europe 3, 55–7, 93, 133,
   137, 153; actor-centred analysis 83,
   85, 85–6, 89; diffusion 125–6;
   economic inequality 100; legacies
   142–3
economic development 99–101
economic equality 100
economic liberalization 70–2
economic reforming variable (reform)
   65–6, 69–72, 74–5; typological
   analysis 79–89, 90–2
Ekiert, G. 114, 141, 142–3
elaborated Dahlian model 25–9, 49–51
elections: free and fair 22–4, 25–7,
   48–9; initial 66–9, 142–3
electoral democracy: gap with liberal
   democracy 11–37; rise of 39–44
elected officials 25–7
Elman, C. 80, 111–12
empirical compression 111–12
equilibriums 139–40
ethnic-linguistic homogeneity 161
European Union 98, 137

Finlay, B. 65
fiscal sociology 145–6
Fish, M.S. 66–7, 68, 69, 70–1, 73–4,
   122–5, 160
flows 129
former Yugoslavia 7
free and fair elections 22–4, 25–7, 48–9
free states 124
freedom *see* liberty
freedom of expression 25–7
Freedom House ratings 123–4, 147,
   149; fourfold typology of political
   regime forms 27–9, 33–4, 38; rise of
   electoral democracy 39–40, 41–3;
   tripartite classification of political
   regime forms 50–1, 59; *see also* civil
   liberties, political rights

French Revolution 145
Frye, T. 73, 74, 127
Fukuyama, F. 1
functional school 4

Gates, S. 139
GDP per capita 101
George, A. 64, 77, 78, 80
Gerring, J. 15, 16, 55, 119, 127
Gini coefficient 100
global setting: fourfold typology of
  political regime forms 30–4;
  tripartite classification of political
  regime forms 51–3
Goldscheid, R. 145–6
gradualism 69–71
Greskovits, B. 100

Hegre, H. 139
Hellman, J.S. 71
Henderson, K. 125
hierarchical cluster analysis 90
Hirschman, A.O. 140
historical sociology 4
Huntington, S.P. 1, 52, 53, 142, 163
hybrid regimes 2, 40–1, 43, 47, 124,
  133–4, 137–8, 154; actor-centred
  analysis of post-communist political
  pathways 81–9; guidelines for
  typological analysis 79–81;
  structural analysis of post-communist
  political pathways 103–9; tripartite
  classification of political regime forms
  48–59; typological analysis of
  packages 114–18

illiberal autocracy 23–4, 25–9, 31, 32,
  35, 36, 38, 43, 44, 47–8
illiberal democracy *see* electoral
  democracy
inclusive suffrage 25–7
indexing 111–12
indicators 17; conceptualizing
  democracy 25–9; tripartite
  classification of political regime forms
  49–51
initial election 66–9, 142–3
Italy 143

Jones, M.P. 139
Jowitt, K. 1–2, 141, 142

K-means analysis 87, 90–2
Karatnycky, A. 28

Karl, T. 6
Kaufmann, D. 147
Keohane, R.O. 65, 75–6
King, G. 65, 75–6
Kitschelt, H. 2, 5, 76–7, 94, 95, 96–7,
  120, 121, 138, 140, 142, 143, 144,
  146, 163
Kopstein, J.S. 98–9, 128–9, 162
Kurtz, M.J. 101
Kyrgyzstan 56, 57, 93, 126

ladder of abstraction 16–17
law 21; rule of *see* rule of law
Lazarsfeld, P. 111
legacies 95, 96–7, 102, 141;
  approaches to post-communism
  141–4; post-communist political
  pathways 102–11; taxation and
  liberty in post-communist setting
  146–50
legislature *see* constitutional engineering
  variable
Leninist legacy 141, 142
liberal autocracy 23–4, 25–9, 31, 32,
  35, 38, 43, 44
liberal democracy/electoral democracy
  gap 11–37
liberal hegemony 97–8
liberal rights 22–4, 25–7, 48–9, 146–50
liberty 20–1; Montesquieu's 'General
  Rule' 144–6, 147; and taxation in
  post-communist setting 146–50
Lijphart, A. 63–4, 75–6, 159
Limongi, F. 99, 101
Linz, J.J. 4, 11, 21–2, 72, 95, 97
Lipset, S.M. 4, 95, 99
logical compression 111
logical problem 127–30

Macedonia 7
McFaul, M. 94
Mahoney, J. 46, 81
Mair, P. 11
Malesky, E. 120
measurability problem 25, 27–9, 50–1
Meciar, V. 125
membership problem 25, 25–7, 49–50
Mirabeau, Comte de 145
modernization variable (modern) 95,
  99–101, 102, 141; post-communist
  political pathways 102–11
Mongolia 57, 93, 106, 109, 137, 162
Montesquieu's 'General Rule' of
  taxation and liberty 144–6, 147

Moore, B. 4
Munck, G.L. 47
Murrell, P. 70

national-accommodative communism
    96–7, 144
necessary and sufficient causation 81,
    88–9, 109
neo-modernization theory 99–100

O'Donnell, G. 4, 11, 12, 21, 23, 93, 97,
    154
Offe, C. 2
Ogden–Richards Triangle 15
optimists 1, 133
origins of diversity 138–9

paradigmatic thinking 140
Parliamentary Power Index 73–4,
    122–3, 123–4
parliamentary systems 124, 125–6
participation 19–20
partly free states 124
patrimonial communism 96–7, 144
pessimists 1–2, 133
political competition variable
    (displacement) 65, 66–9, 74–5;
    typological analysis 79–89, 90–2
political legacies variable *see* legacies
political rights 50–1, 59; fourfold
    typology of political regime forms
    27–9, 33–4, 38; rise of electoral
    democracy 39–40, 41–3
POLITY IV index 27
polyarchy 19–20
Pop-Eleches, G. 95
post-communist political pathways:
    actor-centred analysis 81–9;
    structural analysis 102–9
post-communist setting: fourfold
    typology of political regime forms
    34–6; regime forms 1992–2007
    55–7; tripartite classification of
    political regime forms 53–7
pragmatic compression 111
pre-communist legacies 141–4; *see also*
    legacies
Presidential Power Index 74
presidential systems 72–3, 124, 126
proximate explanations 5–6; *see also*
    actor-centred analysis
Przeworski, A. 2, 99, 101
pseudo-democracy 13, 45
Puddington, A. 52

Putnam, R. 22, 143

qualitative vs quantitative approach
    75–7

reduction of a property space 111–12
reform *see* economic reforming variable
regional effects 123–5; *see also*
    diffusion
Reilly, D.A. 98–9, 128–9, 162
Reinicke, W.H. 46
reliability 27
rentier state 146
rescaling 111
reverse wave of democratization 52–3
right to run for office 25–7
rights 22–4, 25–7, 48–9; and revenue in
    post-communist setting 146–50
robustness tests 87, 90–2, 147, 149
Roland, G. 70
Romania 104, 106, 108, 109, 137
Ruggiero, G. de 145
rule of law 22–4, 25–7, 48–9; and
    liberty in the post-communist setting
    146–50
Russia 57, 108, 109
Rustow, D. 4

Sachs, J. 70
Sartori, G. 11, 15–16, 25, 49, 64, 118,
    135, 155, 159
Schmitter, P.C. 4, 6, 11, 93, 97
Schumpeter, J.A. 18, 19, 20–1, 145–6
sectoral analysis 146
self-interest 99
semantic field test 158
sequencing of reforms 71
Serbia-Montenegro 7
shallow explanations 4–6; *see also*
    actor-centred analysis
Shleifer, A. 70
shock therapy 69–71
Slovakia 125–6
Social-Democratic Consensus 70–1
spuriousness 123–5
stability 139–40
state capacity 146
state formation 146
state–society relations 146
statistical cluster analysis 87, 90–2
statistical vs comparative approach
    75–7
Stepan, A. 11, 21–2, 72, 95
Stiglitz, J. 70

stock 129
Strand, H. 139
structural analysis 5, 63, 76, 93–109,
   134–5, 137–8; diffusion 128–30,
   131; full typology with empirical
   referents 103–8; identifying
   structural factors 94–102; integrating
   package with actor-based package
   118–22, 130; modernization variable
   95, 99–101, 102, 141; overview of
   scoring 101–2; package based on
   111–18, 130, 136; political legacies
   variable 95, 96–7, 102, 141; post-
   communist political pathways
   102–9; vicinity to Western Europe
   variable 95, 97–9, 102, 141
structural autocracy 103–9, 135
structural democracy 103–9, 135
systematized concept 17;
   conceptualizing democracy 19–24;
   tripartite classification of political
   regime forms 47–9

tabula rasa approach 163
taxation: liberty and in post-communist
   setting 146–50; Montesquieu's
   'General Rule' 144–6, 147
third wave of democratization 11;
   reappraisal 29–36
time 114–17, 119, 128, 130
Transitology 1, 4, 93
tripartition 3, 45–59, 133–4; counting
   rules for classification 59; global
   setting 51–3; indicators 49–51;
   post-communist setting 53–7;
   systematized concept 47–9
Turkmenistan 74

typological analysis 135–6; actor-
   centred analysis 81–9; guidelines for
   79–81; packages 112–18; structural
   analysis 102–9
typological theory 77–9
typologies 77–9
typology of political regime forms
   22–4; counting rules for 38;
   Diamond's typology 13–15; global
   setting 30–4; post-communist setting
   34–6; tripartite *see* tripartition

unfree states 124

Vachudova, M.A. 98, 137
validity 27–8
Verba, S. 65, 75–6
vicinity to Western Europe variable
   (West) 95, 97–9, 102, 141; post-
   communist political pathways
   102–11
Vienna 98–9
Vishny, R. 70

waiting rooms: actor-centred analysis
   81–8; structural analysis 103–8
Washington Consensus 70–1
West variable *see* vicinity to Western
   Europe variable
Whitehead, L. 11
World Bank: Aggregate Governance
   Indicators 147; *World
   Development Indicators* 101,
   147, 151, 164

Zakaria, F. 12, 39–44
zone of instability 139–40

For Product Safety Concerns and Information please contact our EU
representative GPSR@taylorandfrancis.com
Taylor & Francis Verlag GmbH, Kaufingerstraße 24, 80331 München, Germany

9 780415 850100